MILITARY HISTORY FROM PRIMARY SOURCES

THE CRIMEAN WAR
1853-1856

THE ILLUSTRATED EDITION

BY GENERAL SIR EDWARD HAMLEY, K.C.B.

EDITED BY
BOB CARRUTHERS

C⊕DA
BOOKS LTD

This book is published in Great Britain in 2013 by

Coda Books Ltd,Office Suite 2, Shrieves Walk, Sheep Street, Stratford upon Avon, Warwickshire CV37 6GJ.

www.codabooks.com

Copyright © 2013 Coda Books Ltd

ISBN 978-1-78158-352-4

A CIP catalogue record for this book is available from the British Library.

This book was first published by Seeley and Co. Limited, London, in 1891 as "The War in the Crimea" by General Sir Edward Hamley, K.C.B.

CONTENTS

FOREWORD

Caricature of Lieutenant-General Sir Edward Hamley K.C.B., K.C.M.G., M.P.
Originally published in Vanity Fair, 1887.

THE CRIMEAN War (October 1853-February 1856) between the Russian Empire and an alliance of the British, French and Ottoman Empires and the the Kingdom of Sardinia, was part of the long-running struggle between the major European powers for influence over the territories of the declining Ottoman empire. It took place mainly on the Crimean peninsula, but there were smaller episodes in the Caucasus, western Anatolia, the Baltic Sea, the Pacific Ocean and the White Sea of Russia.

The war in the Crimea is often considered the first 'modern' war, because of its use of modern military tactics, such as trench warfare and blind artillery fire, as well as its utilisation of railways and improvements in communication with the telegraph. As well as the devastation of the Charge of the Light Brigade and the courage of the Thin Red Line, the war is also famous for the pioneering nursing work of Florence Nightingale and Mary Seacole. The suffering of the injured soldiers would not have come to light, however, if it were not for the reports of war correspondents such as William Russell of the Times and the photographs of Roger Fenton, some of which appear in this book. This was the first war where the public were informed via telegraph of the daily realities of death and injury and the success or failure of the strategies of those in command.

The author, Lieutenant-General Sir Edward Hamley, K.C.B., K.C.M.G., was born in Cornwall in 1824 to a military family, and joined the Royal Artillery in 1843. He served throughout the Crimean War as aide-de-camp to Sir Richard Dacres, officer commanding the artillery. He took part in all the operations with distinction and was promoted successively to major and lieutenant-colonel by brevet. Throughout the war, he wrote accounts of the Crimean campaign which were published in Blackwood's Magazine. In 1859, his military prowess and literary skills secured him the professorship of military history at Sandhurst.

In 1879 he was British commissioner involved in the delimitation of the frontiers of the Ottoman Empire and was awarded the Knight Commander of the Order of St Michael and St George. By 1882, he became a lieutenant-general and commanded the 2nd division of the expedition to Egypt, and led his troops in the Battle of Tel el-Kebir for which he received the KCB (Knight Commander of the Order of the Bath), the thanks of Parliament and the 2nd class of the Order of Osminieh. He became a conservative Member of Parliament for Birkenhead in 1885 until his death in 1893.

As well as this comprehensive book about the causes and the events of the war, which was reprinted ten times, he wrote his famous 'The Operations of War' in 1867, which became a military text-book and was praised by the German General Helmuth von Moltke. He also wrote pamphlets about national defence, contributed widely to many magazines and wrote novels.

Please note all original spellings and place names have been preserved.

The Editor.

CHAPTER I

EVENTS WHICH LED TO THE WAR IN THE CRIMEA

Why Russia covets Constantinople—Why other Powers oppose her Desire—Why the Time seemed Favourable—The Czar's Confidence in his Design—The Quarrel of the Churches—The Sultan accedes to the Czar's Claim—Russia puts forth Fresh Pretensions—The Vienna Note—Turkey declares War with Russia—How England was drawn into War—How the Czar was misled into War—His False View of the English Spirit—England supports Turkey—Why Louis Napoleon joined with England—Result of sending Allied Fleets to the Bosphorus—Russia chafes the Western Nations—France and England declare War—The War at first on the Danube—Austria's Summons to the Czar—The Russians leave the Danube—The Allies turn their Designs to the Crimea—Feeling excited in England.

IN CONSIDERING the Empire of Russia it might at first sight appear that a country at once so vast and so backward in civilisation would find ample employment for the wisest and most energetic ruler in endeavours to develop in all directions—physical, intellectual, and moral—its latent resources, rather than in the maintenance of great armies for designs of conquest. And that this course would greatly increase the wealth and influence of Russia, and the happiness of its people, cannot be doubted. But there are other considerations which have prevailed to dictate a policy of aggression.

In the first place, what we call progress is opposed to absolutism. If the immense populations of such vast portions of the earth were imbued with the ideas of the peoples of Europe, they would no longer submit to the will of one man; and when under these circumstances a Czar should become impossible, no one can say what kind of government, or what number of separate governments, might replace him. For the maintenance of his power it is necessary to keep the people ignorant, and, further, to divert their attention from their own lot by fixing it on the alluring spectacle of foreign conquests.

Yet, besides this motive, it must be confessed that a great temptation stands for ever before the eye of a Czar when he looks towards Turkey. He sees there all that Russia wants to give her power and prosperity commensurate with the extent of her dominion. He sees the beautiful harbours of the Bosphorus, whence a Russian navy, secured from all enemies by the narrow passage of the Dardanelles, might dominate the Mediterranean; and he sees, too, a city marked out by nature to become a splendid capital, and an overflowing emporium of commerce. Possessed of these, he need set no limit to his dreams of the greatness of Russia. It is not surprising, therefore, if a race of rulers, not less unscrupulous and ambitious than autocrats in general have proved to be, should always have looked on Constantinople as what ought to be their own.

Fortunately for Turkey, and the world, there are many difficulties in the way of the realisation of these aspirations. No other Power can desire that a rival should attain to such an overshadowing height. Neither England, nor France, nor Italy, nor Germany, could with indifference see Russia acquire such means of bringing her huge force to bear. And Austria has an interest beyond others in preventing the design. For Russia, if established in Turkey, would enclose within her new territory a large portion of the Austrian Empire, producing there a state of permanent insecurity and alarm, and would, moreover, include and control the lower Danube.

It is, therefore, only at some favourable conjuncture that Russia can hope to prosecute her cherished design. And in the beginning of 1853 circumstances seemed to be exceptionally promising. The Emperor of Austria, almost a boy, repaid with affection and reverence the kindness evinced for him by the potent and experienced autocrat. He was, too, under an obligation of the most onerous kind to his great neighbour, who, when Austria was almost crushed by Hungary, had intervened, suppressed the revolt, and restored the discontented kingdom to its allegiance. Moreover, the Kaiser had allowed himself just then to assume an attitude menacing to the Porte, for, in suppressing an insurrection in Montenegro, the Turkish troops, operating near the Austrian frontier, had received from him a peremptory notice to withdraw. The Czar had readily joined in enforcing the demand, and thus it happened that Austria found herself acting with Russia against Turkey—a position which illustrates the consequences that may ensue when a State allows itself to be drawn into trivial issues divergent from its main policy. Nicholas, therefore, assumed with confidence that he would meet with no opposition from the Kaiser.

Prussia's interest in the question was not so obvious or pressing as Austria's, while the King (the Czar's brother-in-law) had always expressed for him the utmost deference, a sentiment which was found to be a constant source of difficulty when endeavours were made for the concurrent action of the Four Great Powers.

As to France, it was not easy to foresee what policy might commend itself to Louis Napoleon. New to the throne, and engaged in feeling around for support in that as yet precarious seat, no indications were visible of the ·course to which his interests might incline him. But whatever his tendencies might prove to be, it seemed very unlikely that the Empire would begin its career as a belligerent either by singly opposing Russia, or by ranging itself against England, who, in the course of the summer, gave proof, in a great naval review, of her ability to bring a paramount influence into any military enterprise in which command of the sea would be a main condition.

Assuming, then, that Austria were favourable, or neutral, the course which England might take became the prime consideration. Hitherto she had done nothing to encourage the design of Russia, for to maintain Turkey as an independent state was her traditional policy. But, in the long interval of peace since Waterloo, not only had we given no sign of an intention to support that policy by force of arms, but we were believed to be absorbed as a people in those commercial pursuits of the success of which peace is one very favouring condition; while, as if to emphasise this supposed state of feeling, Lord Aberdeen, our Prime Minister, had become noted for his repugnance to any course which might tend to a resort to arms. The Czar was led by all these considerations to believe that the opportunity had come for giving effect to the idea which, during his visit to England in 1844, he had conveyed to the British Government. While expressing his conviction " that it was for the common interest of Russia and England that the Ottoman Porte should maintain itself in a condition of independence," yet "they must not conceal from themselves how many elements of dissolution that empire contains within itself: unforeseen circumstances may hasten its fall"; and thence he came to the conclusion that "the danger which may result from a catastrophe in Turkey will be much diminished if Russia and England have come to an understanding as to the course to be taken by them in common." It was in unison with these utterances that he addressed to Sir Hamilton Seymour, the British Ambassador at St Petersburgh, on the 9th of January 1853, the parable which has become historical.

Meanwhile, a cause of dispute already existed between Russia and Turkey. A jealousy had long been cherished between the monks of the Greek and Latin Churches in the Holy Land—which of these should enjoy most privilege and consideration was a question that, some little time before, had once more risen into prominence. Which of them should enter earliest in the day into the Church of the Holy Sepulchre at Jerusalem, or should have possession of the key of the Great Church of Bethlehem, were the questions of immediate

Prince Alexander Menschikoff, the Russian commander-in-chief in the Crimea.
Portrait painted in 1851 by Franz Krüger (1797-1857)

concern. The Czar took up warmly the cause of the Greek Church, of which he was the head, and which looked to him as its champion; and it may be urged in reply to those who look on the dispute as trivial, that it did not seem so to the Russian people, and, therefore, could not seem so to the Czar. The French Emperor had taken the side of the Latin Church. It is not to be supposed that he could be actuated by any superstitious, or even earnest, feeling in favour of such claims. But he was only following the policy pursued by the French monarchy in 1819, during a similar ferment of the question, when it claimed to act as the hereditary protector of the Catholics in the East since the time of Francis the First, and he must therefore be acquitted of taking his course merely from a desire to do what was hostile or provocative to Russia. Each of these sovereigns endeavoured to put pressure on the Sultan for a decision in favour of his own clients; and that hapless potentate, who could not be expected to evince any warmer sentiment than toleration towards either of the two infidel sects, which every true Mahometan must hold in abhorrence, made it his aim to satisfy both sovereigns, and offend neither. But his attempt, though clever, was ineffectual, and the result was that he only partially satisfied the Latin sect, while he excited such indignation, real or simulated, in the Czar, that Nicholas at once moved two army corps to the frontier of the Danubian Principalities as a menace, and immediately afterwards sent Prince Menschikoff as a Special Envoy to Constantinople, whose instructions must have been such as were quite inconsistent with a desire for an amicable settlement, for the British Ambassador described the language conveying his demands as "a mixture of angry complaints and friendly assurances, accompanied with peremptory requisitions as to the Holy Places in Palestine, indications of some ulterior views, and a general tone of insistence bordering sometimes on intimidation."

Thus the hostile menace was made to appear to turn on the matter of the Holy Places. But, in considering the origin of the war, it must not be forgotten that all the Czar professed to demand was the possession, and possibly the monopoly, of certain religious privileges, whereas the event which he desired to precipitate was something very different, and entirely disproportionate, namely, the dismemberment of Turkey. This was presently made plain when the Sultan put an end to the immediate dispute by acceding to the claims of Menschikoff. The question of the Holy Places, thus settled, could no longer supply the pretext for war; what it did supply was the opportunity for prolonging the quarrel, by confusing fresh demands with the original dispute, and for rousing religious feeling in Russia against Turkey. Accordingly, the Czar's Envoy, instead of accepting the concession as closing the dispute, put forth a fresh and larger pretension, requiring the Sultan to join in a convention which would virtually give Nicholas the protectorate of all the Christian subjects of the Porte. The nature of this demand was thus characterised by our Foreign Secretary, Lord Clarendon: "No sovereign, having proper regard for his own dignity and independence, could admit proposals which conferred upon another and more powerful sovereign a right of protection over his own subjects. Fourteen millions of Greeks would henceforth regard the Emperor as their supreme protector, and their allegiance to the Sultan would be little more than nominal, while his own independence would dwindle into vassalage." And, indeed, there was a terrible precedent to warn Turkey, for the Empress Catherine had claimed a similar protectorate in Poland, in which she had very soon found the means of extending her dominion over its territory.

The Sultan's Ministers, therefore, no doubt counselled and supported by our Ambassador, Lord Stratford, who exercised a control over our relations with Turkey of a singularly independent character, promptly refused to entertain Menschikoff's proposal. To this refusal the Czar responded by causing his troops, on the 2d of July, to pass the frontier river, the Pruth, and occupy the Danubian Principalities; and next day he issued a manifesto, stating that in doing so "it was not his intention to commence war, but to have such security as would ensure the restoration of the rights of Russia."

This invasion might have been justly met by the Sultan with a counter declaration of war, and the martial spirit of his people was so thoroughly roused as to render the step imminent. But the Western Powers, in their solicitude to preserve peace, stayed it for a moment, while the representatives of France, England, Austria, and Prussia, met in conference at Vienna, in the hope of finding a means of averting war. They framed a diplomatic instrument known as the Vienna Note, which, in their eagerness to soothe the Czar, was couched in terms that might be interpreted as sanctioning his pretensions, and which indeed (as the Austrian Government had taken means to ascertain) he would accept. On receiving this Note he at once signified his readiness to assent to it. The reply of the Turkish Government was not so speedily given, and the Mediatory Powers strongly urged it to signify acceptance. But when its reply came, it was found to point out that the Note could be construed as re-embodying the dangerous pretensions of the Czar, and that, unless certain specified modifications were introduced, the Porte must refuse its assent; while Lord Stratford advised his Government that these objections were well founded. This made fresh correspondence necessary, in the course of which it slipped out that the Russian interpretation of the Note confirmed the apprehensions of the Porte. The Mediatory Powers, at last aware of their singular error, perceived that their Note could be held to affirm new rights of interference on the part of Russia, and not merely (as the Czar had hitherto pretended) the confirmation of old privileges. They could no longer, therefore, support their original Note; the Czar, on his part, refused to accept the Turkish modifications of it, and the Porte felt itself compelled to demand the evacuation of the Principalities within fifteen days, with war as the alternative. This summons being disregarded, a state of war between the two countries ensued on the 23d October 1853; but for some time no acts of hostility took place beyond the assembly and movement of their respective forces.

The course of events that led to war between Russia and Turkey having been thus traced, it remains to follow the steps by which the Western Powers were drawn on to join in it. It has often been said that England drifted into the war. This was so far true that there was for us no sharp crisis, no clash of great national interests, which only the appeal to arms could compose. Our part in the war was the result of a state of feeling gradually aroused by observation of what was passing in the East, and of the steps which the British Government, with intentions anything but warlike, had slowly taken, tending to commit it to the active support of Turkey. Up to the time (after the issuing of the Turkish ultimatum) when the French and English fleets were ordered to move to the Bosphorus, it had been possible for England to restrict her part to the field of diplomacy. And that she should have committed herself to the side of Turkey was not due to her traditional policy only, for the ostensible grounds of quarrel between the two Eastern Powers were not such as necessarily to draw her from her attitude of mediator. What had impelled her on her course was the knowledge that below these grounds lurked the true design of the Czar. This had been made clear by his own words to the British Ambassador, already adverted to, and in various conversations in January and February 1853. "We have on our hands a sick man, a very sick man.... If your Government has been led to believe that Turkey retains any elements of existence, your Government must have received incorrect information. I repeat to you that the sick man is dying, and we can never allow such an event to take us by surprise. We must come to some understanding." But this view was not left to stand alone; it was enforced by an inducement. "I can only say, that if, in the event of a distribution of the Ottoman succession, upon the fall of the Empire, you should take possession of Egypt, I shall have no objection to offer. I would say the same thing of Candia: that island might suit you and I do not know why it should not become an English possession." The voice which uttered this was the voice of the one potentate who had an interest in precipitating the catastrophe, and who was then taking such a course as might immediately lead to it. Vain indeed the effort to spread his net in the sight of those whom he had thus himself enlightened. But it seems likely—indeed there is no other explanation—that he had forgotten, or dropped out of sight, this complete showing of his hand. As was natural in an autocrat whose faculty for rule lay in the strength of his will, not of his judgment, he had accustomed himself to confound what he desired with what he believed in; and absorbed for the moment in his parade of sympathy with the Christians in Turkey, he had come to consider this as his true motive, and expected others to adopt that view also. So complete was this illusion, that it was long before he had begun to realise the possibility of being opposed by England. At first he had assumed her toleration, if not her concurrence, to be certain. And even when he was at war with Turkey, and the fleets had been despatched to the Bosphorus, he sent an autograph letter to the Queen, expressing surprise that there should be any misunderstanding between the Queen's Government and his own as to the affairs of Turkey, and appealing to Her Majesty's "good faith" and "wisdom" to decide between them. Thus it is evident that it was Russia that had been the first Power to "drift" into war, and this was owing to the false view taken by the Czar. Starting with the belief that Turkey would be left unsupported, he had gone on to assume that he would, by the display of his forces, coerce her into compliance with the measure which would give him the means of, at any time, quarrelling with and crushing her, that England would acquiesce, and that, if she did, he might disregard the other Powers; and thus he had been led into a position from which he could not recede without war. And the delusion under which he took these steps contains one of the important lessons that render history of value as a guide and a warning. There is a general concurrence that he confided in the belief that England was entirely absorbed in the pursuit of wealth, through manufactures and commerce, and could no longer be induced to fight for a principle, a sentiment, or an ally. Even after Lord Aberdeen had been impelled to take action directly tending to war, the Czar still believed that a community which made the exaltation and worship of trade the mainspring of its policy, and which listened complacently to the denunciation of war as an unmixed evil, would never be roused into armed resistance to his projects. How far a more determined tone on the part of our Ministry, at an early stage of his course of aggression, would have effectually checked it, may be matter of speculation. But there can be no doubt, judging from his own language and his own acts, that his not unreasonable persuasion of the degeneracy of our national character was a main element in producing the state of mind which rendered him so fatally domineering and precipitate in the pursuit of his ends, and so regardless of the decencies of public law.

At the time of Menschikoff s mission, Lord Stratford, having resigned his post, was in England. But the difficulties which that mission was creating seemed again to demand his commanding influence on the spot, and he had been desired to resume his functions. The instructions given to him, conceived in a spirit of conciliation to Russia, in a matter which, on the surface, did not vitally concern us, were to admonish the Porte to show increased consideration for its Christian subjects. But, at the same time, remembering what lay under the surface, the Government empowered him, in case of imminent danger to Turkey, to request the Commander of our Mediterranean Squadron, then lying at Malta, to hold it in readiness to move, though he was not to call it up without orders from the Home Government. But when Menschikoff, on

The Battle of Sinope, 1853, by Ivan Aivazovsky (1817–1900)

the removal of his first grievance, put forth his other and more dangerous claim, the British Government perceived that it could no longer rest in any degree on the good faith of the Czar. At the end of May 1853, when Menschikoff departed from Constantinople, breathing war, Lord Clarendon instructed Lord Stratford that it was indispensable to take measures for the protection of the Sultan, and to aid him by force, if necessary, in repelling an attack upon his territory, and in defence of the independence of Turkey, which England, he declared, "was bound to maintain." At the same time, in a despatch to St Petersburgh, he required to be informed what object the Czar had in view, "and in what manner, and to what extent, the dominions of the Sultan, and the tranquillity of Europe were threatened?" A few days afterwards the Allied squadrons moved up the Mediterranean, and anchored in the neighbourhood of the Dardanelles, which the Sultan was bound by treaty to keep closed to the fleets of other Powers so long as Turkey was at peace. On the 22d October, the day before Turkey declared war, the fleets entered the Dardanelles. The Ambassadors had been instructed to call them up to Constantinople, "for the security of British and French interests, and, if necessary, for the protection of the Sultan." The step was precipitated by the apprehension of fanatical disturbances in the Turkish capital.

It has been generally assumed that the circumstances under which the French Empire had recently come into existence demanded that its chief should make war on somebody, in order to divert attention from the origin of his power, and to give employment to an army which might otherwise become dangerous. It may be readily granted that it was most expedient, both for him and his people, to make his influence immediately felt. But that, in allying himself with England on the Eastern question, he was seizing on an opportunity for war is only a surmise for which it would be difficult to adduce proof. It was inevitable that he should throw his weight into the question, and he could hardly hesitate, in his choice of a side. It was scarcely possible for the champion of the Latin Church in the East, who had just stood forth in defence of its claim, to abet the Czar in his demand for the protectorate of the Christian subjects of the Porte. Moreover, Nicholas, in his arrogant way, had given just offence both to Louis Napoleon and the French people by refusing to address him, as all other reigning potentates did, as "Mon Frere;" as if he, the choice of the French people, were not entitled to be admitted to the brotherhood of sovereigns; which was one of those gratuitous and unprofitable affronts which wise men are careful not to offer. On the other hand, the advantage was obvious of arraying himself by the side of, instead of against, the great Sea-Power his neighbour; while as for individual predilections he had acquired, in his long residence in England, a hearty esteem for our institutions and our people, and the kindnesses which he had received as an exile were always cordially acknowledged by him as a sovereign. But the evidence points altogether to the view that at first his design in associating himself with England was, while gaining the benefit of the alliance, to make use of it for peace, and not for war. Martin, in his Life of the Prince Consort, says, "Amity with England, and a close political alliance, had been uniformly declared to be the Emperor's dearest wish." On ascending the throne he had said, "Certain persons say the Empire is only war. But I say the Empire is peace, for France desires it." At the time of the Vienna Note, the Prince Consort, discussing the parties to it, said, "Louis Napoleon wishes for peace, enjoyment, and cheap corn." On the 8th August 1853 the Queen's speech said, "The Emperor of the French has united with Her Majesty in earnest endeavours to reconcile differences the continuation of which would involve Europe in war." And after the fleets were in the Bosphorus, the Prince Consort wrote: "Louis Napoleon shows by far the greatest statesmanship, which is easier for the individual than the many; he is moderate, but firm; gives way to us even when his plan is better than ours, and revels in the advantages he derives from the alliance with us." No conjectures can hold their ground against this testimony, and it may be taken for certain that the Emperor faithfully co-operated with our Government throughout in its endeavours to settle the quarrel by diplomatic pressure, backed by the display of force.

When, however, they took the last step of sending their fleets to the Bosphorus, the control of events passed out of their hands. If Russia should choose to disregard the moral pressure of their presence, and, resenting their entry into the Bosphorus, to avenge it on the Turks, the Allies could no longer preserve a mediatory attitude. They must become principals. This was foreseen by the Queen when she wrote thus to Lord Clarendon: "It appears to the Queen that we have taken on ourselves, in conjunction with France, all the risks of a European war, without having bound Turkey to any conditions with respect to provoking it." The justice of this view of the matter was presently made evident. The Turks, while keeping most of their fleet in the Bosphorus, had left a squadron of light war-vessels in the Black Sea. On the 30th November it was at anchor in the port of Sinope, when Admiral Nakimoff attacked it with six ships of the line, and absolutely destroyed it, with its crews to the number of 4000 men.

It is not necessary to argue that the Russians were exceeding their rights as belligerents in order to show the impolicy of this stroke. While the disparity of force deprived it of all glory, it roused public feeling, hitherto not too favourable to the Czar, to a pitch which, certainly in England, could only be appeased by arms. For long the English people had been chafing at the wrongs inflicted on the Turks, aggravated by the patience with which they were endured. Each successive step of the Czar had aroused deeper indignation. In the original difficulty, the position of the Sultan, pressed by such powerful rivals for an award which could bring him only unmitigated trouble, seemed to entitle him to special indulgence. But Menschikoff's bearing throughout his mission was arrogant and provocative. The setting up of the second pretext, on the failure of the first, revealed the real intention of grinding Turkey to dust. The seizure of the Principalities showed contempt for public law and common justice so gross that the popular mind could easily appreciate it. His manifestoes, outrageous in tone and matter, had been fuel to the flame; and now the crash at Sinope, under the very shadow of our ships, was of a character thoroughly to exasperate a people whose element was the sea. The French could probably in no case have endured to see their fleet return without some substantial triumph, but a reckless utterance of the Czar effectually roused them from what had hitherto been a somewhat supine view of the situation. The French Emperor had addressed to him, as a final attempt, a letter suggesting a scheme of pacification, and assuring him that if it were rejected the Western Powers must declare war. In his reply, among other taunts, Nicholas said, "Russia will prove herself in 1854 what she was in 1812." This allusion to the disasters in Russia, so ruinous to the first Napoleon's power, and so humiliating to France, effectually dispelled the apathy of the French people.

When Louis Napoleon proposed to our Government that the fleets should enter the Black Sea, and if necessary compel all Russian ships met with

Russian ships at the battle of Sinope, 1853. Painting by Ivan Konstantinovich Aivazovsky

there to return to Sebastopol, the measure hardly kept pace with the feelings aroused in both countries. On the 27th February 1854 France and England demanded the evacuation of the Principalities by the 30th April as their ultimatum. No answer was vouchsafed, and a in March they declared war. If any further stimulus had been needed for the British people, it was now supplied in the publication of the Czar's conversations with Sir Hamilton Seymour, hitherto held in official secrecy. His parable of the sick man then proved much more striking and suggestive than he could have desired. It caught the popular fancy—it was seen to have indicated a foregone conclusion—and he who could foretell the sick man's dissolution, and arrange for the distribution of his possessions, was judged to have been intent ever since on fulfilling his own prophecy.

At this time everything pointed to a campaign on the Danube. When the Turks declared war, the Russians in the Principalities, not yet ready to advance, remained on the defensive along the river. Omar Pasha, facing them, crossed and seized Kalafat, and desultory combats, much more calculated to exalt the military repute of the Turks than of the Russians, had gone on there during the autumn and winter. But it was obvious that it could serve no purpose to the Czar that it must rather destroy his military along with his diplomatic repute, to let the war drag on in this way. Accordingly, by May 1854 Russian troops had been concentrated in the Principalities in sufficient force to begin an offensive movement. The preliminaries to the passage of the Balkans, in the march on Constantinople, were to be the sieges of the Turkish fortresses of Silistria and Shumla; and the invasion of

Turkey began with the passage of the Danube by the Russians, who opened their first parallel before Silistria on the 19th May. Thus it happened that the troops of England and France, as they arrived in Turkish waters, were at first conveyed to Varna, and were now encamped between that place and Shumla, in the expectation of defending the fortresses by fighting the army in the field. But now another influence intervened, which entirely changed the aspect of the war.

On the 13th January 1854 the Four Powers, none of them at that time at war with Russia, had obtained the agreement of Turkey to fresh terms to be submitted to the Czar, and were sending back his envoys with an avowal of their intention to oppose his acts of aggression. Kinglake says that Nicholas had been so slow to believe that the young Kaiser could harbour the thought of opposing him in arms, that on receiving the assurance of their alienation he was wrung with grief. This is a fresh proof that his autocratic temper had been so fostered by long exercise of irresponsible power that he could no longer read facts truly where his wishes were strongly concerned; that he believed only what he desired to believe; and that his faith in the friendship of the Kaiser, and the pacific temper of England, had been of paramount effect in blinding him to the difficulties in his path. Well might the Prince Consort write, just after Sinope, "the Emperor of Russia is manifestly mad."

On the 3d of June, Austria, with the support now finally secured of Prussia, summoned the Czar to evacuate the Principalities. In February she had moved 50,000 men up to the frontier of the territory seized by the Czar. Her territorial position on the north bank of the Danube is such as to enable her effectually to check a Russian invasion of Turkey in that direction. The operation can only be persisted in by first repelling the Austrian advance. For this the Czar was not pre-pared. He continued his operations on the river just long enough to give a victorious aspect to the valiant defence of Silistria, and to a subsequent passage of the Danube at Giurgevo by the Turks, led by English officers. Austria was on the point of war, and had sent an officer to the English headquarters to form a joint plan of operations, when the Czar at last perceived that the pressure on him could not be resisted. The siege of Silistria was raised; the Russians immediately began to withdraw from the Principalities, and on the 2d August they recrossed the frontier. The Austrian troops thereupon occupied, in the interests of Turkey, the territories thus abandoned.

Now Austria did not then, or afterwards declare war against Russia. But, as has been related, France and England had done so in March. It may be, and has been, said that had the Western Powers gone step by step with Austria, leaving it to her, who had most concern in a war on the Danube, to give the word for the commencement of hostilities, the Czar would, as the event proved, have been forced to abandon his prey and the final settlement of the quarrel between him and Turkey might still have been effected by negotiation. It is impossible to deny this, but at the same time it is impossible absolutely to affirm it. For no negotiations could have been satisfactory which did not provide some compensation for Turkey; and it is very unlikely that the Czar would have conceded this without the compulsion of arms. But the determining cause may well have been the savage blow delivered at Sinope, which roused the impatience of the Western peoples to a pitch beyond control.

But now, with the abandonment of the Principalities, that which had hitherto been the ground of contention had suddenly vanished, and with it had vanished also the immediate concern in the quarrel of Austria and Prussia, whose alliance for the coercion of the Czar had been formed expressly "in defence of the interests of Germany." But English views had for long gone against the acceptance of a drawn game. To withdraw the Allied fleets from the Euxine without having fired a shot, while its waters were still strewed with the wrecks of the Turkish ships; to leave the shores of Turkey unprotected, while opposite to them stood the embodied menace of Sebastopol, with its forts and arsenal, from whence had just issued the destroying squadron; and to abandon the Ottoman Empire to the impulses of so grasping, so unscrupulous, and so vindictive a personality as that of Nicholas, had not in this latter period been included within the range of possibilities. On the first declaration of war the French Emperor had sketched, and our Ministry had approved, a plan for the attack of Sebastopol. "In no event," said Lord Lyndhurst in June, "except that of extreme necessity, ought we to make peace without previously destroying the Russian fleet in the Black Sea, and laying prostrate the fortifications by which it is defended." On the 24th July the Times wrote, "the broad policy of the war consists in striking at the very heart of the Russian power in the East, and that heart is at Sebastopol." And its editor, Mr. John Delane, who had gone to Constantinople to observe events, told Lord Stratford that if our army were to perish before Sebastopol, the first thought of the nation at home would be to raise another, and go on. And this state of feeling had been aroused by the sense entertained in this country of the dangerous nature of the Czar's designs, and of the dishonesty which had marked his pursuit of them. "It is," wrote the Queen, in discussing the causes of the war, "the selfishness, and ambition, and want of honesty of one man and his servants which has done it." Such were the circumstances in which France and England prepared to transfer their armaments from Turkey to the Crimea.

CHAPTER II

THE LANDING IN THE CRIMEA

Prospect of the Invasion—Instructions to the British Commander—A Siege contemplated—Preparations for Invasion—The Cholera— The Fleets and Flotillas—Composition of the English Army—Its Commanders—The French Generals—Description of the Crimea—Its Products and Population—The Coast reconnoitered—The Landing Place—The Troops landed—Transport obtained.

THE LAND which the armies were about to invade was that known to the ancients as the Tauric Chersonese. It was quite beyond the range of the ordinary tourist; it led to nowhere, and had little to tempt curiosity. Thus it was as completely an unknown country to the chiefs of the Allied armies as it had been to Jason and his Argonauts when they voyaged thither in search of the Golden Fleece. It was known to contain a great harbour, and a city with docks, fortifications, and arsenal; but the strength and resources of the enemy who would oppose us, the nature of the fortifications, and even the topography, except what the map could imperfectly show, lay much in the regions of speculation. It was believed, however, that any Russian force there must be inferior to that of the Allies, that the country would offer no serious impediments to the march, and that, with the defeat of the defensive army, the place would not long resist the means of attack which would be brought to bear on it There was no thought of a protracted siege; a landing, a march,-a battle, and, after some delay for a preliminary bombardment, an assault, were all that made part of the programme.

These anticipations were by no means so ill-founded as, after the many contradictions by the event, they were judged to have been. It was unlikely that a large Russian army should be permanently kept in a spot not easy of approach by land, and where its supply would be difficult, at a time when Sebastopol was not imminently threatened; and, since the sudden cessation of operations on the Danube, there had been little time for preparation against so formidable an attack as was now impending. The command of the sea conferred on the assailants inestimable advantages, and there was very fair reason to expect that, long before Russia could bring her huge numbers to bear, the conflict would be decided in closed lists by the armies which should at first enter them. In any case, it would have been very difficult to point to any more vulnerable spot on Russian territory.

It must not, however, be thought that no siege of Sebastopol was contemplated. Immediately after the Russians had retreated from the Danube, the Duke of Newcastle, Secretary for War, wrote thus to the Commander of the British Forces, on the 29th June 1854:—

"I have to instruct your Lordship to concert measures for the siege of Sebastopol, unless, with the information in your possession, but at present unknown in this country, you should be decidedly of opinion that it could not be undertaken with a reasonable prospect of success. The confidence with which Her Majesty placed under your command the gallant army now in Turkey is unabated, and if, upon mature reflection, you should consider that the united strength of the two armies is insufficient for this undertaking, you are not to be precluded from the exercise of the discretion originally vested in you, though Her Majesty's Government will learn with regret that an attack from which such important consequences are anticipated must be any longer delayed.

"The difficulties of the siege of Sebastopol appear to Her Majesty's Government to be more likely to increase than diminish by delay; and as there is no prospect of a safe and honourable peace until the fortress is reduced, and the fleet taken or destroyed, it is, on all accounts, most important that nothing but insuperable impediments, such as the want of ample preparations by either army, or the possession by Russia of a force in the Crimea greatly outnumbering that which can be brought against it, should be allowed to prevent the early decision to undertake these operations. . . .

"It is probable that a large part of the Russian army now retreating from the Turkish territory may be poured into the Crimea to reinforce Sebastopol. If orders to this effect have not already been given, it is further probable that such a measure would be adopted as soon as it is known that the Allied armies are in motion to commence active hostilities. As all communications by sea are now in the hands of the Allied Powers, it becomes of importance to endeavour to cut off all communication by land between the Crimea and the other parts of the Russian dominions."

This despatch had been preceded by a private letter containing this passage:—

"The Cabinet is unanimously of opinion that, unless you and Marshal St Arnaud feel that you are not sufficiently prepared, you should lay siege to Sebastopol, as we are more than ever convinced that, without the reduction of this fortress, and the capture of the Russian fleet, it will be impossible to conclude an honourable and safe peace. The Emperor of the French has expressed his entire concurrence in this opinion, and, I believe, has written privately to the Marshal to that effect."

A siege, then, was in the programme, but it is certain that even a probability that it would last through the J winter would have put an end to the project.

While awaiting embarkation, the troops were employed in making fascines and gabions for the siege works, the material for which, abundantly supplied by the woods around them, might not be found on the plains before Sebastopol; and great quantities of these were collected, ready for conveyance, on the south side of Varna Bay.

It was at this time, while the armies were expecting to begin the enterprise, that the cholera broke out among them. Cases had occurred among the French troops while on the voyage from Marseilles; the pest followed them to their camps, and late in July it reached the British army. Out of three French divisions, it destroyed or disabled 10,000 men and our own regiments in Bulgaria lost between five and six hundred. It then attacked the fleets, which put to sea in hopes of thus baffling it, but it pursued them, and reduced some ships almost to helplessness. This was a main reason, among others, why the stroke, which could not be dealt too swiftly, was delayed.

Meanwhile the preparations went on. In order that the guns might be available immediately on landing, it was desirable that they should be conveyed complete as for action, and, to this end, boats, united in pairs, were fitted with platforms bearing the guns ready mounted on their carriages; and steamers were bought and chartered for the transport of other material. And now the naval resources of England showed forth in their superiority. The French, in default of sufficient transport, crowded their war-ships with troops, thus unfitting them for battle; so did the Turks; while the sea was covered with the small sailing-vessels of both loaded with material. But in one great compact flotilla of transports, in which the steamers were numerous enough to lend the propelling power to all, a British force, of all arms, namely, four divisions of infantry, the Light Brigade of cavalry and sixty guns, with all that was necessary to fight a battle, was embarked; and our war-ships, thus preserving all their efficiency, were left in condition to engage the enemy's should they issue from Sebastopol.

It was at Varna that the huge multitudinous business of embarkation went on. Piers had been improvised by the engineers, but of course the operation was accomplished under difficulties vastly greater than would have been met with in home ports. The troops moved down slowly from their camps; the poison in the air caused a general sickliness, and the men were so enfeebled that their knapsacks were borne for them on packhorses during even a short march of five or six miles, all they could at once accomplish. As they were embarked, they sailed for the general rendezvous in the Bay of Balchick, about fifteen miles north of Varna. The mysterious scourge still pursued them on board ship, and added a horrible feature to the period of detention, for the corpses, sunk with shot at their feet, after a time rose to the surface, and floated upright, breast high, among the ships, the swollen features pressing out the blankets or hammocks which enwrapped them.

After all were assembled, an adverse wind still delayed them: but on the 7th September the whole armament got under weigh in fine weather. Each great British merchant steamer wheeled round till in position to attach the tow-rope to a sailing transport (most of these were East Indiamen of the largest class), and then again wheeled till the ship in rear attached itself to a second; then all wheeled into their destined positions for the voyage. They were formed in five columns, each of thirty vessels, and each distinguished by a separate flag; and the five columns carried the four divisions of infantry, with their artillery, namely, the Light, the First, Second, and Third, complete, and the Light Brigade of cavalry. Few sights more beautiful could be seen than the advance, and the manoeuvres which preceded it, of this orderly array of ships, all among the largest in existence, on the calm blue waters, under the bright sky. The French and Turks, notwithstanding the use of their men-of-war for transport, were unable to carry any cavalry. Our flotilla was commanded and escorted by Admiral Sir Edmund Lyons in the Agamemnon. Our naval Commander-in-Chief, Admiral Dundas, directed the British Force that was held ready to engage the enemy, including ten line-of-battle ships, two screw-steamers, two fifty-gun frigates, and thirteen smaller steamers carrying powerful guns. The French fleet numbered fifteen line-of-battle ships and ten or twelve war-steamers, and the Turkish eight line-of-battle ships and three war-steamers.

The Russian fleet had, since the first entry of the Allies into the Black Sea, remained in the fortified harbour of Sebastopol. It consisted of fifteen sailing line-of-battle-ships, some frigates and brigs, one powerful steamer, the Vladimir, and eleven of a lighter class. Considering the encumbered condition of the French and Turkish squadrons, it seems clear that if, with a fair wind and good officers, the Russian armament had issued from its shelter, it might in a bold attack (though of course at heavy cost) have inflicted tremendous havoc on the transports and troops.

It is to be noted that the Fourth Division of infantry, the Heavy Brigade of cavalry, and five or six thousand baggage horses belonging to the English army, were still at Varna awaiting embarkation, and the siege train was also there in the ships which had brought it from England. Of these the greater part of the Fourth Division was immediately embarked, and landed in the Crimea in time to advance with the army.

Our five infantry divisions were formed each of two brigades, each brigade of three regiments, and each division numbered about 5000.

The First Division was commanded by the Duke of Cambridge, and was formed of the brigade of Guards, viz., a battalion each of the Grenadiers, Scots Guards, and Coldstream, under General Bentinck; and the 42d, 79th, and 93d Highlanders, under Sir Colin Campbell; with two field batteries.

The Second Division was commanded by Sir De Lacy Evans, and composed of the brigades of Penne-father, 30th, 55th, 95th, and Adams, 41st, 47th, 49th; with two field batteries.

The Third Division was under Sir Richard England, with Brigadiers Campbell and Eyre, 1st, 38th, 50th; 4th, 28th, 44th regiments; with two field batteries.

The Fourth Division was at first incomplete, its 46th and 57th regiments being still en route. It was under Sir George Cathcart, having the 20th, 21st, 63d, 68th regiments, and the first battalion of the Rifle Brigade; with one field battery.

The Light Division was commanded by Sir George Brown, with the 7th, 23d, and 33d, under General Codrington; and the 19th, 77th, and 88th, under General Buller; also the second battalion of the Rifle Brigade; with one troop of horse artillery, and one field battery.

The Light Brigade of cavalry, under Lord Cardigan, included the 4th and 13th Light Dragoons, the 8th and 11th Hussars, and the 17th Lancers; with one troop of horse artillery.

Lord Raglan, Commander of the English Army, was sixty-six years old. He had served on Wellington's staff, and lost his arm at Waterloo. Since those days his sole military experience had been in the office of Military Secretary at the Horse Guards. He was so far well acquainted with military business, but he had never held any command, and while no opportunity had been afforded to him of directing troops in war, his life, for forty years, had been no adequate preparation for it. But he was a courteous, dignified, and amiable man, and his qualities and rank were such as might well be of advantage in preserving relations with our Allies.

Sir George Brown had distinguished himself in the Peninsula as an officer of the famous Light Division— the reason, perhaps, for now giving him the command of it—and had been severely wounded at Bladensburg; since when his military life, like his chiefs, had been passed chiefly n office work. He had held many posts, including that of Adjutant-General at the Horse Guards.

Sir De Lacy Evans had a brilliant record from the Peninsular, American, and Waterloo campaigns, and had been Commander of the British Legion in Spain in two very honourable campaigns and many battles.

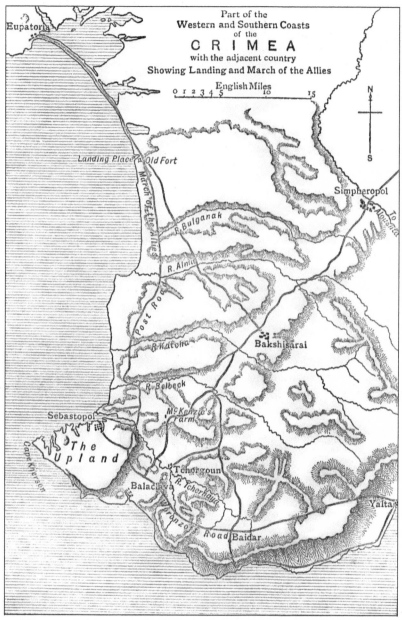

Map no. 1. Part of the western and southern coasts of the Crimea with the adjacent country,
showing landing and march of the Allies.

Sir George Cathcart had in his youth, as aide-de-camp to his father, British Commissioner with the Russian Army, been present at the chief battles in 1813. He was also on Wellington's staff at Quatre Bras and Waterloo. He was favourably known as the writer of commentaries on the campaigns of 1812 and 1813 in Russia and Germany; he had commanded various regiments of cavalry and infantry; and, as Governor of the Cape, had recently conducted successful campaigns against the Kaffirs and the Basutos. On these grounds, his reputation stood so high that a "dormant commission" had been given to him, entitling him to command the army in case Lord Raglan should cease to do so.

Of the Brigadier-Generals the best known was Sir Colin Campbell, who had established a great reputation as a commander of large forces in our Indian wars, after very honourable service in the Peninsula.

Most of the French generals had seen much active service in Algeria. St Arnaud was a gallant man, experienced in the warfare suited to that country, but frothy and vainglorious in a notable degree—and much too anxious to represent himself as taking the chief part to be a comfortable ally.

Though part of the English army had seen service in India, though a large portion of the French troops had made campaigns in Algeria, and though the Russians had for years carried on a desultory war in Circassia, yet the long European peace had left them all with little except a traditional knowledge of civilised war. No change of method had taken place since the Napoleonic era. But the British and French had both abandoned the musket for the rifle, ours being the Minié; both it and the French arm were muzzle-loaders; some Russian regiments had a rifle, but a large proportion of them were still armed with the old brass-bound musket which had served them throughout the century; the artillery also of all remained as before.

As the fleets sailed eastward from Varna across the Black Sea, their course was crossed at right angles by the coast on which they were to land, and of which they might almost be said to, know as little as knight-errants, heroes of the romances beloved by Don Quixote, knew of the dim, enchanted region where, amid vague perils, and trusting much to happy chance, they were to seek and destroy some predatory giant.

Crim Tartary, better known now as the Crimea, forms part of the Government of Taurida, a province of Southern Russia. From the coast of the Euxine it stretches southward, as an extensive peninsula, into the midst of that sea. Its neck is the Isthmus of Perekop, five miles wide, and its length from thence to Balaklava at its southern end is, in direct line, 120 miles. All the northern and middle portion is a flat and arid steppe, where are sprinkled at wide intervals small villages inhabited by Tartars, whose possessions are flocks and herds; but the remaining and southern end of the peninsula is different indeed in aspect, and in climate. Here begins a mountain region sheltering from the northern blasts the slopes and hollows, the lesser hills of which, covered with pine and oak, enclose valleys of bounteous fertility. Multitudes of wild flowers spring up amid the tall grass; the fig, the olive, the pomegranate and the orange flourish, and the vine is cultivated with success on the southern slopes. The seaward end runs out into capes resting upon high cliffs, and is indented on its western side by the deep and sheltered harbour of Sebastopol, which, as the chief and indeed only large and safe harbour of the Black Sea, had by the work of generations been converted into a great arsenal and dockyard, defended towards the sea by strong forts, and affording ample anchorage for the Black Sea fleet, and around these works had sprung up a city. The area of the whole peninsula is nearly twice that of Yorkshire, and its population at the time of the invasion numbered something short of 200,000. Going along the road from Sebastopol to Perekop, the first considerable town reached, sixteen miles distant, is Bakshisarai, "the Garden Pavilion," and in another sixteen miles, where the road quits the hills for the steppe, is Simpheropol, the nominal capital. The part of the country with which the reader has at present to do is included in a parallelogram, one side of which is a line outside the western coast from Eupatoria to the level of Balaklava, and the opposite side passes through the hill region, south from Simpheropol to the sea.

In this region the mountains have subsided into hill ranges of some 400 feet high, and through these the watershed pours five streams flowing westward into the Black Sea, all of which formed features in the campaign. The first of these is the muddy rivulet called the Bulganak; seven miles south of it is the valley of the Alma (Apple River); another space of seven miles divides the Alma from the Katcha; four miles further the Belbek is reached; and five miles from that the Tchernaya, northwesterly in its course, flows into and forms the head of the harbour of Sebastopol.

The distance from Varna to Eupatoria is about 300 miles. The armament arrived on the 9th at the rendezvous first assigned, "forty miles west of Cape Tarkan." It remained anchored there throughout the 10th, while Lord Raglan and General Canrobert, with the Commanding Engineer, Sir John Burgoyne, and other English and French officers, naval and military, reconnoitered the coast for a landing-place, and observed its character throughout. At dawn, in a swift steamer, the Caradoc, escorted by the Agamemnon, they were off Sebastopol, and could look through the entrance of the inlet upon the forts, the ships, and the city; then, rounding Cape Kherson, they passed the cliffs on which stood the plateau destined to bear the camps of the besiegers, and arrived off the inlet of Balaklava, deep down between its two ancient high-perched forts. Then, turning back north, they took note of the rivers already enumerated, from the Belbek to the Bulganak, and the coast thence to Eupatoria, when the space for the landing was fixed on, south of that town, in Kalamita Bay. All the 11th and 12th the Turkish and French fleets, great part of which was not propelled, as was ours, by steam, were drawing together, and on the 13th nearly all were opposite the beach, while those still at sea were coming on with a fair wind.

The considerations which had been main elements in the question of the selection of a point of disembarkation were, first, a space sufficient for the armies to land together, and in full communication with each other; and secondly, that the ground should be such as the fire of the ships could protect from the possible enterprises of the enemy. Ship's guns are so formidable in size and range that no batteries capable of rapid motion can hope to contend with them. No ground fulfilling these conditions was found on the southern coast; where the cliffs stand up steep and high out of the water, nor did the mouths of the rivers afford the necessary advantages. On the other hand, the western coast north of Sebastopol offered no harbour of which the armies could make a secure base, or even a temporary depot; while, south of Sebastopol, the inlet of Balaklava, though small, was deep and well-sheltered, where large steamers could unload close to the shore, and the small bay of Kamiesch was capable of being made a base. These facts will tend to throw light on some questions raised during the progress of the war.

The piece of beach selected to land on, five or six miles north of the Bulganak, was very happily adapted for the purpose.

Two small lakes at the foot of the sea-banks are separated from the sea by strips of beach, and from these strips roads went up the banks. Thus, when the troops were landed here, no attack could be made on them (by night, let us suppose) except by penetrating into the narrow and easily defended space between the lakes and the sea; while, on the other hand, full facilities existed for their movement to the plains above. Here the disembarkation, quite unopposed, began on the 14th, the French and Turks landing about two miles lower down the coast, on a similar strip. In the afternoon a ground swell arose, to a degree so violent that many boats were hurled on the strand, and several rafts were dashed to pieces, the troops, drenched with rain, making fires of the fragments. Next day the surf abated, but it was not till the 18th that the whole of the forces were landed, and in condition to advance.

The Fourth Division having arrived and landed, the British force numbered about 26,000 infantry, sixty guns, and the Light Brigade of cavalry, about 1000 sabres. The French had 28,000 infantry, and the Turks 7000, with sixty-eight guns, but with no cavalry. In order that the men might march lightly, especially when so many were still low in strength from the effects of the atmosphere, the knapsacks of the British were left on board ship, the more indispensable articles being taken from them and carried by the soldier, wrapped in the blanket which was to cover him at night. No tents were landed except for the sick and for general officers. Except such part of the pack-horses as could be conveyed in the flotilla, there was no transport landed, but some convoys of the enemy were intercepted, and a number of country vehicles were procured from the Tartars. In this way were collected 350 arabas (the waggons of the country, a rude framework of poles surmounting the axle), and a thousand cattle and sheep, with poultry, barley, fruit, and vegetables.

CHAPTER III

BATTLE OF THE ALMA

Operations open to the Russians—The Bulganak reached—The Valley of the Alma—The Russian Bank—Omissions of the Russian Commanders—The French ascend the Heights—Position in Front of the British—Russian Forces there—Delay to allow French to gain Heights—English ordered to advance—First Onset of the English—The Light and Second Divisions—The Russian Heavy Guns withdrawn—Our First Onset fails—Advance of the Guards and Highlanders—English Artillery in the Action—General Retreat of the Russians—The Losses—Tactical Views of the Battle—General Advance wanting in ensemble—The Cavalry.

O N THE 19th the advance of the armies began. The French were on the right, next the sea. The fact that we had cavalry and they had none indicated the inland flank as ours. The four French divisions were ranged in lozenge form, the apex heading south for Sebastopol, the four points marked each by a division with its guns; and in the space thus enclosed were the Turks, and the convoy of provisions; ammunition, and baggage. The British were formed in two columns of divisions, that next the French of the Second Division followed by the Third; the other of the Light Division followed by the First and Fourth; the batteries on the right of their respective divisions. The formation of the divisions was that of double companies from the centre, giving them the means of forming with readiness either to the front or the left flank, which was also the object of placing three of the five divisions in the left column. If the Russians, after leaving a sufficient garrison in Sebastopol, were to keep an army in the field, it might, from its natural line of communication with Southern Russia, namely, the road thither by Bakshisarai and Simpheropol, assume a front at right angles to the front of the Allies, and advancing thus, might attack either their flank or rear without risk to its own. On this account, also, the Cavalry Brigade was divided, two of its regiments covering the front, the other two the left flank, while the fifth closed the rear. If the Russians were to threaten that flank, the three divisions of our left column would be the first to confront them, with the other two in second line, while the French and Turks must come up on their right, or left, or both, according to the direction of the Russian attack, and with fair

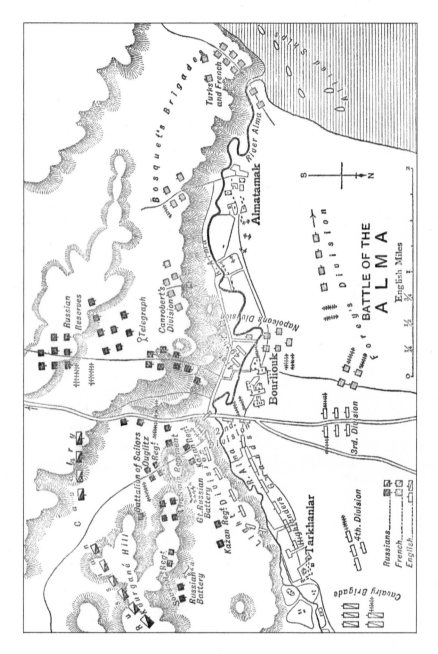

Map no 2.
The Battle of
the Alma

chance, on those open plains, of meeting it in time, and also, if forced to retreat with their backs to the sea, they might expect effectual support from their ships. But, at the best, persistent attacks on this side by the Russians, with such a wide space to manoeuvre on at pleasure, and with cavalry in superior force (as, with our deficiency in that arm, it was certain to be) would greatly, perhaps decisively, embarrass our advance unless we should succeed in inflicting on the enemy a crushing defeat.

The combined armies, then, were moving, in sufficiently compact formation, straight for Sebastopol, about twenty-five miles distant from the starting point of the British; through their front ran the post-road to that city from Eupatoria; but roads were needless, for the ground was everywhere smooth, firm, grassy, and quite unenclosed. In rear of the divisions moved the cattle, sheep, the close array of arabas, and the pack-mules with the reserve ammunition, while the cavalry regiment in rear kept all in motion. In this order the Bulganak, an insignificant sluggish stream, was reached early in the afternoon. It was while our divisions were crossing its bridge that they first saw the enemy. A force of the three arms, about 2000 cavalry, 6000 infantry, and two batteries of artillery, was drawn up among the hills, at some distance beyond the stream; insufficient for a battle, but capable of an action with an advanced guard. It appeared to have been brought there only to effect an armed reconnaissance, for after a short and distant exchange of shots with our foremost batteries, with some trifling loss on either side, it retired without any noteworthy collision of foot or horse. The army thereupon bivouacked on the stream (for the sake of water), with its front some hundred yards on the further bank; the British right wing parallel to the stream, and the left thrown back to the rivulet, in case of an attack on that side. But it passed the night unmolested.

Next morning, the 20th, the troops were under arms early, but did not move for some time. Marshal St Arnaud, returning from a visit to Lord Raglan, passed along our front; a tall, thin, sharp-visaged man, reduced by illness, but alert and soldier-like, and manifestly much pleased as he saluted our ranks in return for the cheers with which they greeted him. In less than ten days he was a dead man.

Between nine and ten o'clock the army moved forward, surmounting a succession of grassy ridges. It was well known that we were to try conclusions with the Russians that day. About noon a steamer, coasting along on our flank, began to fire towards the land, just where a sharp, steep cliff ended the shore, and where, in fact, was the mouth of the Alma. When the British surmounted the next ridge, they looked down on the arena of battle.

The valley of the Alma lay before them, at the foot of a smooth, sloping plain. The river, as it flows at the foot of this plain, makes somewhat of an angle, enclosing the Allies; and the apex just marks the junction of the French left with the English right. Just within the apex is the village of Bourliouk, and noting that as the place where the two Allied armies touched, the share of each in the battle becomes clear.

The ground on the Russian bank was, as befitted a defensive position, much more difficult and commanding than on the other. Beginning at the sea, for more than a mile and a half thence up the stream, there rises close to it a perpendicular rocky wall, as if the sea-cliff were bent backward. Then comes another mile where the cliffs have receded somewhat, and subsided into hills, still steep and difficult, though not forbidding ascent. Near the mouth of the Alma the stream was fordable, and from thence a path led up the cliff.

Three-quarters of a mile up the stream from its mouth there is on the Allies' bank the village of Alma Tamack; and opposite this a cleft in the cliff allows of a road practicable for guns, which ascends the heights. A mile further up is a farm, opposite which the cliff has subsided and receded, and here is another road. Finally, at another half mile up the stream, a few hundred yards to the right of the village of Bourliouk, where, on the Russian side, the hills have still receded and become more practicable, another road crosses, ascending the heights to a telegraph tower. Everywhere, the hills, whether standing up in cliffs, as near the sea, or receding from the stream, were the buttresses which supported on their tops a high plain stretching away towards the next river that crossed our line of march on Sebastopol.

The part of the stream thus described marks the front of the French and Turks, who may be said to have faced south-south-west.

The other face of the angle made by the stream marks the British front, which may be said to have faced south-south-east. And now the character of the Russian side of the river changes materially. Here the crest line has receded much farther back, and the ground is easy of ascent for all arms. Just opposite the centre of the British front it shoots up to a pinnacle, called the Kourgané Hill, from the sides of which long, smooth, wide slopes descend to the river. The one of these which chiefly concerns us, that on our right front, is broken in its even descent from the summit by a high knoll surmounted by a terrace, at some hundred yards from the river. Remembering that ground is good for defence, not so much because of the difficulties it opposes to movement, as because of the facilities it affords for bringing the fire of the defenders to bear on the assailants, and for counter-attacks, it will be understood why Menschikoff had occupied this part of his line most strongly both with infantry and artillery.

The great post-road from Eupatoria to Sebastopol, on each side of which the British had been marching, passes the river by a bridge a little to the left of the apex of the angle formed by the stream, and then ascends to the plateau, through the hollow between the Telegraph Hill on the right and the Kourgané Hill on the left. There was good reason for Menschikoff to take position across the road. But in doing so he had of course to consider what extent of ground was suited to his force, very inferior to that of the Allies. Bearing in mind the inaccessible nature of the cliffs, and also that troops ascending them would be very near the edge of the precipitous face above the sea—remembering too that the ships, as he presently found, could throw their big projectiles on to that part of the ground—he massed the chief part of his force about the Kourgané slopes, and nearly all the remainder between the Sebastopol road and the Telegraph Hill. And this arrangement would have been so far unimpeachable had he done what he easily could have done to debar the enemy from the roads leading up the cliffs, either by breaking them up, or by placing works at the points where they reached the plateau. With the aid of other fieldworks on his front and flanks he might have justly considered himself as occupying, despite his inferior numbers, a strong position for the direct defence of Sebastopol. But no such means were taken of adding to the strength of the ground, for the two bits of trench work made by him were not intended as defences.

A halt of some length was made by the Allies on coming in sight of the enemy, while Lord Raglan and St Arnaud, moving out to the front, concerted the general order of the attack. When the advance was ordered, about one o'clock, it was begun by Bosquet's division, which was next the sea, and faced the cliffs. After laying down their knapsacks, one of his brigades crossed the Alma near its mouth, and ascended the path there, followed by the Turks; and the other entered the road through the cliff opposite Alma Tamack, by which passed also the divisional artillery. At the same time French ships near the mouth of the stream threw their projectiles on to the plateau, the surface of which they could see. The remainder of the French forces followed in a line of columns at some considerable distance in rear of Bosquet. Next to his division was Canrobert's, which entered the road opposite the farm, and debouched on the plateau nearly a mile west of the Telegraph; but he was obliged to send his guns by the road followed by Bosquet's left brigade. Next to Canrobert's came Prince Napoleon's division, and behind both was Forey's in second line. All these troops then were directed on the right face of the angle formed by the stream, and all were on the right of the post-road to Sebastopol. The ground may be at once cleared for the battle by saying that Bosquet's right brigade and the Turks, passing at the mouth of the stream, found themselves far from the enemy, on whom they never fired a shot; and his other brigade was a mile west of Canrobert's division, which, it has been said, was nearly a mile from the Telegraph, while all its artillery was following Bosquet's left brigade. Prince Napoleon's division bore directly on the ground immediately around the Telegraph. All this makes it plain that a little engineering science on the part of Menschikoff would have almost neutralised the action of the French and Turks in the battle. As it was, the chief result achieved by St Arnaud was that he gained a position threatening Menschikoff s left flank at the moment when his front was assailed by the English.

The British divisions moved down abreast of the French, at first in column formation, the Second Division on the right, the Light Division on the left, in first line: the Second followed by the Third, the Light by the First, in second line, and the Fourth in echelon in rear of the left. Beyond the left moved four regiments of the Light Brigade, while the remaining one closed the rear. As they advanced, the Russian forces became more clearly discernible, as did also the ground our line was to occupy. It was marked on the right by the village of Bourliouk, already mentioned, and on the left, about two miles up the stream, by the village of Tarkhanlar, to which, however, the left of our infantry did not quite attain. Between the two were gardens and vineyards, enclosed by low stone walls, stretching down to the stream, which proved fordable nearly throughout. Right opposite our centre, as we moved, was the slope of the Kourgané Hill, with its terraced knoll a few hundred yards from the river, on which appeared an earthwork of some kind, with twelve or fourteen guns, some of them bearing on the post-road, some directly on our front, some on our right wing, and thus sweeping our whole front A thousand yards from this battery, and facing our left, another earthwork with guns was visible. As already said, these works were not intended for defence, for they were easily surmounted, being banks of earth only two or three feet high, so that the guns looked over them; they were probably intended to prevent the pieces from running down the slope, and also might afford some slight shelter to the gunners. Behind the battery on the Kourgané and on its flanks, the Russian battalions were thickly posted, their front extending to the battery facing our left; and on the other flank they were massed on the knolls close to the post-road. The columns in reserve were higher up on the slopes, where also were drawn up the 3400 cavalry of Menschikoff's army. Besides the battery on the knoll, he had on this part of the field nine field batteries (the Russian battery is of eight guns), of which one was in the earthwork on his right, another supported the twelve-gun battery, two in reserve on the upper slope, two across the post-road, bearing on the bridge, and three attached to the cavalry. The force confronting the English may be taken as 21,000 infantry, 3000 cavalry, and eighty-four guns; those opposing the French as 12,000 infantry, 400 cavalry, and thirty-six guns: making the totals of Menschikoff's army 33,000 infantry, 3400 cavalry and 120 guns. Part of the

French troops during the Battle of Alma.

British Fourth Division had been left behind at the place of disembarkation to clear the beach, and did not arrive till after the battle. Our force engaged was 23,000 infantry, 1000 cavalry, and sixty guns. The French and Turks together numbered about 35,000 infantry, with sixty-eight guns. Deducting the column that passed the Alma at its mouth, they had 25,000 infantry, and sixty-eight guns; these when brought to bear would of course overwhelm the force opposed to them, which, moreover, only came by degrees on the French part of the field, where no attack had been provided for by the Russians. It is impossible, therefore, that the French could have met with any very strong opposition.

As the skirmishers on our right approached Bourliouk they were met by the fire of Russian light troops and light guns in the village; while the skirmishers in front of the Light Division (four companies of its rifle battalion), encountered a large number of the enemy's skirmishers in the vineyards; but, as our columns advanced, these retired across the stream, first setting fire to Bourliouk, the conflagration of which was a notable incident of the battle. It was now that the twelve-gun battery on the Kourgané Hill gave our people a taste of its quality; shot and shell, of a size far greater than that of field-artillery, began to tear the ground, and to burst in the air. The Light and Second Divisions began thereupon to deploy; but our right was much too close upon the French, and a great deal of marching and countermarching now took place, without mending the fault, for too little ground was taken, and our troops were crowded in their advance to a most damaging degree.

The delay was not accidental, however, but was according to the plan, in pursuance of which the advance against the front of the strongly occupied part of the position was only to take place when Bosquet's movement against the left should begin to take effect. His voltigeurs, and afterwards those of Canrobert, had been seen swarming up the heights, and some guns (Bosquet's twelve) had been heard, along with the Russian batteries opposing them. But, as already said, the French artillery had all to advance by one road; the process was slow, and Canrobert's main body of infantry, as well as Prince Napoleon's division, waited for the support of the guns—hence the delay. Kinglake says that, while their movement was still incomplete, a French staff-officer came from St Arnaud to ask Lord Raglan to advance. The order to attack was thereupon given to the Second and the Light Divisions.

Having issued this command, the English general took a course too extraordinary to remain unnoticed. Accompanied by some of his staff, he rode round the right of the burning village, and descending to the Alma, crossed it by a ford close to the left of the French Army. Proceeding up the opposite bank, he reached a knoll between the Telegraph Hill and the post-road, from whence he looked from a distance, which was at the moment beyond the effective range of field-artillery, upon the flank of the Russian position on the Kourgané' Hill, and also, on his right front, on the columns of the Russian reserves. He was thus in the singular position for a commander of occupying, with a few officers, a point well within the enemy's lines, and beyond the support, or even the knowledge, of any of the rest of his army; and Kinglake, the historian, who accompanied him in this excursion, and who records it with applause, says, also, he was too far from the scene of the main struggle on which his army had now entered to be able, for the time, to direct the movements of his own troops.

It was fortunate, in these circumstances, that the divisional commanders had so plain a task before them. On receiving the order, the Second and Light Divisions had at once begun their advance; but Evans's being delayed by the burning village, and having to pass round both ends of it to the river, Brown's, forming the left of our line, was the first to attack. Passing the low wall of the vineyards which occupied this bank, pushing before it the Russian skirmishers, and losing some men as it went, it made its way, much disordered by the tangling vines, to the stream, whose clear current was in most places shallow, but in others formed pools where the men were in water to their necks. Wading through, they found themselves, at a very few yards from the stream, standing beneath an almost perpendicular bank about six feet high, in which the long slope abruptly ended, and where they were for the moment out of the view of the enemy's battery above them on the hill. A pause was made here, ended by Sir George Brown himself riding up the bank and calling on his regiments to follow. The whole division thereupon gained the slope, and began the attack—not in orderly lines, for, besides insufficiency of space, it was impossible under such a fire as now assailed it to form these, but with such attempts at lines as the men themselves, instinctively seeking their own companies, succeeded in making, that is to say, a line chiefly of groups and masses. But, whenever they were able to form, our regiments attacked in a two-deep line, according to our custom, and were met by the Russians in deep columns, formed of two or more battalions, so that the front of a British line was of greater extent than that of the double or quadruple force in the enemy's column engaged with it. Three regiments of the Light Division, with one of the Second Division, gallantly led by General Codrington, went straight up the slope, their too dense front torn by the great heavy battery, only three hundred yards in front of them, and firing down a smooth natural glacis. On our right of that battery the 7th regiment had become engaged with a Russian column formed by the left wing of the Kazan regiment, and numbering 1500 men; while the two left regiments of our Light Division had been halted on the slope near the river, because General Buller, perceiving a formation and advance of infantry and cavalry on his left front, formed a corresponding front to meet it. The regiment of the Second Division (95th) which had joined Codrington was one of four led by Evans himself across the river near the bridge, and which then, bearing considerably to their left, partly prolonged and partly supported the Light Division, while his other two battalions (41st and 49th), under General Adams, passing round the right of the burning village, crossed by a ford below into the hollow space, garnished with knolls, between the Telegraph and Kourgané' Hills, where stood part of the Russian left.

The First Division, formed in second line to the Light, embraced much more ground, so that the brigade of Guards extended from near the post-road to quite beyond the rear of Codrington's brigade, while the Highlanders, forming abreast of them, were prolonging the front of the army. After remaining for some time, lying down in line during the advance of the Light Division, the First Division followed it through the vineyards and across the Alma.

Codrington's brigade continued its brisk advance, and now occurred a singular event that was a turning point of the battle, which was nothing less than the sudden retreat of the great heavy battery which had been so formidable a feature of the Russian position. This withdrawal was very discreditable. Whether it was owing to the menacing aspect of the advancing troops, or to anxiety to avoid the loss of guns (and Kinglake says it was well known that such loss would draw down the displeasure of the Czar), it was a disgrace to such a powerful battery, so important to the battle, so surrounded with supporting battalions, to save itself just when, by continuing in action, it might cause heavy and perhaps decisive loss to the enemy. It vanished with celerity just as Codrington's men were touching the earthwork in front of it.

Lieutenant General Sir George Brown G.C.B. and officers of his staff: Major Hallewell, Colonel Brownrigg, orderly, Colonel Airey, Captain Pearson, Captain Markham, Captain Ponsonby. Photograph by Roger Fenton, 1855

Cavalry horses, equipped with lasso harness, came up hastily, were hooked on, and drew the guns away, except two which were captured.

Relieved from the tremendous stress of fire which had poured such huge missiles, at such close quarters, through their ranks, Codrington's regiments, after entering the earthwork, lined the low parapet, and extended on both sides of it. Those on the right were in some degree protected by the 7th, still holding the left Kazan column fast; and on the left, by the two battalions that had been held back there. Facing Codrington were the four battalions of the Vladimir regiment, 3000 strong, supported by the Ouglitz regiment, of the same strength (though it never got down into the conflict), and the right wing of the Kazan regiment; the Vladimir was closely supported by the fire of the field battery, already said to be in support of the great battery. And had our attack been so ordered that the supporting divisions were now taking part in it, the conflict, assuming large proportions, might have drawn into its active area the whole of the forces on both sides, and have issued in a result more decisive than a mere victory. But the troops with Codrington, without close support, seeing before and around them fresh masses of the enemy, being a target for their guns, and threatened by a great body of cavalry, gave way and descended the hill. On arriving at its foot the four regiments, and the four companies of rifles, were less in number than when they went up by forty-seven officers, fifty sergeants, and 800 rank and file, killed and wounded; and, in addition, the 7th lost twelve officers, and more than 200 men. But they had inflicted far heavier losses on the enemy.

Had they but clung to the ground they held a few moments longer, they would have received effectual support, for the Guards, after gaining the farther bank of the stream in good order, had already begun the ascent, and their centre battalion, the Scots Fusiliers, was disordered and swept down by the retreating troops, with a loss of eleven officers and 170 men. But the Grenadiers on its right, and the Coldstreams on its left, continued to advance in lines absolutely unbroken, except where struck by the enemy's shot. Such French officers on the hills on the right as, in an interval of inaction, were free to observe what our troops were doing, spoke of this advance of the Guards as something new to their minds, and very admirable.

At this time the whole of our troops were being brought to bear on the position. The three regiments remaining with Evans (55th, 30th, and 47th) had been engaged chiefly on the left of the post-road, against the battalions and batteries drawn up for its defence, and had undergone heavy losses. His two other regiments (41st and 49th), which had moved to the stream on the other side of Bourliouk, were towards the close of the battle brought up to the knoll where Lord Raglan stood. The Third Division was moving across the stream in support, and on the left of the Guards the Highlanders were advancing against the Russian right flank, while beyond them again moved our Cavalry Brigade. It was, then, upon troops shaken by heavy losses, and dispirited for the want of a forward impulse, that our whole army was now closing.

Our artillery had also taken an effective share in the fight. At first, till ground was gained on the further bank, some batteries of the Light, Second, and First Divisions had, from the space behind and around the burnt village, brought their fire to bear on the men and guns defending the post-road, but as the infantry advanced they began to cross the river. The battery of the First Division, already in action, now passed at a shallow ford just below the bridge, and going some way up the road, ascended a knoll to the left, where it found itself on the right of the 55th, and in full view of the field. The guns had outstripped the gunners, who followed on foot, and the gun first to arrive was loaded and fired by the officers, who dismounted for the purpose. The rest of the battery immediately came up, and its fire bore on and turned back a heavy Russian column (the only one at that time within view) which was descending the hill. Two batteries from other divisions also came into action here, and on the ground where Lord Raglan stood two guns, called up by him, had been so placed as to bear on the flank of the batteries guarding the post-road, causing them to retire, while the two troops of horse-artillery, advancing with the cavalry on our left, were finally directed on the masses still held in reserve by Menschikoff.

The two battalions of the Guards, with some men rallied from the Scots battalion, went up the hill on each side of the gap in their centre, and were met by the four battalions of the Vladimir regiment, and the two Kazan battalions, much shattered in the fight, which had hitherto been engaged with the 7th. This new phase of the battle was not of long duration. The columns could not stand before the close fire of the lines. Moreover, at this moment the Highland regiments, after receiving the badly aimed fire of the field-guns in the earthwork on the flank (which then rapidly withdrew from the action), had now approached the right of the Russian position. The brigade was in echelon, the right battalion leading and already past the earthwork defended by the Vladimir. This Russian regiment, after undergoing heavy loss, still hotly assailed in front by the Guards, and its rear threatened by the Highlanders, retreated to its right rear towards the right Kazan column, upon which it endeavoured to form, and both came under the fire of the leading Highland regiment (42d). At the same time Campbell's other regiments attacked the columns hitherto in reserve high up the Kourgané Hill. These did not maintain the contest; the Russian forces all over the position were quitting it. No attempt was made by their cavalry or artillery on this side of the field to cover the retreat; they seemed to have shifted for themselves, leaving the infantry columns to make their way off the field, which they did without panic, though shattered as they went by our most advanced field batteries. The English, moving over the whole field, from the eastern slopes of the Kourgané on the extreme left to the slopes of the Telegraph Hill now occupied by the French, once more completed the connection of the Allied Forces. Lord Raglan proposed to push the enemy in his retreat with the untouched troops of the two armies; but the French Marshal declined to join in that step, on the ground that his men had divested themselves of their knapsacks before ascending the heights, and that it was impossible to advance till they had resumed possession of them. The leading English batteries continued, however, to pursue the enemy with their fire for some little distance on the plateau, where some of them bivouacked at nightfall, covered by a few companies detached for the purpose.

In the battle the English lost 106 officers, of whom twenty-five were killed; nineteen sergeants killed, and 102 wounded; of rank and file, 318 killed, 1438 wounded; and nineteen missing, supposed to be buried in the ruins of Bourliouk; total 2002. The French lost only three officers killed, yet their official accounts placed their total loss at the disproportionate number of 1340; but there were good reasons for believing that this was a great exaggeration. Lord Raglan (says Kinglake) believed that their whole loss in killed was sixty, and in wounded 500, and there was a general belief in our army that the French losses were slight. The Russians stated their own losses at 5709.

As to the tactics of the Allies, they had before them a position very difficult of access on their right, very advantageous for defence in the centre, and with open and undefended ground on their left. Supposing they had neglected the part so difficult of access near the sea, and carried their whole line inland, till their right was across the post-road, and their left extending far beyond the Russian right, in that case, if the Russians had held their position, with a powerful attack prepared against their front, and a large force turning their right, a defeat would have been to them absolute destruction. If, seeing the manoeuvre, Menschikoff had marched out of the position, and formed across our left, backed on the Simpheropol road, he would have gained a tactical advantage largely compensating for his numerical inferiority, and great chances would have been afforded to an able tactician thus operating on a flank with his own retreat assured; in fact, there Would have been a large field open for skilful manoeuvres on both sides, and the Allies would at least have had the advantage of drawing him from his position, when they might well have hoped that, with ordinary equality of skill, they would have forced him back, and gained the road to Sebastopol. On the other hand, they had to consider whether they would run any serious risk in thus leaving a space between their right and the sea. Now a Russian force could only have operated there by traversing the plateau swept by the guns of the fleet, descending the difficult paths through the cliffs, crossing the stream, and forming for attack with its back to the sea, and with a retreat across the Alma and up the cliffs impossible, except in case of the most absolute defeat of the Allies. This, therefore, need not be taken into the account and all considerations point to this suggested movement of the Allied Army away from the sea as the right one.

The battle, as fought, showed a singular absence of skill on all sides. The Russian general showed great incompetency in leaving the issues of the cliffs unclosed, in keeping his reserves out of action, in withdrawing his artillery when it might have best served him, and in leaving absolutely unused his so greatly superior force of cavalry on ground very well adapted to its action.

The part played by the French was not proportionate either to their force, or to their military repute. Of the two divisions brought at first on to the plateau, one brigade, that nearest the sea, together with all the Turks, never saw the enemy, and had no effect on the action; and another division of the front line, with easier ground, only arrived very late to the support of the others. Though these others (three brigades) were opposed by no overwhelming force, they hung back, and never, up to the end of the battle, seriously engaged the Russians. No favourable impression was left on the minds of the English by their Allies' share in the action.

The English divisional generals were, as we have seen, left to themselves, except for the order given to two of them to attack; and it was inevitable, in their relative position to the French, that they should advance straight to their front. This they did, in the face of a formidable resistance, and with a gallantry to which their losses testify. But when it had become evident that no great operation against our flank was to be attempted, and that the enemy was altogether committed to a direct defence, our attack should have been so strong, so concerted, and so fed and maintained, as to bring our whole force to bear on the enemy. Thus, if the Highland Brigade had crossed the river along with the attacking divisions and beyond them, supported by the Fourth Division and the cavalry, then the Light and Second Divisions, secure on their flanks, and closely supported by the Guards, could have brought their whole strength at once to bear, while the Russian reserves would have found too much to do in meeting the onset on their flank to reinforce the defenders of the principal battery. But as there was no unity and no concerted plan, our troops suffered accordingly. The artillery, too, instead of being left to come into action according to the views of its different commanders, should have had its part in supporting the attack distinctly assigned to it. All, therefore, that we had to be proud of was the dash and valour of the regiments engaged. These were very conspicuous, and worthy of the traditions of the Peninsular days. A French officer, who was viewing the field, where our men lay, as they had fallen, in ranks, with one of our naval captains, observed to him, "Well, you took the bull by the horns—our men could not have done it."

Our cavalry, though so inferior in number, would probably not have been deterred by that consideration from engaging (as indeed it proved on a later occasion) but the part assigned to it was that of observation and defence only. "I will keep my cavalry in a bandbox," was said to have been Lord Raglan's expression; and he was right, for it was all the army had to depend on for the many essential duties which cavalry must in such a case perform.

CHAPTER IV

THE MARCH ROUND SEBASTOPOL TO BALAKLAVA

*March to the Belbec—Question of attacking the North Side—
Menschikoff bars the Harbour—Reasons against Attack of North Side—
Todleben's Strange Contention—Impolicy of moving Allies Inland—The
Flank March begun—Rencontre with Menschikoff's Rear—The English
reach the Tchernaya—First View of Balaklava—Question of Bases
for the Two Armies—Lord Raglan chooses Balaklava—Features of the
South Side—Positions of the Allies.*

THE NEXT two days were passed on the Alma. The many slain were buried by us. In and about the principal battery were about 700 or 800 bodies, of which two-thirds were Russians and the dead lay thick on other parts of the field. The close intermixture of Russian and English bodies showed that all the fighting on this part of the field had been between them alone. Hospitals were established in some empty houses in Bourliouk, where surgeons of the army and navy attended to the wounded before they were borne to the ships. And amidst these scenes of suffering the cholera knew no relenting.

On the 23d the armies marched again, and as before, over dry grassy plains, and passing the Katcha, seven miles from the Alma, encamped on the heights beyond about noon. The village here had been deserted in haste by the inhabitants. It had been expected that the enemy might make another stand in the strong position which these heights offered. But their defeat had been too absolute, their retreat too hasty, to admit of such a rally. Kinglake says it became a panic flight for the shelter of Sebastopol. On the other hand, it must be observed that this panic was not evident at the close of the battle, and that our march on the footsteps of Menschikoff's army did not show us marks of such complete disorder. At the mouth of the Katcha the Scots Greys and the 57th regiment (of the Fourth Division) were disembarked, and joined the army.

The next day a march of six miles carried us across the Belbek. Here the character of the country changed from grassy plains to hills clothed with coppice, and here the army halted during the 25th. These heights were waterless, and the cavalry and horse-artillery led a hard life while covering the army; the horses had neither forage nor water for forty-eight hours, all which time they remained accoutred and harnessed; and the men and officers did not, for these and two other days, taste meat.

The army was now so close to the prime object of the enterprise that, by going about a mile and a half beyond the halting place, the towers and fortifications were seen at no great distance in the basin below. And it was during the halt here that the question arose whether the army should at once attack the north side of Sebastopol. It may be doubted whether it was ever seriously considered. The harbour of Sebastopol is from 1000 to 1200 yards wide. On the north side, besides some storehouses and a factory, the only constructions were forts at the entrance; others on the cliffs, looking on the sea outside; and on the heights inland a large permanent work, known to us afterwards as "the Star Fort," which, supported by earthen works and batteries, recently thrown up on either flank, dominated all the ground within range of its guns. It was on the south side that the city stood, with its public buildings, the quarters of the garrison, the docks, and the arsenal. The harbour between these was filled with the ships of war, whose broadsides could, of course, be brought to bear on either side, but which were at first disposed with the object of resisting an attack on the northern bank, where they swept the ground over which an enemy would advance. It is asserted that on the 21st, the day after the battle of the Alma, Sir Edmund Lyons, second in command of the fleet, urged Lord Raglan to follow up the success, and "try to take the northern forts by a coup de main." But, from what has just been said, this was manifestly not only a quite desperate but a fruitless enterprise, except on one condition, namely, that the Allied Fleet should take a principal part in the attack; and it was only in such a case that the view of a naval commander need have been an element in he question. Had some of our ships engaged the forts, had the rest passed in and attacked the vessels of the enemy, while the Allied Army stood on the heights above ready to descend, it is conceivable that Sebastopol might have fallen in a storm of battle as tremendous as the world has ever witnessed. But those who assert that this opportunity continued to exist when the armies were on the Belbek (23d and 24th September) ignore the change which had taken place in the problem. Menschikoff, singularly inefficient as a tactician, seems to have possessed both sagacity and decision in other fields of the military art. Immediately on entering Sebastopol after his defeat, he perceived two measures to be necessary. The one was to keep open, by means of an army in the field, his communications with Russia, while leaving a sufficient garrison in Sebastopol; the other was to bar the harbour against his enemies' fleet. Therefore, contrary to the advice of his admiral, he caused seven ships of war to be sunk across the entrance of the harbour, in line with the forts, on the night of the 22d. On the 23d our vessels in observation off the port perceived that this had been done, and it was reported to St Arnaud the same evening. Thus an attack would now be made under very different conditions, for the rest of the Russian Fleet, thus rendered secure against attack, could still bring an exterminating fire to bear on the north side. The proper person for Lord Raglan to consult on the subject (if it was any longer matter for consultation) was his chief engineer, Sir John Burgoyne, who always denied that the proposition was ever seriously entertained, or that Lord Raglan had ever discussed it with him. And in support of this it is to be remembered that, as has been already said, the shore north of Sebastopol offered landing-places, but no harbours. The only point it afforded for the disembarkation of supplies was the mouth of the Katcha, open to every wind, and the communications with which would have been liable to be intercepted at any time by a Russian army in the field. Finally, supposing all the success possible to be achieved, the Allies in possession of the north side, and the ships in the harbour by some miracle got rid of, it may be asked—what next? How were we to compel the surrender of the south side by means of our field-artillery, across an interval of 1200 yards, against an enemy who, besides the artillery in his great stone forts, could from an inexhaustible arsenal line the whole southern shore, as well as the Inkerman heights on our left flank, with heavy guns? It may safely be said that, after driving the enemy off the north side, we should have found ourselves in a position of greatly augmented difficulty.

It would not have been necessary to dwell upon this but or the support afforded to the theory which Todleben, the engineer who became so famous for his defence of Sebastopol, has set forth in his ample, and in most respects excellent, account of the siege. Unfortunately, not only his opinions but his facts are frequently more than questionable, and he gives but too much reason to infer that he exaggerated the insufficiency of the means of resistance in order to exalt the importance of his own splendid services in enabling the garrison to make so memorable a defence.

For example, he desires to show that the Allies, upon reaching the Belbek, ought to have made an assault on the north side. On the highest part of the ground there was the Star Fort, with the trenches and batteries in extension of it. To carry this by assault Todleben represents as an easy matter. This fort was a permanent work of 700 yards extent round the lines of fire; it had escarps of masonry, and a glacis, and was surrounded by a ditch twelve feet deep and eighteen feet wide. It was armed with forty-seven guns. The ground over which the assailants must have advanced was swept by the broadsides of the ships below. Is it possible that an engineer could have looked on such a scheme as practicable? But he says the enemies' ships, approaching the shore, could batter the fort almost with impunity. The impossibility of this is best shown by the fact that, in the subsequent engagement between the fleets and forts, one of the batteries on the cliffs (100 feet high) of the north side disabled several of our ships without receiving a shot in return, although they made it the object of their fire, and that the Star Fort is distant inland from this battery 1000 yards. Thus, according to Todleben, the ships, while themselves under the fire of the coast batteries, which they could not injure in return, were to bombard a fort a thousand yards beyond these batteries, and which would be invisible from the sea.

The second alternative suggested by Todleben is that the Allies should have established a force on the road to Bakshisarai, thus intercepting the communications between Russia and Sebastopol, which would, he says, have brought the campaign to an end. Now the nearest point at which the Allies could have touched the Russian communications was Mackenzie's Farm. But the heights there were waterless, therefore the intercepting force could not have remained there; it must have gone farther, to the Upper Belbek. It would then have been some seventeen miles from its base on the Katcha—one so precarious that a strong breeze from the wrong quarter would render it useless. This long line of supply must have been covered by the rest of the army, throughout its length, from attacks which might be directed on any part of it either by the garrison of Sebastopol on the one side, or by Menschikoff's army in the field on the other. The reduction of a fortress by pressure of this kind must of course be slow in its operation, and had the Allied commanders been reck- less enough to put a force into such a position, it would have been impossible to maintain it, under the stress of such enterprises against their communications and their line as the enemy showed himself capable of undertaking shortly afterwards at Balaklava and Inkerman.

On the afternoon of the 24th Lord Raglan visited Marshal St Arnaud, and the arrangements for the flank march were then agreed on. The French commander sat rigidly in his chair during the interview, and his manner and looks showed that his sickness was gain- ing on him. On leaving the French camp, Lord Raglan said to one of his staff, "Did you observe St Arnaud? — he is dying."[1] When the visit was repeated next morning, the Marshal was no longer able to take part in discussion.

On the morning of the 25th the heavy cavalry, a troop of horse-artillery, and a battalion of rifles, were sent as an advanced guard on the road

1 Kinglake

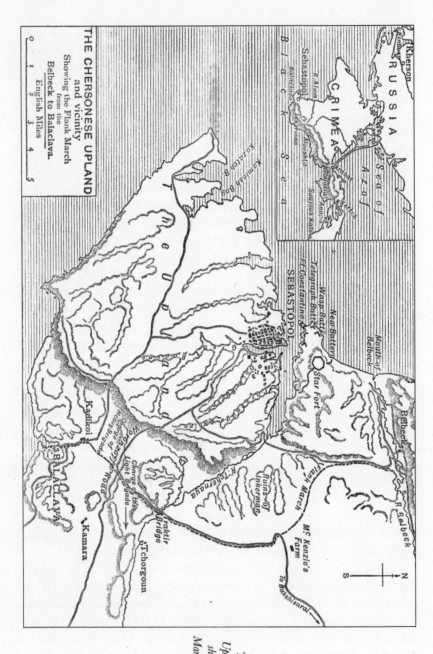

Map no. 3.
The Chersonese
Upland and vicinity,
showing the Flank
March from the Belbek
to Balaklava

48

through the woods leading to Mackenzie's Farm. Towards noon the march of the main body began. Four field batteries advanced up one of the roads leading to Sebastopol. Outside a small house by the roadside Lord Raglan and General Airey were seated with a map before them, and Lord Raglan himself indicated to the officer at the head of the column the direction in which it was to strike through the wood on the left of the road, and called out to him to go "south-east." Thereupon the guns, with their waggons and carriages, in long procession, plunged into the narrow wood path, the wheels crashing through the coppice, and steering by the sun when there was a divergence of ways, kept the main path for about an hour, passing as they went some of the heavy cavalry, small bodies of which were drawn up on their right, on the edge of the heights that looked down on Sebastopol. Their further progress was stopped by the troop of horse-artillery which was halted in the path in front. The cavalry and rifles, either by accident or design, had diverged to the right, and the troop thus found itself leading the advance of the army in ground where it could do nothing effectual for its own defence, and was devoid of all proper protection or support. Presently Lord Raglan rode up with his staff, demanding sharply why the troop had halted, and ordered it immediately to proceed, himself leading the way. The march was continued in this extraordinary manner, the headquarter staff first, then thirty guns in long procession, through a thick wood, and moving round an enemy's fortress and army. What this might have portended was presently made evident, for in an open space Lord Raglan came suddenly on a Russian column moving at right angles to his own course.

This singular rencontre had come about in this way: Menschikoff, after sinking his ships, and making arrangements for the defence of the fortress, had left Sebastopol that morning, with the army which had fought on the Alma, in pursuance of his design of keeping open his communications with Russia by means of holding a position in the open country. The highroad from Sebastopol to Bakshisarai, after ascending steeply from the valley of the Tchernaya, crosses the end of the plateau on which the English were moving at the open space on which stand the buildings and fields of Mackenzie's Farm, before again descending to the plain on the way northward towards the Upper Belbek. He had begun his movement before dawn on the 25th, and the halt we made in the wood had enabled his army to pass by, except some of the baggage and its escort. Prince Menschikoff, with the leading troops, had at this time reached the village of Otarkoi on the Belbek, and thought so little of keeping himself informed of what might be passing near his army (being probably altogether intent on transporting it unobserved into its new positions), that he remained for several days in the belief that the irruption on his rear had been made only by a patrol. Some of his baggage train was captured, but many of the vehicles hurried off, on the one side towards Bakshisarai, on the other towards Sebastopol. We had been absolutely unaware of this march of an army across our front till we stumbled on it; while Menschikoff remained in such complete ignorance that the Allied Army was defiling within four or five miles of him, that even on the 28th a messenger from him arrived in Sebastopol, part of whose errand was to get news of the movements and position of the enemy.

The English forces gradually assembled on the ground around the farm, and then resumed their march, descending to the Traktir Bridge, where the road to Balaklava crosses the Tchernaya. There, on the banks of the stream, the leading troops bivouacked after nightfall, while the rear divisions and batteries did not arrive till some hours afterwards. Looking back to the heights we had quitted, the glare in the sky showed that our allies, following in our steps, were bivouacking there.

Cathcart had been left with his division on the Belbek to send the sick to the embarking place on the Katcha, and to cover the march of the armies. A messenger sent by him succeeded in reaching the British headquarters, and returned with news of the progress of the movement, which Cathcart sent on to the Katcha; and Lyons despatched a naval officer, who also managed to reach Lord Raglan, and to return with a message to the Admiral. Thus the fleet was prepared to co-operate next day in the seizure of the port of Balaklava. On the 26th Cathcart followed the march of the armies, and arrived unmolested on the Tchernaya.

This same day, the 26th, the British resumed their march, crossing the valley of the Tchernaya towards the low hills which separated it from that of Balaklava. It was, perhaps, partly in consequence of the long, fatiguing march of the day before that men seized with cholera began to strew the roadside directly the advance began. Troops moving on the enclosing hills right and left of the valley protected the flanks of the main column, and some guns which accompanied them opened fire, while other and heavier shots were heard from the sea. On passing the ridge which divided the valleys right athwart our path, we looked down on the object of the whole movement, and very insignificant it seemed. At the end of a piece of richly cultivated garden ground was seen a pool lying deep between enclosing cliffs, which were crowned by walls and towers. From thence there presently came a shell travelling towards us at a height which showed it had been fired from a mortar. At the same time some companies of our rifles running along the hills on the left of the lake clambered over the walls, along which the garrison was seen to run, and from whence they presently made signs of surrender. Thereupon a small English steamer appeared suddenly in the piece of water below, assuring us that the harbour was our own, and the communication with the

Field Marshal Lord Raglan during the Crimean War, c.1855. Photograph by Roger Fenton.

fleet reestablished. On this occasion four shots only were fired by the garrison (composed of militia of the place), and their commander, in excusing himself for provoking an assault by firing at all, said he thought he was bound to do so until summoned to surrender. Nobody was wounded on either side. But the following account appears in Todleben's official narrative:—"The enemy opened against Balaklava a powerful cannonade. Twenty ships approached the coast and bombarded the old ruins. The mortars, however, only ceased fire after having exhausted their ammunition. This imperceptible garrison had defended itself even to the last extremity. There remained only Colonel Minto, six officers, and sixty soldiers, all wounded in many places." What are thus described as having "remained" were all that had been in the place—the account belongs altogether to the regions of fiction.

This day the French Army crossed the Tchernaya and bivouacked on the Fedukhine heights.

A question entailing momentous consequences now arose. It was whether the English or the French should occupy as a base the harbour of Balaklava. Hitherto on the mere evidence of the map, it had been counted on as available for both armies, but now that it lay before their eyes, a mere pool, already crowded, with one straggling row of poor houses for a street, it was seen that it would not bear division. The French had a strong ground of contention on their side, for the right of the Allied line had hitherto been conceded to them, and whoever took the right now must hold Balaklava. General Canrobert, who had succeeded Marshal St Arnaud in the command, took a course very considerate towards us. Seeing that we were already in possession, and that it would be difficult in many ways for us to move out, he gave Lord Raglan his choice whether to keep the left of the line, and give Balaklava to the French, or to take the right and keep that harbour. Admiral Lyons counselled strongly for keeping Balaklava, as the place best adapted for securing a due communication between the army and its base on the sea. It was an occasion which a Greek poet would have represented, after the event, as one in which the chooser, blinded by some angry god, had made choice of calamity. Lord Raglan took the right, and Balaklava, and with them brought untold miseries on his army.

We have now reached the point in the drama where the main action begins to which all that had passed was merely preliminary. The armies thenceforward assumed that position towards the enemy which they were to keep up to the final act of the war. Above them stood the broad Upland of the Chersonese, on which for nearly a year their lives were to be passed, and for the most part ended, and to which, after a time, they were chained by necessity until their task should be accomplished. It becomes necessary, therefore, to describe the conditions in which the forces opposed were operating.

The outer harbour or roadstead of Sebastopol is a creek about four miles long from the point where it breaks, nearly at right angles, the coast line to its extremity where the Tchernaya flows into it. It maintains a great depth throughout, even close to the shore. On the points which mark the entrance stood two stone forts, that on the north named Constantine, on the south Alexander. Outside Alexander, looking out to sea was the Quarantine Fort. After entering the roadstead, the Artillery Fort was passed on the south; and about a mile from the entrance the Inner or Man-of-War harbour ran for a mile and a half into the southern shore. On the two points which marked this inlet stood two other forts, Nicholas and Paul. On the western shore of this inner creek stood the city of Sebastopol; on its eastern shore, indented by the inlet on which the dockyards were built, was the Karabelnaia suburb, where stood the extensive barracks for the garrison. Nearly half way between this inner harbour and the head of the roadstead was another much smaller inlet, the Careenage Creek.

The ground south of the roadstead was marked by very singular features. The plateau or plain, the ancient Chersonese (which, following Kinglake's more descriptive phraseology, will in future be called the Upland), where the Allied Armies stood was marked off from the valley of the Tchernaya by a wall of cliff, which, following up that stream southward for about a mile from its mouth, turns round south-west and defines the valley of Balaklava, passing about a mile north of that place, and joining the sea-cliffs. This plateau is channeled by many chasms or ravines, which, beginning with slight depressions in its midst descend between rocky walls to the shore, and between these rose elevated points, lying all round the town and suburb, which, crowned by such works as the Malakoff, the Redan, the Flagstaff Bastion, and others, afterwards acquired each a fame of its own. Another feature of first-rate importance was the conformation of the coast line at Cape Cherson, where the northern side of its angle was indented by twin inlets, Kazatch and Kamiesch Bays, having a common entrance, which throughout the siege constituted the French base, being most conveniently adapted for the purpose; a road, paved afterwards by the French, and thus placed beyond the vicissitudes of weather, passed from these creeks along the rear of their Divisions as they faced Sebastopol.

The largest of the ravines, dividing the plain from south to north, descends to the head of the inner harbour. It was at first the line of separation between the French and English. Two French Divisions, under General Forey, the Third and Fourth, forming the siege corps, encamped between it and the coast. Kamiesch Bay was immediately filled with their shipping, whose masts looked like a forest; and a wharf was made for landing the multitude of stores which crowded the beach and the environs of a small city of tents. The First and Second French Divisions, and some battalions of Turks, under General Bosquet, were posted on the eastern and south-eastern cliffs of the Upland, to cover the siege against an attack from the Russian field army.

On the right of the great ravine were the Third and Fourth English Divisions; beyond them the Light Division rested its right on the ravine descending to the Careenage Creek; on the other side of which, near the eastern edge of the Upland, was posted the second Division, looking towards the heights of Inkerman, and some hundred yards in rear of it the First

Division was encamped, its right also near the edge of the Upland; and both these were available for mutual co-operation with Bosquet, while, unlike his force, they sent their quota of men to the trenches.

Bosquet set about fortifying the edge of the heights on which he stood; (see map 3) and, so far as the position on the Upland was concerned, the armies there were for the present (that is to say, while their force held its present relation to that of the garrison of Sebastopol and Menschikoff's field army) sufficiently secure. But there were two vulnerable points in our line; that with which we will first deal was caused by the need to cover Balaklava About 4000 yards from that place a row of heights crossed the valley, low on the side of the Upland, but rising into higher and sharper hills towards the heights of Kamara. On these, slight works were constructed, armed with iron twelve-pounders, and garrisoned by Turks. The 93d Highlanders (left there by the First Division) were encamped between these heights and Balaklava; a thousand marines were landed and placed on the hills to our right of the harbour, on the heights before which places were found for guns brought from the ships; and in the valley below the cliffs of the Upland, and on the left front of the Highlanders, were the camps of the two brigades of cavalry. A point of special importance was that the one metalled road, the Woronzoff road, which ascended the cliff of the Upland, and wended thence to the town of Sebastopol, lay, as it crossed the valley of Balaklava, between and along the hills occupied by the Turks. The road continued on to Yalta, the Woronzoff country house and estate on the south-eastern shore of the Crimea; another branching from it crossed the Tchernaya, and went on up the Mackenzie heights to Bakshisarai. The Russians could approach Balaklava quite out of range of the guns and troops on the Chersonese; thus the Allies must be drawn from their heights down to the alley in case of an advance of the enemy in that direction. Therefore, the valley of Balaklava was a vulnerable point, and, if possible, should have been made strong enough to secure the Woronzoff road throughout its extent from Balaklava to the plateau.

The Russians in Sebastopol now knew exactly what they had to face, and were at least delivered from the perplexities which had at first beset them.

The tidings of defeat on the Alma reached Sebastopol about ten or eleven at night on the 20th, when Menschikoff arrived in the fortress. The Prince gave orders to Admiral Korniloff to bar the entrance to the harbour by sinking some of the war-ships. Next morning the Admiral summoned his naval captains, and after telling them of Menschikoff's design, put it to them whether his own proposal would not be preferable, which was to put to sea and, by attacking the Allied Fleet and flotilla, deprive the enemy of their means of subsistence. The council did not concur with him, believing that the time for such an enterprise had gone by, and preferring to bar the harbour by sinking the ships. The same afternoon those which were to be sunk were moved into their places.

During the 21st, Menschikoff's troops from the Alma, after reaching the north side, were transported across the harbour, in accordance with his determination to move his army into the open country, and bivouacked in a field outside the town.

During this day Colonel Todleben was occupied in considering how to meet the attack which he says was expected on the north side. As we have seen, he took a view of the prospect which was entirely unreasonable. He considered the case of 60,000 men, protected from the assault of an equal number by fortifications and heavy artillery, as absolutely desperate. In his book he blames the other 60,000 for not sweeping them off the face of the earth. He communicated his forebodings to Admiral Korniloff, who took command on that side on the 24th, and who made preparations to defend the Star Fort and the adjacent ground in a spirit of absolute despair. But on the 25th the march of the Allied Armies along the Mackenzie heights was discerned from the Naval Library, which occupied a very lofty position in the city. Thereupon all doubt was at an end, the garrison was concentrated on the south side, and the preparation for the long struggle began.

The strength of the garrison was thus: six militia battalions, 4500; gunners at the coast batteries, 2700; marines, 2600; seamen of the fleet, 18,500; workmen, 5000; the Taroutine battalion of Menschikoff's army left in the town, 750; marine battalions landed from the fleet, 1800—total 35,850 men. The Russian sailors were habitually drilled and organised as soldiers in addition to their proper duties, in consideration that (as now happened) the fleets might easily be shut in by a powerful enemy. These men were therefore excellent for their purpose, and could also supply an immense number of trained gunners for the heavy artillery which armed the works. The workmen also, being in Government employ, had received military training, and a very large proportion of the whole force was particularly valuable, far more so than ordinary troops, for constructing works, for handling the machines used in moving and mounting heavy guns, in fact, for the business of creating a fortress.

Lieut-Colonel Todleben, henceforth the inspiring genius of the defence, was thirty-six years old, in the fullest vigour of body and mind. Educated at the military college at St Petersburg, he had been trained and commissioned as an engineer. He had just been employed in the siege of Silistria, and when that was abandoned, had been sent to Sebastopol, strongly recommended to Menschikoff. Placed at first on the general staff, he had begun to act as chief engineer when the invasion was imminent. On the 14th September he had added the earthworks already mentioned to the Star Fort, and, a few days later, took charge of the defences of the South Side. These had been traced, and partially executed, years before. Loop-holed walls of stone and earthen batteries formed a continuous line round the town itself, from the sea to the great ravine, and these he had begun to strengthen. On the other section of the line, extending from the great ravine to the harbour, he had raised extensive batteries on the sites of the Redan, the Little Redan, and the Bastion No. 1, close to Careenage Bay. The Malakoff Tower was semi-circular, of stone, five feet thick, fifty feet in diameter, twenty-eight feet high, prepared for musketry, and having five guns on the top; it was covered at the foot by a slope of earth, but was not yet surrounded with works. These constituted, on the 26th September, very formidable defences against an assault, and were daily growing stronger. The whole line was armed, by that date, with 172 pieces of ordnance, many very heavy, and in great part overwhelmingly superior to field-artillery.

The reader has now before him the means of determining the question whether the Allies were wrong in not at once proceeding to assault the place. It is said that Sir George Cathcart strongly advised it, though it appears that his opinion was formed on too incomplete a view of the enemy's works, and was greatly modified afterwards. What is more surprising is that Todleben is found to maintain, in his official narrative, that Sebastopol could not have been defended against an assault in the last days of September. It must be remembered that part only of the Allied Army could have been available for the purpose. Menschikoff's army, of unknown strength, might have been within six miles of us, for, as we had no troops beyond the Tchernaya it was impossible to know what might be passing in the wooded heights on its further bank. Therefore Bosquet's two divisions and the Turks must remain as a covering force, and even our First and Second Divisions could only have been taken from the same duty at great risk, to say nothing of the necessity of protecting Balaklava. Thus the assaulting forces would be actually fewer in number than the defenders; moreover, it would have been extremely difficult to have supported the attack with artillery, since our field-guns in the open must have been at once crushed by the heavy and long-reaching artillery in the works, while endeavouring to get within their own more limited range. Thus the two French and three English Divisions must have advanced unsupported for 2000 yards, under the fire of the numerous and powerful artillery already described, to attack works defended by forces equal to their own. Their first object must have been limited to seizing these works, and occupying the ground on which they stood, for to advance down the slopes towards the harbour would have been impossible under the broadsides of the Russian ships. Heavy guns must have been brought up and placed in battery to disable the ships before anything further could have

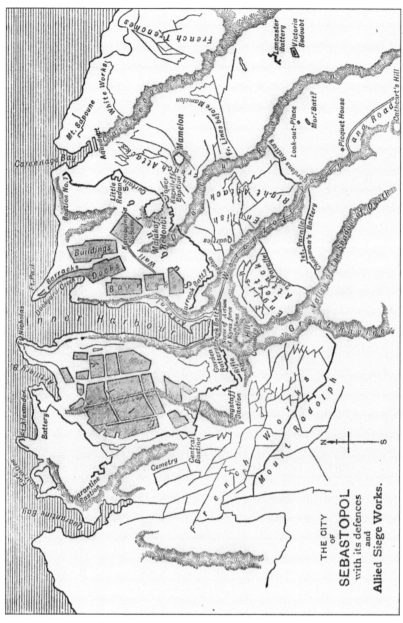

Map no. 4.
The city of Sebastopol
with its defences and
Allied siege works.

been attempted. And, at any stage of these operations, a repulse, which could only have taken place after heavy losses, would have entailed tremendous consequences. Nevertheless, this singularly able engineer represents both himself and Admiral Korniloff as addressing themselves to the business of defence in a spirit of despair. They did all that skill and energy could do, but without the hope of being able to resist the expected attack. And in his official narrative, written long afterwards, he still maintains that an assault must have succeeded; but in supporting the opinion, he represents the garrison (the numbers of which, as stated by himself elsewhere, have just been given) as only 16,000, while he estimates the forces which the Allies could assail them with at 40,000. These miscalculations do not diminish the difficulty of understanding how so accomplished an officer could risk his own repute by persisting in giving expression to conclusions so opposed by facts.

After the commanding engineers and artillery officers French and English, had made a reconnaissance of the Russian works, it was deemed indispensable to endeavour, before proceeding to assault, to silence the Russian artillery with the guns of our siege trains, and the disembarkation of these at the two ports began on the 28th.

On the 2d October, at daybreak, a long train of carriages, escorted by troops, was seen ascending the heights bordering the Belbek. It conveyed the civil inhabitants of Sebastopol, their families, and their goods; under cover of night they had passed along the southern side of the harbour, and crossed the bridge and causeway of the Tchernaya. Thus the garrison, freed from all encumbrance, and from the task of feeding all these noncombatants, was now reduced to a large compact body of defenders, regular troops, sailors, and marines, and workmen necessary for the business of the siege, and was thus, in all respects, in the best possible condition for beginning the struggle which Todleben, disturbed by no anxieties from within the fortress, could now enter upon with the whole force of his rare ability. Every day saw additional strength bestowed on the works, the labour on which never ceased day or night. The Central and Flagstaff Bastions were heightened and thickened, and a new work placed between them, and new batteries above the inner harbour looked up the great ravine and its branches. The Redan received the additions of the formidable Barrack Battery between it and the inner harbour, and of another battery on its other flank. The Malakoff Tower was surrounded with a bastion, from which extended batteries on each side, and a continuous line of trench connected it with the works between it and the harbour. All this was effected by the time of the attack. These works were armed as fast as made with heavy artillery, Also a ship of eighty-four guns, moored at the head of the inner harbour, bore on the mouths of the ravines which issued there.

CHAPTER V

BEGINNING OF THE SIEGE

Sir John Burgoyne—Our First Siege Batteries—Chapman's and Gordon's—The First French Batteries—Co-operation of the Fleets demanded—The Fleets to join in the Cannonade—Ships versus Forts—Risk to no Purpose—Positions of the Fleets—The Cannonade begins—French Fire silenced—English Fire successful—Losses on both Sides—Action of the Fleets—English Batteries still efficient

ALL THIS time the weather had been of the kind called in America the Indian summer—clear, still, and bright, but not sultry, with cool nights. War had as yet shown us none of its uglier features; except for the cholera, the armies were sanguine and cheerful, and the work of preparing for the cannonade was carried on in good spirits. Everywhere the soil of the Upland was firm and fairly even, and vehicles could find plenty of space to move on free from impediment.

The officer upon whom the conduct of the siege operations of the English fell, and who, as we have seen, had already been called on to advise in more than one important crisis, was Sir John Burgoyne. He was the oldest officer in the Crimea, born in 1782. He was the son of the General Burgoyne known in history as the commander who surrendered at Saratoga, and in dramatic annals as the author of the comedy of The Heiress. In the first years of the century the son had served in many climes; afterwards was with Sir John Moore at Corunna; at the passage of the Douro; helped to construct the lines of Torres Vedras; at the sieges and assaults of Badajos and Ciudad Rodrigo; wounded at Burgos and at St Sebastian; present at most of the great battles in the Peninsula; and finally at New Orleans. His mind was of the sedate, deliberative order, keeping a strong hold of facts and principles, and most unlikely to be swayed by the sudden impulses of those around him. As an engineer he had a sound judgment, ripened in an uncommon degree by thought and his large experience. He was entirely and, as preceding pages have endeavoured to show, rightly, in favour of employing our siege trains before attempting to assault, and he also believed that their effect would be such as to render an assault possible. Although so advanced in years, his capacity for military service was hardly impaired. The statue in Waterloo Place is an excellent likeness, though one peculiarity, an upstanding and disordered fell of hair, could perhaps hardly be expressed in bronze. The conditions of the task that lay before him will now be briefly described.

One, who approaches from the south the hollow in which lies the harbour of Sebastopol, finds the ground rising to heights that form an outer line to those on which stood the Russian works. Between these two lines was an interval of about two miles. From our side the slopes descended for more than half way, and then rose again to the opposing ridges. These slopes were cut into longitudinal slips by the ravines which descend from the plateau to the basin in which lies the great harbour. It has been said that the largest of these divides the Upland, descending to the head of the inner harbour. To our right of it is another, which came to be known as the Valley of the Shadow of Death, running into the great ravine 1400 yards from its end; and it was near this point of junction that the left of our earthworks rested on the chasm. At an average distance of 500 yards to the right of these combined ravines another cuts the plain, ending, like them, at the head of the inner harbour; in this lies the Woronzoff road as it enters Sebastopol. It was across the strip of plain, called by us Green Hill, between the great ravine and that of the Woronzoff road, that part of our first batteries, with their connecting line of trench were constructed, known, from the engineer in charge of the works, as Chapman's Battery, and later as the first parallel of the Left Attack. The system of fortification which had been created by the science of Louis XIV.'s engineers had, with some modifications, endured down to this time. It was based on the range of artillery and musketry, and the rules prescribed that the first parallel, with its batteries, should be traced at 600 yards from the enemy's works. Chapman's Battery was at a much greater distance, and for this reason:—The ground sloping constantly downward, was more and more commanded by the guns on the opposing heights, therefore the parapets must needs be higher in proportion as the works descended the hill. The ground here was stony, and a rocky substratum lay very near the surface; hence the labour of trenching was very severe, rendering the construction of high parapets extremely difficult, and advantage was therefore taken of a terrace on the face of the slope to place the battery at 1300 to 1400 yards from the Redan. But the distance was of the less consequence, as our siege-guns were far more powerful than those of an earlier day, and the old rules could not therefore be now considered as applicable. Another cause of difficulty, affecting the English, but scarcely the French, was the power which the Russians possessed of placing guns in position, in the ground between our right and their fortifications, which would enfilade our trenches in proportion as they were pushed forward.

On the other side of the Woronzoff ravine, on the slope between it and the Docks ravine, which, like the other slope, varied from 400 to 600 yards in width, was traced the work called, after the engineer who constructed it, Gordon's Battery, and known later as the first parallel of our Right Attack. The name of the slope was Mount Woronzoff, and this slope or ridge was the only one that led direct to the Redan without intervening obstacles.

Again, on the next slope, which lay between the Docks ravine and the Careenage ravine, our sailors made and armed with heavy guns a work called the Victoria Battery. It was not less than 2000 yards from the enemy's works, at which distance its guns were well within their own range, and almost outside that of the opposing artillery. It was also known as the Lancaster Battery, because armed with Lancaster guns.

Of these batteries, part of Chapman's guns, which were forty-one in number, fired across the great ravine upon the Flagstaff Bastion and its dependencies, that lay between the French attack and the city; part across the Woronzoff ravine, on the faces of the Redan, and the works in extension of it on its proper right. Gordon's guns, twenty-seven in number, bore in parts, according to their position, on the left face of the Redan, on the Malakoff, and on the ships in the inner harbour and the Careenage Creek. The naval battery bore on the Malakoff, which stood on the continuation of the same slope, and one gun was directed on a ship in the Careenage Creek. The task of the French was much easier. The ground on their side was much more easily trenched, and trenches there were not exposed as ours were to be enfiladed (fired into lengthways) by guns outside the fortress. A hill which they named Mount Rodolph gave them the means of opening their trenches against the Central and Flagstaff Bastions at somewhat shorter range than ours, being about 1000 yards, and the proximity of their base enabled them to bring up their siege train with comparative facility.

But, of course, none of the trenches. French or English were begun till the work of bringing up the siege-guns, and their supplies of ammunition, to depots near at hand, was well forward. It was not till the night of the 9th of October, when a fresh wind from the northeast favoured the enterprise, by preventing the enemy from hearing the men at work that the French broke ground on Mount Rodolph and by morning had made a trench there 1100 yards long. On the nights of the 10th and the 11th the English opened their works on Green Hill and Mount Woronzoff. Each day the Russians cannonaded heavily the works of the night, and each night these works were repaired and pushed steadily forward till, by the evening of the 16th, all the siege batteries were complete in guns and ammunition. The French placed fifty-three guns in battery, making with ours 126 in all. To these the Russians opposed 118; besides which, 220 pieces would bear upon attacking troops.

The cannonade which was expected to usher in the final act of the war was therefore to begin on the morning of the 17th. And now a question had arisen which must always be of interest when (as is so commonly the case in England's wars) the navy is in close co-operation with the army. It appeared to the military commanders that the fleets might greatly aid the land attack by standing in and engaging the sea-forts. Writing to Admiral Dundas, on the 13th October, Lord Raglan says, "I know no way so likely to insure success as the combined efforts of the Allied naval and military forces." After pointing out that the recent success on the Alma had led all to believe that the capture of the place would be accomplished, he ends thus: "Not to disappoint these universal expectations, the combined efforts of all branches of the naval and military service are necessary, and none, I am sure, will be withheld. Excuse my pressing these considerations on your attention."

Every reader can perceive how difficult it must be for a commander to resist such an appeal. Dundas consented, but, as he himself said, "with reluctance." At a conference of the Allied admirals, on the 15th, it was resolved that all their ships should make a simultaneous attack upon the sea-forts. But all the English captains considered that the attack of the fleets should be made not at the time of the preliminary cannonade, but at the moment of the intended assault. The judgment of the admirals on this point was that it should be left to the military commanders to say in what stage of the conflict the navy should render the aid of its broadsides, whether all at the time of the land cannonade, all at the time of the assault, or partly at each of these stages.

The military commanders replied on the 16th. They chose the last alternative; they applauded the conclusion the admirals had come to as "a great resolve," and expressed their belief that "moral and material effects" would be produced which must "insure the success of the attack upon Sebastopol."

Now the primary object of the fleets had been to render the passage of the Black Sea secure. This had become less pressing since the sealing up of the harbour—nevertheless the possibility still existed, and must be provided against, of giving to the Russian Fleet still afloat the opportunity of sallying out upon a foe so broken by conflict as to be open to defeat. And the prospects of an engagement between ships and such forts as defended the harbour, solid edifices of hard stone, with casemates for the guns, and armed with a numerous and powerful artillery, were not hopeful for the ships. If such an attack were pushed home by them, no limit could be placed to the damage they might suffer. The chances of being riddled, sunk, set on fire by shell or hot shot, ruined as steamers, and disabled by damage to structure or by loss of men, were absolutely indefinite. On the other hand, the probability

Balaklava, looking towards the sea. Print by William Simpson, c1855.

of ruining the walls of the forts might to some considerable extent be calculated beforehand, and was not promising. Only a very close fire could accomplish this, and that could not but mean unknown damage to the ships. Nevertheless, it might well be worth while to run great risks if the success of the assault could be clearly seen to be thereby assured. But it is impossible to gather from the language of the generals what it was they expected from the co-operation of the fleets. "If," says Lord Raglan to Admiral Dundas, "the enemy's attention can be occupied on the sea front as well as upon that of the land, there will be a much greater chance of making a serious impression upon their works of defence, and of throwing the garrison into confusion." Again: "Their (the fleets') presence would go far to make all feel that victory would be nearly a matter of certainty," and the Allied generals had, as we have seen, talked of "moral and material effects" to be produced by combined action, which must insure the success of the attack. But this brings us, and could have brought the admirals, no nearer to the actual results to be expected. The only way in which the assault could be facilitated would be by causing the withdrawal of Russian troops from the threatened land fronts. But troops could be of no use against an attack by ships upon sea-forts, and no such withdrawal would have taken place. It may be said that the gunners would thus be detained in the sea-forts who might otherwise have reinforced those employed on the land batteries. But that might have been effected equally well only by the menace of a naval attack. Thus the naval commanders must have been, and were, conscious that their fleets were about to run a great risk for no definite end and with the likelihood of being compelled to appear to suffer defeat.

Kinglake, who knew both Dundas and Lord Raglan, and who was then in the Crimea, thinks they might have come to a more satisfactory conclusion in a personal interview. But they were not on cordial terms, and had not met for some time. On the other hand, Sir Edmund Lyons, the second in command in the fleet, was in constant communication with the General. We have seen that he offered advice both as to the expediency of attacking the north side, and of an immediate assault after the flank march; it was owing to his counsel that we took Balaklava for a base; and now it was he who urged that the fleets should join in the attack. It was very unfortunate that he enjoyed such credit with Lord Raglan as to be listened to even when giving opinions about the operations of the armies, concerning which Lord Raglan had legitimate advisers at hand. He was always in favour of unhesitating and adventurous action, a course to which he may have been inclined, more than he was conscious of, by a chance similarity of person to the commander whose whole life was an example of valorous resolve. He was very like Nelson, and was naturally proud of the resemblance, though Nelson was no beauty, and may have secretly felt that a conformity in spirit also would be becoming. In these earlier stages of the war, his rash desire to do something effective rendered him Lord Raglan's evil genius, and how rash his impulses could be was shown a little later when he succeeded Dundas in the command of the fleet; for he who now so hotly urged a naval attack never made the slightest attempt on Sebastopol when he had become responsible for such an action, and had found by experience how fruitless it would be. Dundas must have felt himself placed at a great disadvantage with such an associate, as any commander must feel in having a too self-assertive subordinate, who wants to take the lead, and who fancies he has a popular repute to maintain.

The naval attack was not, however, executed as had been arranged. At the urgent instance of the French, a change was made in the morning. It was decided that the French Fleet should approach to within 1600 to 1800 yards of the coast line, from Cape Cherson to the middle of the mouth of the roadstead, and anchor there, firing on the Quarantine Fort and Alexander; and that the British should prolong the line so as to include in their fire Fort Constantine and the Telegraph and Wasp Batteries, on the coast of the north side. Several hours were occupied in thus anchoring the ships, and the land attack began without them.

Both sides had received reinforcements during the period of preparation. Menschikoff had by the transfer of troops from his army increased the number of soldiers in the garrison by 25,000. On the other hand, the Allied Fleets had sent men, guns, and ammunition to help the armies. More than

3000 seamen and marines were landed by Dundas, and the sailors became, as the Naval Brigade, a well-known feature of the siege. Of the guns already enumerated as arming the English batteries, twenty-nine were manned by the sailors. The French received from their admiral aid of the same kind.

One other circumstance of this period remains to be noticed. The Russians had pushed their outposts considerably in advance of their line of works on the side of the Malakoff, and Sir John Burgoyne had therefore desired, for the better security of his siege batteries (which had indeed been established at such a distance from the enemy's works partly because of the forward positions of these outposts) that the investing armies should be, in the main, pushed nearer to the enemy's lines. Our generals of division did not concur in this desire. They considered that a more advanced position could only be maintained at a perilous risk. But the French took advantage of the shelter afforded by Mount Rodolph to establish close behind it a brigade of infantry, and thus their batteries there were strongly supported, and the troops which would form the head of their column of assault were as near as possible to the Flagstaff Bastion.

At the earliest dawn on the 17th the Russians, as they descried the embrasures in the hitherto blank faces of the batteries, began a desultory fire upon them. At the concerted hour, half-past six, three French shells from Mount Rodolph gave the signal, and the Allied batteries opened throughout their extent, the Russian works replied, and spectators gathering from the camps in rear looked down upon the most tremendous conflict of artillery which, up to that time, the earth had ever witnessed. For four hours it continued almost unabated, while the onlookers could draw no conclusion from the incessant streams of fire which crossed between the opposing works. For although the English batteries had ruined the Malakoff Tower, dismounting the guns on its roof, and disabling the batteries below by the fall of its fragments, and though considerable damage had been done to all the Russian works, yet all except the Malakoff maintained their fire, and on the side of the French attack no superiority had become evident. It was about ten o'clock that an explosion took place on Mount Rodolph. A shell had blown up the principal magazine, killing about fifty men, and silencing the fire of the nearest battery. On the remaining French guns the Russians concentrated their fire, and at half-past ten the batteries of our allies were reduced to silence. Henceforth the hope of delivering a general assault had vanished, and the fire of the English batteries was maintained only to cover the discomfiture of their allies.

On our side things had gone, and continued to go, very well. Great havoc was wrought on the parapets and gorges of the opposing works, on their guns and gunners, and on the battalions drawn up in support. At half-past eleven

Admiral Korniloff was mortally wounded in the Malakoff. The batteries in the earthworks around the tower gradually ceased to fire. By three o'clock a third of the guns in the Redan were silenced, and very soon afterwards we blew up a large magazine there, reducing great part of the parapet and embrasures to a shapeless ruin, killing more than 100 men, and silencing the rest of its guns. Todleben says the defence in that part of the lines was completely paralysed, and that an immediate assault was expected, while the troops drawn up to meet it in rear of the work had become so demoralised that they fell back and sought the shelter of the scarped edge above the inner harbour.

It will be seen, then, that the purpose of establishing the siege batteries had on our side been accomplished. All that was expected from them had come to pass; the way was cleared, so far as it lay in them to clear it, by opening a passage for our troops into the Redan, and silencing its supporting work the Malakoff. But the disaster to the French had put an end to all thoughts of an assault by them on the Flagstaff Bastion, and the two attacks being interdependent, the design could not be executed. Our fire continued till dusk, and then the cannonade ceased everywhere.

The event had thoroughly justified the prevision of Sir John Burgoyne. The Russian heavy batteries opposed to us had been extinguished by our fire, and the assault would probably have been delivered in the hour before dawn next day, or possibly just before nightfall on the 17th, when it seems more than probable that the first step in the capture of the place would have been accomplished, namely, a secure lodgment on the enemy's main works. Had the French been equally successful in clearing the way to the Flagstaff Bastion, the success of the enterprise would have been assured so far as undertakings can be which are so largely imbued with the element of chance.

Our losses were slight, that of the French in killed and wounded about 100 men, the English forty-seven. The Russians lost more than 1100; not only were whole detachments repeatedly swept from the guns by our shot, and 100 men destroyed by the explosion, but their causalities were vastly increased by the necessity of keeping ready behind the works the troops which were to meet the expected assault, who could not be sheltered from the storm of missiles which swept over the fortified line.

As the ships effected nothing which could influence the fortunes of the day, it has not been essential to describe earlier the part they took. At one o'clock they had taken up their positions. The British ships prolonged the line across the outside of the harbour until met by a shoal between them and the coast of the north side. Inside that shoal a channel was found, and was entered by Lyons in the Agamemnon (brought out of Balaklava for the action), followed by the Sanspareil and London. These ships approached Fort Constantine to from 800 to 1000 yards, and their broadsides speedily destroyed the batteries on its roof. But they made small impression on its casemates, and found themselves under a fire from the batteries on the cliff which they were powerless to return. Many other ships entered the channel to help them, but all experienced the power of these small, high-placed batteries, which they were unable to reach with their fire. Nearly all were set on fire, some in many places. All suffered great damage, and considerable loss of men, and all were compelled to withdraw from the action. It was with these facts before him that Todleben ventured, in enumerating the advantages with which, according to him, the Allies would have attacked the north side, to assert that the ships could have silenced the very works which inflicted this damage with impunity, and could also have brought their fire to bear on the Star Fort, 1000 yards farther inland.

After the cannonade had lasted about four hours and a half, the fleets withdrew out of action. They had brought 1100 guns to bear; the forts replied with 152. The French ships lost 203 men; the English, 317; the Russian garrison, 138.

On the 18th the French batteries were still unable to reopen fire, while the English works and guns, little damaged, once more asserted their superiority over the Redan and Malakoff. But dawn had disclosed a new feature in the problem. At nightfall we had looked on works reduced to shapeless heaps, on ruined batteries and disabled guns. Before morning the parapets had been rebuilt, the batteries repaired, and fresh guns from the inexhaustible supplies of the ships and arsenal had occupied the embrasures; and the Allies could now begin to realise how formidable was the opponent who could thus, as chief engineer, wield the resources of the place. The recuperative power of the enemy, taken along with the failure of the French batteries, diminished indefinitely the chances of taking the place by assault. Nevertheless the hope of achieving that result was far from being abandoned, and there was yet a space of time in which the operations of the Allies were concentrated on the preparation for a renewal of the cannonade as the preface to a combined assault on the chief works between the French and the town. It should be noted, to the credit of our engineers, siege - artillery, and seamen, that while explosions frequently took place in the French and Russian batteries, our magazines remained intact; while their works and the occupants of them suffered severely from enfilade, our losses continued to be slight. On the 18th, 19th, and 20th, when we met single-handed the whole weight of the enemy's fire (the French being for so long unable to resume the contest) our aggregate loss in killed and wounded was only seventy-five men. Up to the 25th October our daily average loss was seventeen, while at the same date the aggregate of Russians killed and wounded in their works amounted to 3834 men.

CHAPTER VI

ATTACKED AT BALAKLAVA AND ON THE UPLAND

Outworks before Balaklava—Russians capture Them—Movements of the Heavy Brigade—Charge of the Heavy Brigade—Russian Cavalry defeated—The Orders to the Light Brigade—Russians both sides of Valley—Nolan and Lord Lucan—Charge of the Light Brigade—Charge of the Chasseurs—Return of the Light Brigade—Close of the Action—No Attempt at Recapture—Weak Point in Allied Defences—French Measures too exclusive—First Action of Inkerman—Object of it—The Sandbag Battery—Preparation for an Assault—Assembly of Russian Forces.

THE DRAMA now shifted into a new act, in which the Allies were to be themselves attacked, and forced to fight for their foothold in the Crimea.

Immediately after he quitted Sebastopol, Menschikoff had been joined by the remainder of his forces in the peninsula, hitherto beyond the sphere of action, being stationed in its south-western corner. These amounted to 12,000 men, and he also received the further reinforcements which, as already said, were on their way from Russia. In fact, the troops which might come to him from thence had, practically, no other limit than the means of transporting them. He therefore drew closer to the place, and while keeping his main force beyond our ken, had begun on the 7th October to send parties down to the Tchernaya. Soon afterwards his lieutenant, General Liprandi, established his headquarters at Tchorgoun, on the further bank, and the force of all arms placed under him began to assemble about that place. It gradually grew till it reached, according to Russian official accounts, the number of 22,000 infantry, 3400 cavalry, and seventy-eight guns, when it was considered strong enough for immediate action.

It has been said that the valley between Balaklava and the Tchernaya is crossed by a line of low heights, stretching from the foot of the plateau to the village of Kamara, and that along their course lies the Woronzoff road.

General Pavel Liprandi, Commander of Russian forces at Balaklava.

Four of these hills had earthworks on their summits—mere sketches with the spade; a donkey might have been ridden into some of them—and they had been armed with, in all, nine twelve-pounder iron guns. The extent of this line of works was more than two miles. Their garrisons had no support nearer than the 93d regiment, and the Turks and marines immediately around the harbour, who were 3000 yards off. The Russians had, of course, observed this, and also the weakness of the works, from the high hills above Kamara, and at daybreak on the 25th October their attack began. Crossing the Tchernaya from the Traktir Bridge upwards, and keeping at first altogether on the side of the valley nearest Kamara, their advanced guard came rapidly on, brought ten guns into positions commanding the hill (known as Canrobert's Hill) most distant from us and nearest Kamara, and began to cannonade it. Liprandi's main body was coming up, and he at length brought thirty guns, some of them of heavy calibres, to bear upon Canrobert's Hill and the next to it. These replied from their five twelve-pounders; and about this time a

3rd Earl of Lucan c.1860. Commander of the British Cavalry Division in the Crimea.

troop of our horse-artillery and a field battery, supported by the Scots Greys, were brought up to the ridge, and joined in the artillery combat, till the troop, having exhausted its ammunition, was withdrawn with some loss in men and horses.

When the formidable character of the attack was seen, our First and Fourth Divisions, and two French brigades, were ordered down to the scene of action. Reaching the point where the Woronzoff road descends from the plateau, the First Division made a short halt. If its orders had enabled it to march down to the plain there, followed by the other troops mentioned, the enemy must have hastily withdrawn over the Tchernaya, or have accepted battle with his back to the Kamara Hills. Instead of this, it was marched along the edge of the heights towards the other road down from the plateau at Kadikoi. Moving at a height of several hundred feet above the valley, it saw the plain spread out like a map, and what next occurred there took place immediately below it, and in full view. The Russians had just captured the two assailed outworks. That on Canrobert's Hill was occupied with a battalion of Turks and three of the guns already mentioned, the other with half a battalion and two. After silencing the guns, the Russians had stormed Canrobert's Hill with five battalions, the Turks, thus outnumbered, maintaining the combat so stubbornly that 170 of them were killed before they were driven out. Pushing on, the enemy captured more easily the next and smaller work: and the garrisons of the others, thus menaced by an army, and seeing no support anywhere, hastily left them and. made for Balaklava, pursued by the cavalry, who rode through the feeble earthworks with perfect ease, seven of the nine guns remaining in the hands of the Russians.

Near these hills the ground on either side rises to a ridge which forms their base, thus dividing the valley into two plains, the one on the side of Balaklava, the other stretching to the Tchernaya, and it was these that presently became the scene of two famous encounters.

The Heavy Brigade of Cavalry, under General Scarlett, had joined the army. It included the 4th and 5th Dragoon Guards, and the 1st, 2d, and 6th Dragoons (Royals, Scots Greys, and Inniskillings), and formed with the Light Brigade the cavalry division commanded by Lord Lucan.

Our two cavalry brigades had been manoeuvring so as to threaten the flank of any force which might approach Balaklava, without committing themselves to an action in which they would have been without the support of infantry. The Light Brigade, numbering 670 sabres, was at this moment on the side of the ridge looking to the Tchernaya; the Heavy Brigade, say 900 sabres, on the side towards Balaklava (see map 3). Its commander, General Scarlett, was at that moment leading three of his regiments (Greys, Inniskillings, 5th Dragoon Guards) through their camping ground into the plain; a fourth, the Royals, was for the moment behind, at no great distance, while the 4th Dragoon Guards was moving at the moment in the direction of the Light Brigade. Having witnessed the hasty retreat of the Turks, the many spectators on the Upland, consisting of the French stationed on it, and the English marching along it, next saw a great body of Russian cavalry ascend the ridge. Scarlett, unwarned till then, wheeled the Greys and half the Inniskillings into line; the 5th Dragoon Guards and the other squadron of the Inniskillings were in echelon behind the flanks; the Royals, galloping up, formed in extension of the 5th. The Russians, after a momentary halt, leaving the Light Brigade unnoticed, perhaps unseen, on their right, swept down in a huge column on the Heavy Brigade, and at the moment of collision threw out bodies in line on each flank; the batteries which accompanied them darting out and throwing shells, all of which burst short, against the troops on the Upland. Just then three heavy guns, manned by Turkish men and officers, in an earthwork on the edge of the Upland, were fired in succession on the Russian cavalry, and those troops nearest on the flank of the column losing some men and horses by the first shot, wavered, halted, and galloped back. At the same moment the mass slackened its pace as it drew near, while our men, embarrassed at first by the picket lines of their camp, as soon as they cleared them, charged in succession. All who had the good fortune to look down from the heights on that brilliant spectacle must carry with them through life a vivid remembrance of it. The plain and surrounding hills, all clad in sober green, formed an excellent background, for the colours of the opposing masses; the dark grey Russian column sweeping down in multitudinous superiority of number on the red-clad squadrons that, hindered by the obstacles of the ground in which they were moving, advanced slowly to meet them. There was a clash and fusion, as of wave meeting wave, when the head of the column encountered the leading squadrons of our brigade, all those engaged being resolved into a crowd of individual horsemen, whose swords rose, and fell, and glanced; so for a minute or two they fought, the impetus of the enemy's column carrying it on, and pressing our combatants back for a short space, till the 4th Dragoon Guards, coming clear of the wall of a vineyard which was between them and the enemy, and wheeling to the right by squadrons, charged the Russian flank, while the remaining regiments of our brigade went in ,in support of those which had first attacked. Then—almost as it seemed in a moment, and simultaneously—the whole Russian mass gave way, and fled, at speed and in disorder, beyond the hill, vanishing behind the slope some four or five minutes after they had first swept over it.

While this was going on, four of the enemy's squadrons, wheeling somewhat to their left, made a rush for the entrance of the harbour. The 93d were lying down behind a slope there; as the cavalry approached, they rose, fired a volley, and stood to receive the charge so firmly that the horsemen fled back with the rest of the column.

All this had passed under the observation of Lord Raglan. He does not seem to have made any comment on the strange inaction of the Light Brigade, which was afterwards explained to be due to Lord Cardigan's impression that he was expected to confine himself strictly to the defensive. But Lord Raglan sent the following written order to Lord Lucan: "Cavalry to advance and take advantage of any opportunity to recover the heights. They will be supported by the infantry, which have been ordered to advance on two fronts." The last sentence referred to the two English Divisions on the march,

'The Thin Red Line', painted by Robin Gibb, 1881. This famous painting shows the 93rd Highland Regiment standing firm before the Russian cavalry.

and still at some distance. This order did not commend itself to Lord Lucan's mind so clearly as to cause him to act on it. He moved the Heavy Brigade to the other side of the ridge, where he proposed to await the promised support of infantry, and this, under the circumstances, was not an irrational decision. After a while a disposition seemed manifest on the Russian side to carry off the captured guns, which might very well seem to signify a general retreat of the forces. Therefore a second written order was sent to Lord Lucan, thus worded: "Lord Raglan wishes the cavalry to advance rapidly to the front, and try to prevent the enemy carrying away the guns. Troop of horse-artillery may accompany. French cavalry is on your left. Immediate." This order was carried by the Quartermaster-General's aide-de-camp, Captain Nolan, author of a book on cavalry tactics, in which faith in the power of that arm was carried to an extreme. He found Lord Lucan between his two brigades, Scarlett's on the further slope of the ridge, Cardigan's (see map 3) beyond the Woronzoff road, where it ascends to the Upland, drawn up across the valley and looking down it towards the Tchernaya. D'Allonville's French brigade of cavalry had descended into the plain, and was now on the left rear of the Light Brigade.

In order to appreciate the position of the Russian army at this time, it is necessary to note an additional feature of this part of the field. Rising from the bank of the Tchernaya, close to the Traktir Bridge, and stretching thence towards the Chersonese upland, but not reaching it, is a low lump of hills called the Fedioukine heights. Their front parallel to the ridge, at about 1200 yards, forms with it the longer sides of the oblong valley leading to the Tchernaya. Menschikoff had sent a force of the three arms to co-operate with Liprandi, but not part of his command; and these troops and guns were posted on the Fedioukine heights. The situation, then, was this: the defeated

The Charge of the Light Brigade by Caton Woodville

Russian cavalry had retreated down the valley towards the Tchernaya, and was there drawn up behind its guns, a mile and a quarter from our Light Brigade; Liprandi's troops were posted along the further half of the Woronzoff ridge, enclosing, with those just said to be on the Fedioukine heights, the valley in which the hostile bodies of cavalry faced each other; eight Russian guns bore on the valley from the ridge; fourteen Russian guns from the Fedioukine heights; Russian rifleman had been pushed from those slopes into the valley on each side; also on each side were three squadrons of Russian lancers, posted in the folds of the hills, ready to emerge into the valley; and in front of the main body of the Russian cavalry were twelve guns in line.

Probably anyone viewing the matter without prepossession will think that Lord Raglan's orders to Lord Lucan were not sufficiently precise. For instance, in the last order, "to the front" is manifestly vague, the enemy being on several fronts. Lord Raglan, in a subsequent letter, explains his meaning thus: "It appearing that an attempt was making to remove the captured guns, the Earl of Lucan was desired to advance rapidly, follow the enemy in their retreat, and try to prevent them from effecting their objects." But the enemy were not removing the guns at that time, and not retreating, and the order, thus given by Lord Raglan under a mistake, did not apply.

Here was plenty of room for misinterpretation; and on receiving this order, Lord Lucan, by his own account, read it "with much consideration—perhaps consternation would be the better word—at once seeing its impracticability for any useful purpose whatever, and the consequent great unnecessary risk and loss to be incurred." He evidently interpreted "the front" to mean his own immediate front, and was presently given to understand that "the guns" were those which had retired along with the Russian cavalry. For when he uttered his objections, Nolan undertook to reply, though there is no evidence that he had any verbal instructions with which to explain the written order. "Lord Raglan's orders," he said, "are that the cavalry should attack immediately." "Attack, sir! Attack what? What guns, sir?" asked Lord Lucan sharply. "There, my lord, is your enemy, there are your guns," replied the believer in the supreme potency of cavalry, pointing towards the valley, and uttering these words, Lord Lucan says, "in a most disrespectful but significant manner."

Very indignant under what he held to be a taunt, Lord Lucan thereupon rode to Lord Cardigan, and imparting to him the order as he understood it, conveyed to him the impression that he must charge right down the valley with his brigade as it stood in two lines (presently made three by moving a regiment from the first line), while the Heavy Brigade would follow in support. And it certainly was impossible for Lord Cardigan to know what he could advance against except the cavalry that stood facing him; and though he shared and echoed Lord Lucan's misgivings, he at once gave the order, " The brigade will advance!"

With these words the famous ride began. But the brigade was scarcely in motion when Captain Nolan rode obliquely across the front of it, waving his sword. Lord Cardigan thought he was presuming to lead the brigade; his purpose could never be more than surmised, for a fragment of the first shell fired by the enemy struck him full in the breast. His horse turned round and carried him back, still in the saddle, through the ranks of the 13th, when the rider, already lifeless, fell to the ground. Led by Lord Cardigan, the lines continued to advance at a steady trot, and in a minute or two entered the zone of fire, where the air was filled with the rush of shot, the bursting of shells, and the moan of bullets, while amidst the infernal din the work of destruction went on, and men and horses were incessantly dashed to the ground. Still, at this time, many shot, aimed as they were at a rapidly moving mark, must have passed over, or beside the brigade, or between the lines. A deadlier fire awaited them from the twelve guns in front, which could scarcely fail to strike somewhere on a line a hundred yards wide. It was when the brigade had been advancing for about five minutes that it came within range of this battery, and the effect was manifest at once in the increased number of men and horses that strewed the plain. With the natural wish to shorten this ordeal, the pace was increased; when the brigade neared the battery, more than half its numbers were on the grass of the valley, dead or struggling to their feet.; but, still unwavering, not a man failing who was not yet disabled, the remnant rode straight into the smoke of the guns, and was

The 8th Hussars at rest, photograph c.1854

lost to view. Lord Lucan moved the Heavy Brigade some distance forward in support of the Light; but finding his first line suffering from a heavy fire, he halted and retired it, not without considerable loss. At the same time another and more effectual movement took place. General Morris, commander of the French cavalry, directed a regiment of his chasseurs d'Afrique (the 4th) to attack the troops on the Fedioukine heights, and silence the guns there. The regiment ascended the slopes, drove off the guns, and having accomplished their object, retired, with a loss of ten killed and twenty-eight wounded. Thenceforth the retreat of our cavalry was not harassed by the fire of guns from this side of the field, and the good comradeship implied in this prompt, resolute, and effectual charge of the French was highly appreciated by their allies, and has received just and warm praise from the historian Kinglake.

What the Light Brigade was doing behind the smoke of the battery was of too fragmentary a kind to be here more than touched on. The Russian gunners were driven off, and parties of our men even charged bodies of Russian cavalry; and that these retreated before them is not only recorded by the survivors of the Light Brigade, but by Todleben. But the combat could end but in one way, the retreat of what was left of our light cavalry. They rode back singly, or in twos and threes, some wounded, some supporting a wounded comrade. But there were two bodies that kept coherence and formation to the end. On our right, the 8th Hussars were joined by some of the 17th Lancers, when they numbered together about seventy men. The three squadrons of the enemy's lancers, already said to be on the side of the Woronzoff heights, descended from thence, and drew up across the valley to cut off the retreat of our men. Colonel Shewell of the 8th led this combined party against them, broke through them with ease, scattering them right and left, and regained our end of the valley. A little later, Lord George Paget led also about seventy men of the 4th Light Dragoons and 11th Hussars against the other three squadrons of lancers on the side of the Fedioukine heights, and passed by them with a partial collision which caused us but small loss. The remaining regiment, the 13th Light Dragoons, mustered only ten mounted men at the close of the action. The mounted strength of the brigade was then 195; it had lost 247 men in killed and wounded, and had 475 horses killed, and forty-two wounded.

The First Division, after its circuitous march by the Col, was now approaching the Woronzoff ridge, followed by the Fourth. It could see nothing of what was occurring in the adjoining valley; but it presently began to have tokens of the charge, in the form of wounded men and officers who rode by on their way to Balaklava.[2] Close to the ditch of the fieldwork on the last hill of the ridge on our side lay the body of Nolan on its back, the jacket open, the breast pierced by the fatal splinter. It was but an hour since the Division had passed him on the heights, where he was riding gaily near the staff, conspicuous in the red forage cap and tiger-skin saddle cover of his regiment.

It was now believed that a general action would begin by an advance to retake the hills captured by Liprandi, and no doubt such an intention did exist, but was not put in practice. The Russians were left undisturbed in possession of the three hills they had captured, with their seven guns. At nightfall the First Division marched by the Woronzoff road up to the plateau, and thence to its camp. It was long before that road was used again, for the presence of Liprandi's troops and batteries rendered it unavailable during great part of the winter.

It is easier to point to the faults of the Allies than to say how they should have been remedied. To post men and guns in weak works commanded by neighbouring heights, and having no ready supports in presence of an enemy's army, was to offer them up as a sacrifice. But where were the supports to come from? Then it has been said that the most effective way of bringing the Allied Divisions down from the upland would have been by the Woronzoff road. But that is on the supposition that it was intended to bring the Russians to a pitched battle. That, however, if the English general thought of it, formed no part of Canrobert's design. He believed that his

---

2 The commander of the Royals, Colonel Yorke, rode by the writer with a shattered leg. He died in 1890, while this chapter was being written, at the age of 77.

The Relief of the Light Brigade by Richard Caton Woodville.
The 11th Hussars reach the Russian guns.

part was at present limited to pushing the siege towards the grand object of the expedition, and covering the besieging army from attack; and he was not to be drawn into doubtful enterprises outside of these. This accounted, too, for the failure to attempt the recapture of our outworks—to what purpose retake them when it was proved that we had not troops enough to hold so extended a line? The ruin of the Light Brigade was primarily due to Lord Raglan's strange purpose of using our cavalry alone, and beyond support, for offence against Liprandi's strong force, strongly posted; and it was the misinterpretation of the too indistinct orders, sent with that very questionable intention, which produced the disaster. And yet we may well hesitate to wish that the step so obviously false had never been taken, for the desperate and unfaltering charge made that deep impression on the imagination of our people which found expression in Tennyson's verse, and has caused it to be long ago transfigured in a light where all of error or misfortune is lost, and nothing is left but what we are enduringly proud of.

It has been said that another blot besides Balaklava existed in the Allied line of defence. In front of the Third, Fourth, and Light Divisions, encamped on the strips of plain lying between the several ravines, were the siege works, and a direct attack made on them would be so retarded that the Divisions could have combined to meet it. But, in the space between the last ravine (the Careenage) and the edge of the Upland, the circumstances were different. (see map 5) A force might sally from the town, and ascending the ravine, or the adjacent slopes, without obstacle, would then be on fair fighting terms with whatever troops it might find there. Or the army outside, descending from the Inkerman heights, and crossing the valley by the bridge and causeway, would find itself on ground well adapted for traversing the space between the ravine and the cliff and entering the Upland at that corner. And the result of the establishment of the enemy's army there would be to open to it an advance which would cause all our Divisions engaged in the siege to form to meet it with their backs to the sea, and, in case of being overpowered, to fall back towards the French harbour (if they could), abandoning the siege works, with all their material; in fact, sustaining absolute defeat, possibly destruction.

The post-road going along the causeway, and ascending these slopes, reaches the Upland at a final crest, from whence it passes down and across the plain to join the Woronzoff road. It was on our side of the final ridge that the Second Division was encamped across the post-road. A mile behind it was the camp of the First Division. Then came a long interval of unoccupied ground, to the French camp on the south-eastern corner of the Upland, where Bosquet's covering corps may be said to have been employed in "gilding refined gold and painting the lily," by constructing lines of defence along the edge of cliffs, several hundred feet high, above an almost impassable part of the valley. Accepting the broad principle that a commander can only be expected to make good the deficiencies of an ally so far as may be without throwing a heavy strain upon his own troops, still, in this case, it was the common safety that was threatened, and it was a common duty to provide against the danger. By leaving a small force only in observation on the impregnable heights, and placing the main body near the really weak point, the labour and the forces of the French, superfluous where bestowed, might have rendered the position practically secure. Kinglake rightly characterises the disposition of Bosquet's corps as an example of the evils of a divided command.

The return of the First Division to its camp may have been unnoticed by the Russians, taking place as it did at nightfall. They may have calculated that the advance of Liprandi would cause the weak point on the plateau, for the moment, to be unoccupied; otherwise it is not easy to account for the enterprise of the day following the action of Balaklava. At noon a force of six battalions and four light field-guns, issuing from the town, ascended the ravine and slope which led to the Second Division. Our pickets fell back fighting, when the Russian field-pieces coming within range, pitched shot over the crest, behind which the regiments of the Second Division were lying down, while their skirmishers maintained, with those of the Russians, a desultory combat in the hollow. The two batteries of the Second Division now formed on the crest, and were presently reinforced by one from the

The valley of the shadow of death - caves in the Woronzoff Road behind the 21 gun battery. In the foreground, cannonballs can be clearly seen. Print by William Simpson c1855.

First Division, and before their fire the Russian guns were at once swept off the field. The enemy's battalions then came on successively in two columns, and these, too, were at once dispersed and driven back by the overpowering artillery fire. The men of the Second Division, launched in pursuit, pressed them hard, and they never halted till they were once more within the shelter of Sebastopol. Evans, not knowing of what force these might be the precursors, had determined to meet them on his own crest, and he was not to be drawn from thence till the action was already decided. General Bosquet sent to offer him assistance, but he declined it with thanks, as the enemy were, he said, already defeated. The Russians lost in this action, by their own estimate, 250 killed and wounded, and left in our hands eighty prisoners. We had ten killed and seventy-seven wounded. The attack, therefore, could not be characterised otherwise than as weak and futile. Nevertheless, it had an object. Todleben says it was intended to draw our attention from another attack on Balaklava. But he is, unfortunately, so unreliable in his statements and views that, with another plain interpretation before us, supported by facts, we need not be drawn aside by him. No further serious attack on Balaklava was intended, but preparations for the battle of Inkerman were then well advanced, and it was with these that the attack was connected. The Russians had brought out entrenching tools with them to Shell Hill, and, could they have established and armed a work there, they would not only have immensely strengthened their position in the future battle, but would also have provided for another highly important object, namely, the safe and unmolested passage of the troops outside Sebastopol, across the long causeway in the valley and the bridge of the Tchernaya. That the present attempt was not made with a larger force was probably owing to the desire to avoid bringing on a general action, and so anticipating prematurely the great enterprise which took place ten days later. But the operations of the Russians for opening that memorable battle will be seen to prove how great would have been their advantage had they possessed a strong lodgment on Shell Hill.

The attack on Balaklava, and its partial success, in depriving us of the hills held by our outposts, had effected its purpose of weakening the forces on the Upland. The two other regiments of the Highland Brigade joined the 93d before Balaklava; some companies of the rifle battalion of the Second Division were also posted there; and Vinoy's brigade of Bosquet's corps was so placed as to prevent the enemy from forcing a passage to the Upland by way of the Col. The whole of the forces under Sir Colin Campbell now executed a complete line of defence, strengthened with powerful batteries, around Balaklava, which might at last be regarded as secure. Seeing what a source of weakness the place was to us, by causing the great extension of our line, and the absorption of so much of our outnumbered forces, the question had been seriously considered of abandoning it, and supplying our army from the French harbour of Kamiesch, which would have infinitely lightened our toils and diminished our risks. But the Commissary-General declared that without Balaklava he could not undertake to supply the army, and the necessary evil was retained.

It was in this interval, between the sortie of the 26th October and the battle of the 5th November, that a work was thrown up by us on the field which, useless as a defence, became the object of bloody conflict. It was observed that the Russians were constructing a work on the other side of the valley to hold two guns (probably to support the coming attack), the embrasures being already formed, and the gabions placed in them. On this being shown to General Evans, he had two eighteen-pounders brought from the depot of the siege train, not far off, and a high parapet with two embrasures, made solid with sandbags, was thrown up on the edge of the cliff to hold them. It was placed about 1400 yards from the enemy's intended battery. In a few rounds the Russian work was knocked to pieces, and our guns, as being too far from our lines to be guarded, were then removed from what became afterwards a point, in the history of the battle, known as "the Sandbag Battery."

On the 4th of November the French infantry in the Crimea numbered 31,000; the British, 16,000; the Turks, who were not permitted to develop their value, 11,000. They must have been very different from the Turkish soldiery of the present day if they were not equal in fighting quality to any troops in the Crimea, and superior to all in patience, temperance, and endurance. But it was a tendency of the time to disparage them, partly from

Cornet assistant Surgeon Henry Wilkin, 11th Hussars. He survived the Charge of the Light Brigade. Photograph by Roger Fenton.

their abandonment of the outposts at Balaklava, the valorous defence made by a great part of them being, from some accident, unknown at the time; and they were employed in ways which gave them no opportunity of helping us in battle.

On both the Allied and the Russian side it was known that a crisis was now rapidly approaching; but only the Russians knew that it was a race between them for delivering the attack. The French siege corps, comparatively strong, close to its base, and protected on both flanks, on one by the sea, on the other by the English, was now retrieving its disaster of the 17th October, by diligently pushing its approaches in regular form upon the Flagstaff Bastion. We were strengthening our batteries and replenishing our magazines; as has been said the Russian daily loss in the fortress far exceeded ours in the trenches. We were ready to support a French attack which would now be made over a very short space of open ground. On the 4th November the Allied commanders had appointed a meeting on the 5th for definitely arranging the cannonade and assault which, they hoped, would at length lay the fortress open to us. The Russians were, of course, alive to the peril. But, on the 4th they had completed the assembly of their forces for attack. For long the corps d armee stationed about Odessa had been in motion for the Crimea. It had repeatedly sent important reinforcements to the fortress, and the whole of those, which had reached the heights beyond the Tchernaya by the 4th November, raised the total of Menschikoff's forces in and around Sebastopol, according to Todleben, to 100,000 men, without counting the seamen, so that not less than 110 to 115,000 men were confronting the 65,000 which, counting seamen and marines, the aggregate of the Allied forces amounted to.

Of the Russian troops which took actual part in the battle of Inkerman, 19,000 infantry, under General Soimonoff, were within the fortifications of Sebastopol; 16,000; under General Pauloff, were on the heights beyond the Tchernaya. These were to combine for the attack, accompanied by fifty-four guns of position and eighty-one field-guns. On their left was the force which had been Liprandi's, now commanded by Prince Gortschakoff, stretching from the captured hills outside Balaklava, across the Fedioukine heights, into the lower valley of the Tchernaya. The remainder of the troops formed the ample garrison of the works of Sebastopol. Long before the November dawn of Sunday, the besiegers heard drowsily in their tents the bells of Sebastopol celebrating the arrival in the camp of the young Grand Dukes Michael and Nicholas, and invoking the blessings of the Church on the impending attack, towards which the Russian troops were even then on the march.

CHAPTER VII

BATTLE OF INKERMAN

Rumours before the Battle—Description of the Ground—British Position—The Russian Plan of Battle—How carried out—Proximity of Corps to Battlefield—Soimonoff attacks—Effects of the Fog—Soimonoff's Right in Advance—The British repulse Him—Pauloff's Troops engage—Pauloff also repulsed—Causes of Russian Repulses—Dannenberg's Attacks—Greater Obstinacy of the Attack—Action and Death of Cathcart—The French drive back the Russians—Allies defeat another Resolute Attack—Allied Artillery begins to prevail—What delayed Bosquet—Crisis before the French arrived—Gortschakoff's part—Close of the Battle—Terrible Carnage—The Operations discussed—The Attack suitably met—The Sandbag Battery—Russian Exaggeration—What was at Stake—Consequence of Victory

WHEN THE Czar Nicholas received the news of the battle of the Alma, he was, Kinglake tells us, terribly agitated. A burst of rage was followed by a period of profound dejection, when for days he lay on his bed, taking no food, silent and unapproachable. But a speedy reaction must have followed when his military counsellors showed how hopeful was the situation. For his enemies were now definitely lodged in a small corner of the Crimea, and bound to it by their dependence on the fleet; Sebastopol was amply garrisoned, and the fortifications daily grew stronger; the field army assured the concentration of the troops which were crowding the roads of Southern Russia; behind them the resources in men and material were almost boundless. Only there was this limitation that a season was near when the march of troops towards and along the Crimea would be almost impossible. But there was ample time to do all that was needful to raise the Russian Forces to an overwhelming preponderance; and then point of attack, offering at once the greatest advantages for entering on the battle, and the most complete results as the fruits of victory, was so obvious that it might almost be fixed, and the details arranged, at St Peters-burgh. Probably it was so arranged; rumours began to pass through Europe of a great disaster

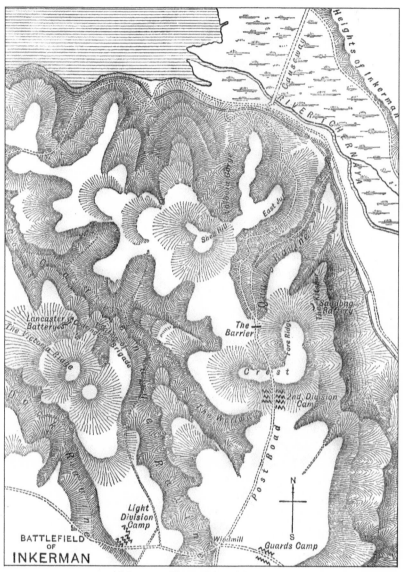

Map no. 5. The battlefield of Inkerman.

impending over the invaders, and a paper was communicated to our Foreign Office, purporting to be a copy of a despatch from Menschikoff for transmission to the Czar, and believed to be authentic, which said, "Future times, I am confident, will preserve the remembrance of the exemplary chastisement inflicted upon the presumption of the Allies. When our beloved Grand Dukes shall be here, I shall be able to give up to them intact the precious deposit which the confidence of the Emperor has placed in my hands. Sebastopol remains ours." This confidence was amply justified by the situation. But while such were the views of the enemy, only a few in the Allied Armies foresaw this particular danger. Evans, whose apprehensions were intensified by his responsibility as commander of the troops on that part of the ground, had indeed for long felt uneasy at our want of protection there, and had even begun a line of intrenchment to cover his guns; but it was not more than begun, and on the day of battle the ground was marked only by two small fragments of insignificant intrenchment, not a hundred yards long in all, and more like ordinary drains than fieldworks, one on each side of the road as it crossed the crest behind which the Second Division was encamped.

Inkerman was not the name of the ground on which the battle was fought, and which probably had no name, but was taken from the heights beyond the Tchernaya. Opposite the cliff which supports the north-eastern corner of the Upland rises another, of yellow stone, honey-combed with caverns, and crowned with a broken line of grey walls, battlemented in part, and studded with round towers. These are the "Ruins of Inkerman," and around them masses of grey stone protrude abruptly through the soil, of such quaint, sharp-cut forms that in the distance they might be taken for the remains of some very ancient city. From these the hill slopes upward to a plateau, mostly invisible from our position, where Menschikoff's field army was assembled. It is from this locality, the features of which are so striking to the eye when viewed from the British position, that the corner of the Upland, bounded on the west by the Careenage ravine, and on the north by the harbour, has received the name of Mount Inkerman.

The Second Division camp stood on a slope, rising beyond it to a crest, which, nearly level for most of its width, bent down on the right to the top of the cliffs above the Tchernaya, on the left to the Careenage ravine, the extent from the one boundary to the other being about 1400 yards. On ascending to this crest, and looking towards the head of the harbour, the ground beyond was seen bending downward into a hollow, and again rising to a hill opposite, which, with its sloping shoulders, limited the view in that direction to about 1200 yards. This opposite summit was Shell Hill, the post of the Russian artillery in the engagement, and the space between that and our crest comprised most of the field of battle, the whole of which was thickly clad with low coppice, strewn throughout with fragments of crag and boulders. A very few natural features marked the field. About 500 yards from its right boundary, our crest, instead of sloping down to the front as elsewhere, shot forward for about 500 yards, in what Mr. Kinglake calls the Fore Ridge, and from the spine of this eminence the ground fell rapidly, still covered thickly with stones and coppice, to the edge of the cliffs, where, at a point abreast of the northern end of this Fore Ridge stood the famous Sandbag Battery on a point (called by Kinglake the Kitspur), isolated to some extent by a small ravine plunging north-east to the valley. Two other natural features complete the general character of the field, namely, two glens, which half way between our crest and Shell Hill, at the bottom of the dip, shot out right and left, narrowing the plateau between them to half its width, till it expanded again as they receded from it at the bases of Shell Hill.

Menschikoff, whose plans of battle always showed how vague were his ideas about tactics, gave general orders to this effect: General Soimonoff was to assemble within the works his force of 19,000 infantry and thirty-eight guns, and issue from them, near the mouth of the Careenage ravine; at the same time, General Pauloff, with his 16,000 infantry and ninety-six guns, was to descend from the heights, cross the causeway and bridge of the Tchernaya, and "push on vigorously to meet and join the corps of Lieutenant-General Soimonoff." In another paragraph of the orders the object of the operation is stated to be to attack the English "in their position, in order that we may seize and occupy the heights on which they are established." The forces in the valley, lately commanded by Liprandi, now by Gortschakoff, were "to support the general attack by drawing the enemy's forces towards them, and to endeavour to seize one of the heights of the plateau." The garrison of Sebastopol was to cover with its artillery fire the right flank of the attacking force, and in case of confusion showing itself in the enemy's batteries, was to storm them. This being the general directions, the execution of them was left to the different commanders, namely, for the main attack to Soimonoff and Pauloff, for the auxiliary operations to Gortschakoff and the commandant of Sebastopol.

If these orders had been destined to be carried out under Menschikoff's own superintendence, their vagueness might be excusable. But, regarding himself apparently as the commander of all the forces in the locality, he committed the direction of the two bodies who were to make the main attack to another officer, General Dannenberg, who was to take command of them "as soon as they shall have effected their junction." This general only received his orders at five o'clock in the evening of the 4th, and neither he nor Menschikoff appears to have been then aware of the obstacle which the Careenage ravine—the sides of which were nearly inaccessible—offered to the combined action of troops astride of it, and both of them dealt with the ground on both sides of it as one clear battlefield. After many perplexing orders had been issued, Dannenberg seems to have at length realised the nature of the chasm that would intersect his front, and he therefore made further arrangements for the advance of his two generals on the two sides of it. But Soimonoff had interpreted the orders of the Commander-in-Chief as directing him to advance on the eastern side of the ravine; he had framed his plan for the movement, and submitted it to Menschikoff, who, though he must have seen how it conflicted with Dannenberg's scheme, seems to have made no attempt to decide between them. Soimonoff, therefore, followed his own idea, and thus it came to pass that 35,000 men, with 134 guns, were crowded into a space insufficient for half their numbers, while Dannenberg, who possibly only learned on the field of this wide departure from his design, was left to conduct an enterprise the plan of which he could not approve.

Here a moment's pause may be made to point out that, when two bodies of troops, separated by a distance of several miles, were to move by narrow issues to the ground where they were to join forces, it would have been an immense advantage to possess a commanding fortified point between them and the enemy. Shell Hill would have been such a point, and that circumstance will be seen to be amply explanatory of the Russian design in the action of the 26th of October.

Against the formidable attack in preparation, the menaced ground was then occupied by very nearly 3000 men of the Second Division, placed on the alert by the attack on their outposts. On the adjoining slope, the Victoria was Codrington's Brigade, which, with some marines, and three companies brought in the course of the action from Buller's Brigade, numbered 1400 men, and, as these might be regarded as partly the object of the attack, they remained throughout the action on the same ground. Close to them was the Naval Battery, which had been placed to fire on the Malakoff, but four of its heavy guns had been withdrawn to the siege works, and only one remained, which could not be brought to bear till the close of the battle.

Three-quarters of a mile in rear of the Second Division was the brigade of Guards, which was able to bring into action 1331 men.

Two miles in rear of the Second Division were the nearest troops of Bosquet's army corps, stretched round the south-eastern corner of the Upland.

Buller's Brigade, on the slope adjoining Codrington's, was a mile and a half from the Second Division. Cathcart's Division (Fourth), two miles and a half from the Second Division, and England's (Third), three miles, were on the heights in rear of our siege batteries.

Soimonoff issued from the fortress before dawn, crossed the Careenage ravine, and ascended the northern heights of Mount Inkerman, where at six o'clock he began to form order of battle. For some reason never explained, he disregarded that part of the plan which prescribed that he should combine with Pauloff, and act under the orders of Dannenberg. Waiting for neither, he at once commenced the attack. Spreading 300 riflemen as skirmishers across his front, he formed his first line of 6000 men, and the second, in immediate support, of 3300. The advance of these would cover the heavy batteries, numbering twenty-two guns, which he had brought from the arsenal of Sebastopol. These, corresponding to our eighteen-pounder guns and thirty-two-pounder howitzers, were posted on Shell Hill, and the high slopes which buttressed it right and left. Behind them came his 9000 remaining infantry, as a general reserve, and the light batteries (sixteen guns) which formed the remainder of his artillery. These operations were completed by about seven o'clock, when the heavy batteries opened fire, and his lines of columns descended the hill.

The pickets of the Second Division, each of a company, and numbering altogether 480 men, were at once pressed back fighting. But the main body of the Division, not ranged on the crest as in Evans's recent action, was pushed in fractions at once down the hill to support the pickets, by Pennefather, who commanded in the temporary absence of Evans, then sick on board ship. He was probably less impelled to this mode of action by any tactical reasons, though these, too, favoured it, than by his fighting propensity, which always led him to make for his enemy. Consequently, the crest was held only by the twelve nine-pounder guns of the Division, and a small proportion of its infantry. The large Russian projectiles not only swept the crest, but completely knocked to pieces the camp on the slope behind it, and destroyed the horses tethered there.

The morning was foggy, the ground muddy, and the herbage dank. The mist did not, however, envelop the field. Shell Hill was frequently visible, as well as Codrington's troops across the ravine, and columns could sometimes be descried while several hundred yards off. It was chiefly in the hollow that the mist lay, but even here it frequently rose and left the view clear. No doubt it was favourable to the fewer numbers, hiding from the Russians the fact that there was nothing behind the English lines, which came on as boldly as if strong supports were close at hand. It needs some plausible supposition of that kind to account (however imperfectly) for the extraordinary combats which ensued, where the extravagant achievements of the romances of chivalry were almost outdone by the reality.

On reaching the point of the plateau where it was narrowed by the glens, the Russian battalions halted to give their guns time to produce their effect. When they resumed their march, the battalion columns on the right passed first, and thus our left was the part of our line which received the first attack. It is to be noted as a feature of the field that at the point where the post-road enters the Quarry ravine, and where we had a picket, a wall of loose stones, crossing the road and stretching into the coppice on each side, had been thrown up as a slight defence, and to mark the ground, and this was known as "the Barrier."

Here it must be remarked that the indefatigable inquiries of Kinglake, and the care with which he arranged the information thus obtained, first disentangled the incidents of the battle from the confusion which long hid them, and rendered them intelligible, as they had never been before, even to those who fought in the action.

The enemy, unable to advance through the narrowed space on a full front, such as would have enabled him to make a simultaneous attack all along our position, entered it with his right in advance of the centre and left, and the first attack therefore took place on our left. Only his foremost battalions being visible, the nature of the attack was not at first fully appreciated, and might have been supposed to be merely a very formidable sortie. His battalions advanced, some in a column composed of an entire battalion, some split into four columns of companies, but the broken nature of the ground dissolved all these more or less into dense crowds which had lost their formation. One of these, on the extreme Russian right, preceding for some unexplained reason the others, pressed on till it came in contact with a wing of the 49th, which, delivering a volley, charged, drove it back, and pursued it even on to the slope of Shell Hill. Soimonoff then led in person twelve battalions, numbering 9000 men, against our left and centre, while a column[3] moved up by the Careenage ravine beyond our left flank. At the same time there were arriving on our left 650 men of the Light Division, and a battery from the Fourth Division, raising Pennefather's force on the field to exactly 3600 men and eighteen field-guns. About 400 of Buller's men (88th), which had at first passed over the crest, fell back before the Russian masses, and three guns of the battery which was following them fell into the enemy's hands. At the same time the Russian column in the ravine, after surprising a picket of the Light Division, was making its way to the plateau in rear of our line, and close to our camp, by a glen which led in that direction. It was only just in time that Buller himself arrived with the remainder of his 650 men (77th), who were at once pushed into the fight. Part of them attacked the head of the turning column just emerging from the glen, while a company of the Guards, on picket on the other bank, fired on it from thence, and the column, which had so nearly attained to success that might have been decisive, was driven back, and appeared no more on the field,, Soimonoff's right battalion, advancing on the plateau, was encountered by a wing of the 47th, spread out in skirmishing order on a wide front, which harassed it by so destructive a fire that it broke up and retreated, and two other battalions of the same regiment (the same which had just captured our guns) came to a halt, having before them the troops which had pursued the Russian battalions that first met us to the slope of Shell Hill, and had then fallen back. Passing these on

---

3 Kinglake says this column was composed of sailors, and therefore not included in the numbers of the army.

The ruins of Inkerman and the city of caverns. Print by William Simpson c1855.

the right, Buller's companies (260 men of the 77th) entered the fight, met two Russian battalions, fired, charged, and drove them quite off the field. Seeing this discomfiture of their comrades going on so near, the other battalions just spoken of as halted on our left of these, followed them in their retreat, leaving the captured guns to be recovered by our men. It was about this time that Soimonoff was killed. On our side General Buller was disabled by a cannon shot which killed his horse.

Five of the twelve battalions, besides that other which attacked first, and the turning column in the ravine, were thus accounted for. Seven of Soimonoff s still remained. One of these diverged to the Russian left, where it joined part of Pauloff's forces, then arriving on the field. The remaining six advanced by both sides of the post-road upon our centre, and were defeated like the rest, partly by the close fire of the battery on our left of the post-road (that on the right had been silenced by the fire from Shell Hill), partly by the charge and pursuit of some companies of the 49th, and the pickets which had halted here, and which held the ground beside the guns.

The part of Pauloff's corps, eight battalions, which preceded the rest had meanwhile crossed the head of the Quarry ravine, and, picking up the stray battalion of Soimonoff, and raising the whole force employed by the two generals in the first attack to twenty battalions, numbering 15,000 men, made a simultaneous but distinct onset. They had formed opposite our right, their left on the Sandbag Battery, their right across the post-road where it enters the Quarry ravine.

The four battalions composing the regiment on the right had begun to approach the Barrier, when a wing of the 30th, 200 strong, sprang over it, and charged with the bayonet the two leading battalions. A short and very serious conflict ensued—many of our men and officers were shot down; but the charge proved decisive, and the leading battalions, hurrying back in disorder, carried the two others (of the same regiment) with them, and the whole were swept off the field, some towards Shell Hill, some down the Quarry ravine to the valley.

Finally, it remained to deal with the five battalions still left of the attacking force. Against these advanced the 41st regiment, under its brigadier, Adams, numbering 525 men. Approaching from the higher ground of the Fore Ridge, the regiment, in extended order, opened fire on the 4000 Russians before it, drove them over the declivities, and from the edge pursued them with its fire till they reached and descended the bank of the Tchernaya.

Thus, in open ground, affording to the defenders none of the defensive advantages, walls, hedges, or enclosures of any kind, which most battlefields have been found to offer, these 15,000 Russians had been repulsed by less than a fourth of their numbers. But, in truth, to say they were repulsed very inadequately expresses what happened to them in the encounter. All the battalions which did not retreat without fighting left the field so shattered and disorganised, and with the loss of so many officers, that they were not again brought into the fight. This was in great measure owing to the density of the formations in which the Russians moved, and the audacity with which our slender bodies attacked them. Seeing the British come on so confidently, on a front of such extent as no other European troops would, at that time, have formed without very substantial forces behind them, the Russians inferred the existence of large numbers, and remained convinced that they had been forced from the field by masses to which their own were greatly inferior. This was a moral effect; but there was also a material cause conducing to the result. The Russian riflemen, as we soon had good reason to know, were armed with a weapon quite equal to our Minié; but the mass of the infantry still wielded a musket not superior to the old Brown Bess firelock, which the Minié had replaced, whereas our troops, except those of the Fourth Division, had the rifle. Therefore, long before a Russian column had got near enough to make its fire tell, it began to suffer from a fire that was very destructive, not only because of the longer range and more effective aim, but because the bullets were propelled with a force capable of sending them through more than one man's body. But these reasons are merely palliative; nothing can veil the fact that, supported by an overwhelming artillery, which frequently reduced ours to silence, these great bodies, once launched on their career, ought by their mere impetus to have everywhere penetrated our line; and that had even a part been well led, and animated by such a spirit as all nations desire to attribute to their fighting men, they would never have suffered themselves to be stopped and turned by the imaginary enemies which the mist might hide, or which the intrepid, gallant, audacious bearing of our single line caused them to believe might be following in support of it.

It was half-past seven when this stage of the action was finished, and a new one commenced with the arrival on the scene of General Dannenberg. All Pauloff's battalions were now ranged on Mount Inkerman, and with those of Soimonoff which had previously been held in reserve, and were still untouched, raised the number of fresh troops with which he could recommence the battle to 19,000 infantry and ninety guns. Ten thousand of these were now launched against our position, but this time they were massed for the attack chiefly in and about the Quarry ravine, and, neglecting our left, bore against our centre and right, upon which also was now turned the weight of the cannonade. The reason for this, no doubt, was that closer co-operation might be maintained with Gortschakoff, whose troops had extended down the valley till their right was nearly opposite the right of our position, and who, in case of Dannenberg's success in that quarter, might at once lend a hand to him.

At the same time Pennefather also had received reinforcements. The Guards, turning out at the sounds of battle, had now reached the position; so had the batteries of the First Division; and Cathcart was approaching with 2100 men of his Division, set free by the absence of any sign of attack upon the siege works.

The troops which had at first so successfully defended the Barrier had been compelled, by the large bodies moving round their flanks, to fail back, and the Russians held it for a time. But these were driven out and the barrier was reoccupied by detachments of the 21st, 63d, and Rifles, when, from its position, closing the post road, it continued to be a point of great importance. The troops there, reinforced from time to time, held it throughout the battle, repelling all direct attacks upon it; and it is a singular fact that the enemy's masses, in their subsequent onsets, passed it by, both in advancing and retreating, without making any attempt upon it from the rear.

The first attack was made on Adams, with five Russian battalions, numbering about 4000 against the 700 that opposed them, and took place on the slopes of the Fore Ridge, and about the Sandbag Battery. The Guards, already on the crest, were moved to the support of Adams. Whether the troops of Pauloff were superior in quality, or better led, or whether the lifting of the fog revealed their own superiority in number, the spirit they displayed was incomparably fiercer and more resolute than had yet marked the attack. The conflicts of the first stage of the battle had been child's play compared with the bloody struggle of which the ground between the Fore Ridge and the edge of the cliffs east of it were now the scene. Useless for defence on either side, the Sandbag Battery may be regarded as a sort of symbol of victory conventionally adopted by both, leading our troops to do battle on the edge of the steeps, and the enemy to choose the broken and difficult ground on which this arbitrary standard reared itself to view for a main field of combat. Although the disparity of numbers was now diminished, the Russians, instead of shrinking from difficulties which their own imaginations rendered insurmountable, or accepting a repulse as final, swarmed again and again to the encounter, engaging by groups and individuals in the closest and most obstinate combats, till between the hostile lines rose a rampart of the fallen men of both sides. For a long time the part played by the defenders was strictly defensive; with each repulse the victors halted on the edge of the steeps, preserving some continuity of front with which to meet the next assault, while the recoiling crowds, unmolested by pursuit, and secured from fire by the abruptness of the edge, paused at a short distance below to gather fresh coherence and impetus for a renewal of the struggle. It was with the arrival of Cathcart, conducting part of the Fourth Division, that the combat assumed a new phase. Possessed with the idea of the decisive effect which an attack on their flank must exercise on troops that, however strong they might still be in numbers, had already suffered so many rebuffs, he descended the slope beyond the right of our line. The greater part of his troops had already been cast piecemeal into the fight in other parts of the field where succour was most urgently needed, but about 400 men remained to him with which to make the attempt. And at first it was eminently effective, insomuch that Cathcart congratulated his brigadier, Torrens, then lying wounded, on the success of this endeavour to take the offensive. But that success was now to be turned into disaster by an event which it was altogether beyond Cathcart's province or power to foresee. While advancing in the belief that he was in full co-operation with our troops on the cliff, he was suddenly assailed by a body of the enemy from the heights he had just quitted, and which had either turned or broken through that part of our front which he was endeavouring to relieve from the stress of numbers. Thus taken in reverse, his troops, scattered on the rugged hillside, suffered heavily, only regaining the position in small, broken bodies, and with the loss of their commander, who was shot dead. This effort of Cathcart's changed the restrained character of the defence, and was the first of numerous desultory onsets, which left the troops engaged in them far in advance, and broke the continuity of the line. For the downward movement had spread from right to left along the front; the heights of the Fore Ridge, left bare of the defenders, were occupied by Russians ascending the ravine beyond their left; and our people, thus intercepted, had to edge past the enemy, or to cut their way through. The right of our position seemed absolutely without defence; a body of Russian troops was moving unopposed along the Fore Ridge, apparently about to push through the vacant corner of the position, when, in order to enclose our fragments, it formed line to its left, facing the edge of the cliffs. It was while it stood thus that a French regiment, lately arrived, and thus far posted at the English end of the Fore Ridge, advanced, took the Russians in flank, and drove them back into the gorges from whence they had issued.

The next attack was made by the Russians with the same troops, diminished by their losses to 6000 men, while the Allies numbered 5000. The disparity in infantry for the actual encounter (for the Russian reserve of 9000 was still held back) was thus rapidly diminishing, but the enemy preserved his great predominance in artillery. Again the hundred guns, which by this time they had in action, swept our crest throughout its extent. The right of our position, from the head of the Quarry ravine to the Sandbag Battery, was now held by some of our rifles, and by a French battalion. Leaving these on their left, the enemy's columns issued from the Quarry ravine, and this time pushed along the post-road against our centre and left. Two of their regiments (eight battalions) were extended in first line, in columns of companies; behind came the main column, composed of the four battalions of the remaining regiment. This advance was more thoroughly pushed home, and with greater success, than any other which they attempted throughout the day. They once more made their right the head of the attack and with it penetrated our line on the side of the Careenage ravine, drove back the troops there, and took and spiked some of our guns. The other parts of their front line, coming up successively to the crest, held it for a brief interval, while the main column, passing by our troops at the Barrier, moved on in support. But meanwhile, before it reached the crest, the regiments of the front line had been driven off by a simultaneous advance of French and English, and, after suffering great loss, the main column also retired. It was pressed by the Allied troops, part of whom reinforced those already at the head of the Quarry ravine, while the French regiment, which had defended the centre, moving to its right, took up, with the other already there, the defence of the ground where the Guards had fought. Here the French had yet another struggle to maintain, and with varying fortunes, for once they entirely lost the advanced ground they had held; but their last reinforcements arriving, they finally drove the Russians immediately opposed to them not only off that part of our front, but off the field.

It was now eleven o'clock, and the battle, though not ended, was already decided. For not only had the Allies, after deducting losses, 4700 English and 7000 French infantry on the field, against the broken battalions and the 9000 unused infantry of Dannenberg's reserve, but the balance of artillery power, for long so largely against us (the Allies had in action at the close only thirty-eight English and twenty-four French field-guns) had now been for some time in our favour. At half-past nine the two famous eighteen-pounders had appeared on the field. Forming part of the siege train, they had as yet been left in the depot near the First Division camp, and were now dragged on to the field by 150 artillerymen. Their projectile was not much larger than that of the heavy Russian pieces; but the long, weighty iron gun, with its heavy charge, was greatly more effective in aim and velocity. The two, though not without heavy losses in men, spread devastation among the position batteries on Shell Hill and the lighter batteries on its slopes; while two French batteries of horse-artillery, passing over the crest on the right of our guns, had established themselves on the bare slope fronting the enemy, and had there gallantly maintained themselves under a shattering fire. For long this combat of artillery was maintained on both sides, though with manifestly declining power on the part of the enemy, while our skirmishers, pressing forward on the centre and left, made such way that they galled the Russian gunners with their bullets.

The menace of an attack by Gortschakoff on the heights held by Bosquet had not been without its effect. For an hour, while the real fight was taking place at Inkerman, the French troops were kept in their lines. At the end of that time Bosquet sent two battalions from Bourbaki's Brigade, and two troops of horse-artillery, to the windmill on the road near the Guards' camp, and accompanied them himself. He was there met by Generals Brown and Cathcart, to whom he offered the aid of these troops, and expressed his readiness in case of need to bring up others. The generals took the strange, almost unaccountable, course of telling him that his support was not needed, and asking him to send his battalions to watch the ground on the right of the Guards' camp left vacant by the withdrawal of the Guards to take part in the battle. Bosquet had thereupon returned to his own command; but receiving fresh and pressing communication from Lord Raglan he had directed the troops already despatched again to march on Inkerman. Thus it was not till the battle had been going on for between two and three hours that Bourbaki's two battalions, numbering 1600 men, arrived near the crest, when they were posted for some time in rear of it, the 6th of the Line on the right of the Fore Ridge, the 7th Leger near the post-road, and it was at these points that they first entered the fight.

The next French reinforcements, consisting of four companies of chasseurs, and part of D'Autemarre's Brigade, 1900 men, arrived with Bosquet himself about ten o'clock, closely followed by the rest of the brigade, numbering 2300 more, with two other batteries of field-artillery; and more than half of these troops took an important part in the engagement. Finally, the French reserve, of 2400 men came on the field at eleven o'clock, when the attacks of the Russian infantry had come to an end.

An officer so experienced in war as Bosquet must have frequently considered what part he should take in defending Mount Inkerman against a pronounced attack while he should himself be threatened from the valley. Seeing how closely his own fate was bound up in that of the British troops in that quarter, he cannot be said to have rightly appreciated the problem. The view he took of it was much too exclusively a French view. According to all reasonable calculation, he would have found 20,000 Russians, followed by 15,000 more, with an immense force of artillery, advancing on his left rear long before he had moved a man to support us. In that case, to have continued to watch Gortschakoff would only have insured his own ruin. The most tremendous risk was incurred, by French as well as English, first when he placed all his troops so far from the point of danger, and next when he so long delayed to move sufficient forces thither; and not even his own manifestation of goodwill, and the strange reception given to his battalions by Generals Brown and Cathcart, can altogether exonerate him. That he at last felt himself free to lend effectual aid (and that it was effectual was owing to circumstances beyond calculation) was due to his perception of the fact that Gortschakoff's advance and cannonade was a transparent feint. A commander can hardly be set on a more difficult task than to execute a feigned attack in open ground against a commanding position. All the Russian movements in the valley were as clear to view from the plateau as if performed on a map. Either Gortschakoff's share of the action fell short of the orders given to him, or those orders ought to have directed him to make a real attack. About this Mr. Kinglake says: "With respect to Gortschakoff's instructions, the general order was worded as though it meant to direct against Bosquet's position an actual, unfeigned attack; but on authority which I regard as indisputable, I have satisfied myself that the orders really given to Gortschakoff were of the kind stated in the text," that is, he was "to menace Bosquet by feints." In actually assaulting the heights he would no doubt have lost many men; but they would have been the price of that victory, which could scarcely have been bought too dear. A real attack would undoubtedly have kept Bosquet from parting with his troops; Dannenberg, in their absence, would have penetrated our line, and opened the road to the valley, when Gortschakoff would have joined him on the Upland. It was in expectation of such an effort on Gortschakoff's part that Dannenberg remained on the field long after he had abandoned the intention of resuming his independent attacks. He held his ground, though suffering heavy losses, trusting that the storming of the heights lately held by the French, but now comparatively bare of troops, would open a road for him, and straining his ear for the sound of his colleague's guns on the Upland. At last the decline of the autumn day forced him to begin that retreat which the declivities in his rear rendered so tedious and so perilous, encumbered as he was by a numerous and disorganised artillery. Canrobert has been blamed for not attacking him with the 8000 troops he had assembled on the field, the greater part still unused; and doubtless had the French general taken a bold offensive, the enemy's defeat would have become a signal disaster. But if Dannenberg was looking towards Gortschakoff, so, no doubt, was Canrobert. He could not but remember that the 20,000 troops whom he had watched so anxiously in the morning were still close at hand in order of battle; the policy he had declared at Balaklava of restricting himself to covering the siege, no matter what successes a bold aggression might promise, governed him now; and this seems, in the case of a gallant, quick- spirited man like Canrobert—one, too, whom we had often found so loyal an ally—a more plausible explanation of his almost passive attitude at the close of the battle, than either a defect of resolution or a disinclination to aid his colleague.

This extraordinary battle closed with no final charge nor victorious advance on the one side, no desperate stand or tumultuous flight on the other. The Russians, when hopeless of success, seemed to melt from the lost field; the English were too few and too exhausted, the French too little confident in the advantage gained, to convert the repulse into rout. Nor was there among the victors the exaltation of spirit which usually follows the gain of a great battle, for the stress of the conflict had been too prolonged and heavy to allow of quick reaction. The gloom of the November evening seemed to overspread with its influence not only the broken battalions which sought the shelter of the fortress, but the wearied occupants of the hardly-contested ground, and descended on a field so laden with carnage that no aspect of the sky could deepen its horrors. Especially on the slopes between the Fore Ridge and the cliffs had death been busy; men lay in swathes there, as if mown down, insomuch that it was often impossible to ride through the lines and mounds of the slain. Of these, notwithstanding that the Allies, especially the English, had lost heavily in proportion to their numbers, an immense and almost unaccountable majority were Russians; so that of no battle in which our nation has been engaged since Agincourt could it be more truly said,—

"When, without stratagem,
But in plain shock, and even play of battle,
Was ever known so great and little loss,
On one part and on th' other?—Take it, God,
For it is only thine!"

The Russian losses in the battle were four times as great as the number of the troops with which the Second Division met the first attack. They lost 12.000, of which an immense proportion were left dead on the field, and 256 officers. The English lost 597, of whom thirty-nine officers, killed, and 1760, of whom ninety-one officers, wounded; the French, thirteen officers and 130 men killed, and thirty-six officers and 750 men wounded.

The present writer does not doubt that Dannenberg's plan of attacking by both sides of the Careenage ravine was the right one. It is true that to have attacking troops divided by an obstacle is a great disadvantage. It is also true, as Kinglake says, that "the camps of the Allies were so placed on the Chersonese that, to meet perils threatening from the western side of the Careenage ravine, they could effect a rapid concentration." But they could only effect it by robbing the eastern side of what was indispensable for its defence. If, instead of one part of the enemy's army attacking while the other was coming up in its rear, and therefore exercising no effect upon the battle, both had attacked simultaneously, it is hardly credible that one (and if one, both) would not have broken through. And if it is a disadvantage that the front of attack should be divided by an obstacle, it is a still greater evil to restrict the attack, especially against very inferior numbers, to too confined a space. By crowding on to the eastern slope only, in numbers amply sufficient to have attacked both, the Russians were choosing the ground which best suited our numbers and our circumstances, and which least suited their own.

It has been already remarked that as the mode of fighting the action by us differed radically from that of the 26th of October, so did the circumstances on the two days. On the 26th we had a great superiority in artillery, and plenty of room on the crest for the eighteen guns and the small force of infantry. On the 5th November nearly half of our narrow position was occupied by the line of batteries. Where, then, were the infantry to be posted? Were they to be close in rear of the batteries? Then the' tremendous fire of the enemy would have swept the crest with double effect, ravaging both guns and infantry. If posted in front of the guns, the result would be the same, with the additional disadvantage that our guns would be firing over the heads of our infantry. By pushing the troops down the slope, they met the enemy before their columns could issue from the ravines and deploy; and even on the extreme right we are by no means certain that to encounter them on the ledge near the Sandbag Battery (a mode of action which Mr Kinglake laments as false policy) was not the best way of dealing with the ground, for if we had withdrawn our line there to the main crest, and left the space between the cliff and the Fore Ridge unoccupied, the Russians, after ascending to the ledge, would have been able to take breath beneath its shelter before gaining the plateau, and when there they would have had the opportunity of solving what was one of their great difficulties throughout the day, namely, finding open space to deploy on at a certain distance from our front. As it was, they came up rugged steeps, in disorder and under fire, to close with us still uphill, while yet breathless with the ascent, and here consequently occurred their severest losses. On the whole, therefore, the manner in which our troops fought the battle may be thought to have been very fortunately adapted to the topography of the field, and to the proportions of the contending forces.

It is natural that a Russian chronicler should seek to extenuate this defeat, and we will not greatly blame Todleben for increasing the strength of the English, in the first phase of the combat, to 11,585 (more than trebling their actual force), for laying great stress on the "fieldworks" which strengthened the position, and for claiming successes which, in some mysterious way that he does not elucidate, were turned into disasters. In his visit to the field, in 1869, Mr Kinglake found the Sandbag Battery still there—very likely it is there now—and his detailed account of it is sufficiently exact. But he and other chroniclers advert to it, when describing the combats of which the area around it was the scene, in terms which would convey to those who have never seen it an altogether exaggerated idea of its importance, and even of its size; and Todleben not only describes a Russian regiment 3000 strong as fighting desperately with our Coldstreams for the possession of it, but as capturing nine pieces of artillery "as the prize of this brilliant feat of arms"; some of which, that imaginative chronicler tells us, were carried off by the victors, and the rest spiked. It is true that some hours later in the day one French gun was carried off from this part of the field, and was afterwards recovered in a ravine, so the Russian historian could at least plead that his version is not in this case, as it is in some others, absolutely without foundation. But all this gives to the battery an importance quite fictitious. It was simply a wall of earth, several feet thick and twelve paces long, with two embrasures cut in it, the parapet, elsewhere considerably taller than a man's head, sloping rapidly for a few feet at each end. Behind it might have stood, in two ranks, thirty-six men in all, of whom twenty, ten of each rank, might have been able to fire through the embrasures and over the ends, while the other sixteen would have been better employed elsewhere. It was conspicuous from its height and position, and the enemy, seeing it from below, might easily have imagined it more formidable than it was; but how could 3000 men be employed in attacking, or a battalion such as the Coldstreams in defending it? Sixty men would have been an ample number wherewith to assail it. As for the intrenchments on each side of the road, a common bank and ditch, such as those which generally border our fields, would have been incomparably stronger for defence. Yet Todleben speaks of this useless mound, and these insignificant banks, as "the enemy's works," and another Russian writer says, "in spite of the accumulated forces of the enemy, our columns succeeded in occupying his batteries and fortifications."[4] The truth is that few battlefields have been so devoid of obstacles of this kind as that of Inkerman. The difficulties of the attack lay in the hindrance which the coppice and crags opposed to regulated advances and deployments, though; on the other hand, these objects afforded to the enemy the not inconsiderable advantage of sheltering his skirmishers.

Those who were children at the time of the Crimean War can scarcely realise how ardent, how anxious, how absorbing was the interest which the nation felt for the actors in that distant field, insomuch that Mr Bright, theoretically a man of peace, publicly said he believed there were thousands in England who only laid their heads on their pillows at night to dream of their brethren in the Crimea. This feeling reached its climax with the news of Inkerman, and it was not, nor indeed could it be, in excess of the magnitude of the stake which depended on the issue of that battle. The defeat of that slender Division on its ridge would have carried with it consequences absolutely tremendous. The Russians, arriving on the Upland, where the ground was bare, and the slopes no longer against them, would have interposed an army in order of battle between our trenches and Bosquet's corps. As they moved on, disposing by their mere impetus of any disjointed attempts to oppose them, they would have reached a hand to Gortschakoff on the one side, to the garrison of Sebastopol on the other, till the reunited Russian Army, extended across the Chersonese, would have found on those wide plains a fair field for its great masses of cavalry and artillery. To the Allies, having behind them only the sea-cliffs, or the declivities leading to their narrow harbours, defeat would have been absolute and ruinous; and behind such defeat lay national degradation. On the other hand, when the long crisis of the day was past, the fate of Sebastopol was already decided. It is true that our misfortunes grew darker and darker, that six weeks afterwards most of the horses that charged at Balaklava were rotting in a sea of mud, most of the men who fought at Inkerman filling hospitals at Scutari, or graves on the plain. Any history of the war would be incomplete that failed to record, as a main and characteristic feature of it, the extraordinary misery which the besieging armies endured. Nevertheless, when Inkerman had proved that the Russians could not beat us in battle, we were sure to win, because it was impossible for us to embark in presence of the enemy. We could do nothing else but keep our hold; and, keeping it, it was matter of demonstration that the Powers which held command of the sea must prevail over the Power

---

4 It is just possible that these writers may have supposed that some of the works placed on that ground long afterwards, were there at the time of the battle.

whose theatre of war was separated from its resources by roadless deserts. Such were the consequences which hung in the balance each time that the Russian columns came crowding on, while their long lines of artillery swept the ridge; and it is not amiss that the nation, which sometimes gives its praise so cheaply, should be reminded how much it owed that day to the steadfast men of Inkerman.

CHAPTER VIII

THE HURRICANE AND THE WINTER

*The Hurricane—Its Effects—Privations of the Troops—Want
of Transport—Transport done by the Men—The Cavalry Horses
starved—Sufferings of the Sick—The Hospitals—Indignation in
England—The French take part of our Duties—Relief begins—Why
a Road was not made at first—Roads now made—Improvement in the
Hospitals—Miss Nightingale arrives—The Influence she acquires—
The Ratio of Deaths—Resignation of the Ministry—The Crimean
Commission—The Commissary-General blamed—Defends himself—
General Airey refutes Charges—Departments have their Proper Limits—
The Fault lay in the System.*

THREE DAYS after the battle of Inkerman, Lord Raglan informed his Commissary-General, Mr Filder, that our Army would winter in the Crimea, and desired him to make provision accordingly.

Up to this time the troops had undergone no great privation. During October the weather had been mild and sunny, with cool nights; the tents stood on dry and level spaces of turf. The surface of the plains had been good for transit. Rations for men and horses had been supplied with sufficient regularity; losses of men from sickness or battle had been repaired; and notwithstanding the excessive work which the disproportion of our numbers to their task forced the men to undergo, and the lingering presence of the cholera pest, both of these causes, which lowered the health of the whole force, had not, as had just been shown, impaired its ability to fight, or even its cheerfulness. Therefore, though in the first half of November mists had begun to overspread the Black Sea, and between these and the blue sky hung a low canopy of cloud, nothing formidable had as yet threatened us.

But we had a sudden and rude awakening. On the 14th of November a violent wind arose from the south, dashing huge billows against the iron-bound coast, and sweeping the Upland. It drove before it a deluge of rain, which lodged in the hollows of the tents, caused by the pressure of the wind, and the weight of both wind and rain, as the storm increased, prostrated

The gale off the port of Balaklava, 14th November 1854. Print by William Simpson c1855.

whole camps, and dispersed them, with their contents, far over the miry plain, so that men returning from duty in the trenches for food and repose found themselves destitute of fuel and of shelter. The hospital tents were at once carried away, along with the blankets of their sick and wounded tenants, who were thus left bare to the mercy of the storm. Quantities of food and forage stored round the camps were spoiled, and the daily communication with Balaklava was stopped because the horses and waggons could not make head against the wind. These evils might have been borne, and in some degree repaired, but worse than these were happening on the sea. Twenty-one vessels, in or near the harbour of Balaklava, were dashed to pieces, and eight others disabled. All these were full of stores urgently needed by the army, and among them was the Prince, a magnificent steamer, "containing," says the Journal of the Royal Engineers, "everything that was most wanted—warlike stores of every description, surgical instruments, Guernsey frocks, flannel drawers, woollen stockings and socks, boots, shoes, watch-coats; in short, all that the foresight of the Government could devise for the equipment and comfort of the troops." All these treasures went with her to the bottom of the sea. Our principal ammunition ship was also cast away, and each of the others bore with it to the deep a part of that which we depended on for existence. "Mr Filder's great fear," wrote Lord Raglan, "is want of forage for the horses. He lost twenty days' hay by the tempest."

Next day the little harbour of Balaklava was full of floating timbers and trusses of hay, through which boats could hardly make their way, and numbers of the drowned were washed about the bases of the cliffs outside. The French lost the most beautiful vessel in their navy, the Henri IV, and the garrison of Sebastopol shared, in less degree, the general misfortune, having many of the houses that sheltered them unroofed, as well as their naval magazines.

With this day began our dire season of calamity. At the close of the storm, the evening had brought snow, and henceforth the soil of the devastated camps afforded in no respect better lodging than the rest of the surrounding wold. The sick, the wounded, and the weary lay down in mud. The trenches were often deep in water, and when night put an end to the rifle fire on both sides, the soldiers sat there, cramped, with their backs against the cold, wet earth. A still worse evil was that men seldom pulled off their wet boots, fearing they might not be able to draw them on again; their feet swelled in them, the circulation was impeded, and on cold nights frost-bite ensued, ending at best in mutilation. Coming from the trenches, the men had to go far afield to seek for roots wherewith to cook their food; it is hardly surprising that many preferred to employ these short intermissions of duty in such repose as was obtainable, and ate their salt pork uncooked; and as, under such diet and such exposure, the numbers of the sick increased, so was more work thrown on those who remained. "Our men," wrote Lord Raglan, "are on duty five nights out of six, a large proportion of them constantly under fire." And all this time their clothing was such as they had first landed in in September. It was not from a continuous lack of food that the troops suffered. Except at the worst time, there was generally forthcoming in most camps the due allowance (not, however, without too many intervals of scanty fare) of biscuit, salt meat, and rum. But there was by no means always forthcoming the fuel wherewith to cook it; and if there had been, the diet, so limited, almost invariably produced scurvy, and other diseases. Yet at this very time there was a sufficiency of fuel stored at Balaklava, and rice, flour, vegetables, and tea, such as might have rendered the diet wholesome. Here, then, seven or eight miles from the camps, were supplies which would have enabled the army to meet on much better terms the evils of overwork, and exposure to wet and cold. But these supplies could only be made partially, and with difficulty, available, for want of transport. As has been seen, we had no transport corps, and the army depended, in its first movements, on the horses and carts which could be seized in the Crimea. From a return prepared by the commissariat, there appears the startling fact that, in January 1855, the whole number of effective animals belonging to that department was 333 pack-horses and mules, and twelve camels. Had the depot which the Commissary-General had attempted to form near headquarters been completed, the task of supplying the troops would have been comparatively easy. But the formation of this depot, which was to have afforded conveyance for future supplies, as well as for those necessary for daily and present use, was interrupted for want of transport. In rear of each Division a scanty group of miserable ponies and mules, whose backs never knew what it was to be quit of the saddle, shivered, and starved, and daily died. Such were the means of transport on which the army depended for subsistence. Yet plenty of horses existed in the surrounding countries, and there was a sufficiency of ships in which to bring them. Why, then, were horses not brought in sufficient numbers to Balaklava? In answer to the question, the Commissary-General stated that "the reason for not increasing the amount of transport was not that a greater number of animals was unnecessary, but that a greater number could not be fed in the Crimea."

Here, then, the primary cause of the sufferings of the army is arrived at—the want of forage. Hay and corn would have enabled us to maintain a land transport sufficient to feed the troops and the horses, to shelter them with huts, to supply ammunition for the siege, and to form a depot against contingencies. Shrewd men at home might have made many guesses before they hit on the source of distress, for the intelligence and foresight must have been rare indeed that could have conducted an inquirer through such a jumble of calamity to so unexpected a conclusion.

Now it has been said that the duties the men had to perform in the trenches, certainly when those of pickets and guards in camp were added to them, were as much as they could bear. But besides, owing to the deficiency of transport, they had to perform much work that ought to have been done by horses and mules. The journey through the quagmire to Balaklava and back, carrying up rations, clothing, huts, or ammunition, frequently took up twelve hours, all which time they were without food, shelter, or rest. Also, they were repeatedly on short rations; in the Fourth and Light Divisions they were often on three-quarters, two-thirds, and sometimes half rations of meat and rum; on two occasions they had only quarter rations, and one day they had none at all. For six or seven weeks they were deprived of their ration of rice at the precise time when it would have been so beneficial, a time when scarcely any vegetables were supplied, and hardly a man in the army escaped the prevailing diseases.

The sufferings of the animals were frightful. They were dying all round the camps, and all along the route to Balaklava, of cold, hunger, and fatigue, and as labour could not be bestowed in burying them, their carcasses formed a dismal feature in the desolate scenery. The artillery horses had so much extra work thrown on them that the efficiency of the batteries was very seriously impaired. Lord Lucan had remonstrated against the position chosen for the cavalry after the battle of Inkerman, as being so distant from the harbour as

Embarkation of the sick at Balaklava. Print by WIlliam Simpson, c1855.

to endanger the supply of forage. Subsequently, the reason appeared to be that General Canrobert, anticipating a second attack on the same point, and thinking that the mere presence of cavalry might, when told to the enemy by their spies, deter them, had persuaded Lord Raglan to post them in that quarter. Lord Lucan's forebodings were quickly realised. Before the end of November the neighbouring artillery camps were invaded by ravenous cavalry horses, galloping madly in at the sound of the feeding trumpet, and snatching, undeterred by stick or stones, the hay and barley from the very muzzles of the right owners. Painful it was to see the frenzy of the creatures in their first pangs of hunger, more painful to see their quiet misery in the exhaustion that succeeded. Remedy (except removing the camp) there seemed none. The labour of toiling through the slough to Balaklava to fetch their own forage was so great that many horses sank and died in each journey; every day saw the survivors weaker and less fit for the effort; every frosty night the cold was followed by the death of numbers.

The effect of all this misery was that at the end of November we had nearly 8000 men in hospital. The journey thither was an ordeal fatal to many. Lifted from the mud of the hospital tent, and wrapped in their wet blankets, the sick were placed on horses, a dismal troop; some with closed eyes and livid cheeks, little other than mounted corpses; some moaning as they went, and almost ready in their weariness to relax their hold of the pommel, and bury their troubles in the mire beneath; some fever-stricken, glaring with wide eyes void of speculation, for whom the passers-by, if they saw them at all in their hurried, insane glances, existed only as more of the phantoms that haunted their delirium. Bound for the great hospital of Scutari, the ghostly train would toil on, wading and slipping past the dying horses, the half-buried bullocks, the skeletons, and carcasses in various stages of decay; past the wrecks of arabas, the squalid men with bundles, who had been down for the clothing they had needed for weeks, the waggon-load of dead Turks going to that yawning pit beside the road which was to be their sepulcher, the artillery waggons, returning at dusk with the forage they set out at daybreak to fetch—and on, always through deep mire, to the place of embarkation.

New miseries lay in that last word. Lying amid crowds of other sick and wounded, on the bare planks, in torture, lassitude, or lethargy, without proper food, medicine, or attendance, they were launched on the wintry sea. Their covering was scanty, the roll and plunge of the ship were agony to the fevered and the maimed; in place of the hush, the cleanliness, the quiet, the silent step, that should be around the sick, were sounds such as poets have feigned for the regions of the damned—groans, screams, entreaties, curses, the straining of the timbers, the trampling of the crew, the weltering of the waves. Not infrequently the machinery of the overladen ship broke down, and they lay tossing for days, a hell upon the waters.

Scutari, the longed-for haven, was for weeks the very climax and headquarters of suffering—crammed with misery, overflowing with despair. In those large chambers and long corridors lay thousands of the bravest and most miserable of men. Standing at the end of any of the galleries that traversed the four sides of the extensive building, one looked along a deep perspective, a long-diminishing vista of woe. Ranged in two rows lay the patients, feet to feet; the tenant of each bed saw his pains reflected in the face of his comrade opposite; fronting each was another victim of war or cold, starvation or pestilence. Or, frequently, the sick man read in the face before him not the progress of fever, nor the leaden weight of exhaustion, but the tokens of the final rest to which he was himself hastening. With each round of the sun nearly a hundred gallant soldiers raved or languished out their lives; as the jaws of the grave closed on the prey of to-day, they opened as widely for that of to-morrow. It might be thought that, at this rate, the grave, so greedy, so improvident, would exhaust its victims—that some day it would gape in vain. But no—the sick flocked in faster than the dead were carried out, and still the dismal stream augmented, till the hospitals overflowed, while still faster poured the misery-laden ships down the Black Sea, feeding as they went the fishes with their dead.

Had Dante witnessed these scenes, he might have deepened the horrors of his Inferno. Told with more or less exactness, but with a skill that suffered none of their pathos to be lost, they shook the nation with a universal tremor of anger and grief. It could not bear to think that the men of whom it had suddenly grown so proud should be perishing of want, while wealth and plenty reigned at home. The feeling found expression in two ways, very different, but both very natural as impulses of a community. The one was an absorbing desire to afford immediate relief; the other a fretful craving to find scapegoats, and make them atone for all this suffering. Inspired by the first of these, the country became a vast workshop for the manufacture of warm clothing, and great quantities of this, as well as of luxurious food and drink, were despatched in steamers, with agents to distribute them. But before these came, early in December, and all through the month, clothing was reaching Balaklava from Constantinople, whither Lord Raglan had despatched an officer to remedy, so far as might be, the loss of the cargo of the Prince, so that at the end of that month 17,000 blankets and 19,000 new great-coats had been issued to the troops (mostly at Balaklava, whither they went to fetch them); and on the 13th January Lord Raglan was able to write: "I believe I may assert that every man in this army has received a second blanket, a jersey frock, flannel drawers and socks, and some kind of winter coat in addition to the ordinary great-coat." These defences did not, however, at once check the progress of sickness; during January and February the numbers in our hospital continued to swell till they reached to nearly 14,000.

But before the aid from England arrived, we had received important relief in another form. The French had been so largely reinforced that General Canrobert at length consented to relieve our troops from the task of guarding the ground beyond our Right Attack. That they should have been able to do so by no means implies that they had not their share of winter troubles. Their greater proximity to their home ports, their organised transport, the convenience of their harbours, the road they had paved from thence along the rear of their camps, rendered their supplies comparatively regular and certain. But there were two circumstances which told heavily on them. Their tentes d'abri, small roofs of canvas, only very imperfectly fulfilling the idea of a tent, were so diminutive that a third part of one was carried by the soldier in addition to the rest of his burdens. Propped on short sticks at each end, the tent admitted the three occupants, crawling like ferrets into a rabbit hole, to a space where they could all lie down. But this was obviously a meagre defence against mud and snow; it afforded no shelter at all except for lying down; and a bell tent like ours would have seemed a vast boon to the French troops. Also, their ration of food and drink was inferior to ours, was calculated on a scale suited to different conditions, and did not suffice to maintain in health men undergoing hardships so severe. Therefore, although the French had comparatively easy work in the trenches, although, at the worst, one of each two nights was a night of rest, and their men, never over tasked, were available for fatigues and camp duties, road making, and other labours, yet their means of meeting exposure to wet and cold were so defective that their losses in sick, especially from frost-bite, were very great. The French horses, too, perished by hundreds, and much of the carrying of supplies to the camps had to be performed by the men. But their great resources in numbers not only made good all losses, but went on rapidly raising the strength of their army. Numbering 45,000 in October, it grew to 56,000 in November, 65,000 in December, and 78,000 in January. In this last month Lord Raglan reckoned the strength of the French Army to be at least four times that of the British. We had then on the Upland, to meet all the exigencies of our siege works, and any enterprises of the enemy, only 11,000 men fit to bear arms. It was these three months, then, November, December, and January, which formed "the winter of our discontent." In February a brighter time set in. It was about the 23d January that the French troops were put in charge of the ground on the right of our siege works. Lord Raglan's proposal had been that the French troops should relieve ours in the trenches one night in three. Canrobert substituted for it the measure which was now effected. It released more than 1500 English troops daily from the duty of guarding our front. Lord Raglan says of it: "The position of our troops is greatly improved by being relieved of part of the harassing duties they have had imposed on them; but, speaking confidentially, I am of opinion, notwithstanding what General 'Canrobert says, that more might have been done, considering that the French Army consists of from 60,000 to 70,000 men."

The spectacle of men and horses floundering between Balaklava and the camp, through a sea of mud, was of a sort to suggest to the least inventive mind that to make a road was the proper remedy. In England, accordingly, the numerous class which becomes clamorously wise after the event brought the omission to make a road as one of the heaviest charges against the staff of the Army, insisting, too, that it should have been one of the first things thought of. But can anyone who now looks dispassionately back to that time point to any period as that in which the step was feasible? When we first took position on the Upland no want of a road was felt, and when every man in both armies was needed to prepare for the bombardment which was to precede the assault, it would have been a strange exercise of foresight to withdraw them from their urgent duties in order to make a road which might never be wanted. Even after the loss of the Woronzoff road, the extent of that misfortune was not felt, for men, horses, and vehicles freely traversed the plains, and the speedy capture of the place was still expected Later, when the battle of Inkerman had shown how scanty was our line of defence, how fatal would be the consequence of a breach in it, not a man could be withdrawn from the position. Sir John Burgoyne computed that to make a road would occupy more than 1000 men two or three months. A body of Turks had been hired to attempt it as soon as it was accepted as a necessity that we must winter on the heights, but they died so fast that the survivors could scarcely do more than bury the dead. The official commissioners subsequently affirmed that "hired labour could not be obtained." Neither, assuredly, could military labour; and the absence of a road was therefore one of those misfortunes which become inevitable amid the uncertainties of war.

But when the pressure on the troops grew lighter, means were found to make the part of the road between Balaklava and Kadikoi; and the French troops stationed there carried it on to the Col. By the time it got so far, a railway, undertaken by private contractors at the instance of the Secretary for War, was in course of construction, and before the end of March had not only reached the same point, but was conveying thither ammunition and stores. Some weeks earlier, lavish supplies had begun to arrive from the deeply-moved community at home, not only of things necessary, like warm clothing, but of luxuries; meat, ale, and wine, and even books were poured profusely into the camps. The first agency of this kind to arrive was the Crimean Army Fund, administered by two gentlemen, who also brought, or procured, the men and horses necessary for the distribution. But besides such organised modes of relief, the quantities of similar stores received for distribution by officers from friends at home were uncounted. While the distress of the troops before Sebastopol was thus being daily alleviated, effective influence for good had begun to pervade our hospitals on the Bosphorus. Even before the great stress was laid on them which ensued from the battles and the coming of winter, they were already teeming with confusion and misery. The Army had not contained enough surgeons other than regimental to meet the unexampled needs of the time; the service had been recruited from the civilians of the profession; and by universal testimony both classes grappled with their formidable duties in the best spirit. Had there been a system of organisation suited to the exigency, had the sanitary conditions been good, the attendants numerous, the supplies ample, then the efforts of the surgeons, dealing as they did with the cases as they presented themselves, would have found a fair field. But none of these conditions existed, and all they could do was to struggle on, not so much like swimmers making some way, as like those contending in vain with a torrent.

In those days there were two chiefs at the War Office. The Duke of Newcastle was Secretary for War, and Mr Sidney Herbert bore the mysterious title of Secretary at War. The medical department of the War Office lay in Mr Herbert's province, and his inquiries into the methods of dealing with sickness on an extensive scale had led him to expect the best results from the co-operation of women, in controlling and administering large hospitals. Therefore, when it became apparent that the establishments on

'The Lady with the Lamp'. Florence Nightingale at Scutari, 1854

the Bosphorus were daily growing less able to contend with their difficulties, he- invited the aid of ladies already possessed of large experience, and who, thus encouraged, formed themselves into staffs, and accompanied by paid nurses, and bearing strong recommendations to the medical as well as to other authorities on the spot, proceeded to Constantinople. "It was seen," says Kinglake, "that the humble soldiers were likely to be the men most in want of care, and the ladies were instructed to abstain from attending upon any of the officers." Thus began to enter into the history of the contest an element which strongly moved the imagination of the community, both from the extraordinary alleviation of suffering and establishment of order which it effected, and from the contrast which its gentle and beneficent character offered to the gloomy tenor of the war.

It was on the 4th of November that Miss Nightingale and her immediate companions arrived at Constantinople. She was accompanied by Protestant sisters and Catholic nuns, eighteen in all, with twenty trained nurses, and to all were assigned quarters in one of the towers that form the angles of the great barrack at Scutari, which the Turkish Government had given over to us for a hospital. Another band, numbering in all forty-six, under Miss Stanley, bestowed themselves at first in a neighbouring hospital for sailors, and afterwards at the military hospital at Kulali, on the Bosphorus.

The ladies and their attendants at first took an altogether subordinate part in the care of the sick, replacing the orderlies withdrawn from their regiments, ensuring obedience to the doctors' orders, administering food and medicine, and making the patients comfortable But it was not long before they began to take part in the management. At first Miss Nightingale's share in this was confined to keeping Sidney Herbert informed of what was noteworthy, and enabling him to act accordingly. But the departmental authorities soon got to understand that her views and suggestions were to be specially considered. A regular correspondence on the subject was also established between her and Lord Raglan. Receiving such support, as well as that derived from the strong interest which the public evinced for her mission, she gradually acquired a powerful controlling influence; and to this the extraordinary improvement in the condition of the hospital which ensued was then, and has continued to be, chiefly ascribed. The excellent medical staff cheerfully accepted her sway, and the skill and energy which they had always given without stint, no longer expended in struggling amidst chaos, were directed to the best ends. She received, too, from an unexpected source, a large accession of power. The conductors of the Times had consented to receive and administer, for the benefit of our sick and wounded, a fund formed by the contributions of their readers. Mr Macdonald, who had come out in charge of it, learning from Miss Nightingale what needs of the sick were most urgent, supplied them, and thus added immeasurably to the benefits attending her presence. Not the least among these was an extensive kitchen which she established close to her quarters, where all that part of the patients' diet that called for special care in preparation was excellently cooked on an enormous scale.

But all these ameliorations took time. In the period of worst distress in the camp, that is to say, in December and part of January, the influence of the ladies had hardly begun to take effect in any way, and not at all in diminishing the sick-list or the death-rate. Even when their care and skill had made patients feel themselves in good hands, and had banished a vast proportion of the misery, the ratio of deaths for some time continued to increase. It kept steadily and largely augmenting all through December, November, January, and February. In these four months nearly 9000 soldiers died in our hospitals, and at the end of February 13,600 men were lying sick there. The causes lay too deep to be touched even by improved method and administration. But early in March a sanitary commission had arrived to examine into the condition of the hospitals, with power to act on the conclusions they might come to. Works of ventilation, of drainage, and of water supply, had in the second week of March already made some progress; the death-rate went down with extraordinary rapidity week by week, till in June it had come to the level of our military hospitals at home.

In the result the evils suffered met some compensation in the form of permanent benefit. At the close of the campaign Mr Herbert presided over a sanitary commission at home and to its recommendations are due many of the improvements which so greatly distinguish our present military hospital system from that which existed at the time of the war.

It has been said that one form taken by the excitement at home was the desire to punish those to whom delinquency was imputed. Strongly pressed by this manifestation of public feeling, and by the calamitous accounts from the East, the Duke of Newcastle began, in the latter half of December, to write letters to Lord Raglan implying censure on him and his staff. Following this up was a letter, on the 6th of January, condemning the staff generally, and the Quartermaster-General in particular, as the member of it in whose department it lay to provide for many of the privations which had proved so calamitous. And it is not easy to avoid the inference that the Ministry was seeking to shelter itself against the indignation of the community by giving it vent against those who had already begun to be the objects of it. Lord Raglan found no difficulty in defending, in a manly spirit, his subordinates. He was soon relieved from the necessity of maintaining a contest with their accusers, for, on the 26th January, Mr Roebuck moved for a committee "To inquire into the condition of our army before Sebastopol, and into the conduct of those departments of the Government whose duty it has been to minister to the wants of that army." The motion was carried by a majority of 157, and the Ministry thereupon resigned. Lord Aberdeen was succeeded by Lord Palmerston, the Duke of Newcastle by Lord Panmure. The new Ministers were naturally bent upon inquiry. They resolved to send a commission to the Crimea to seek a clue to the causes of the sufferings of the army, and Sir John M'Neill, for many years Envoy to Persia, and Colonel Tulloch were selected for the purpose. On the 12th March they arrived in the Crimea, and taking up their residence on board a steamer, at once began to take evidence. In June they issued a first report, dealing with food and transport. It contained a

One of the wards of the hospital at Scutari. Print by William Simpson, c1855

remarkable tribute to the army. "It is doubtful," says the report, "whether the whole range of military history furnishes an example of an army exhibiting, throughout a long campaign, qualities as high as have distinguished the forces under Lord Raglan's command." Their labours, their privations, their spirit, and their discipline, form the subjects of admiring comments. "The Army," says the report, "never descended from its acknowledged military preeminence." Again, "Both men and officers, when so reduced that they were hardly fit for the lighter duties of the camp, scorned to be excused the severe and perilous work of the trenches, lest they should throw an undue amount of duty upon their comrades; yet they maintained every foot of ground against all the efforts of the enemy, and with numbers so small that perhaps no other troops would even have made the attempt. . . . The officers have not only shared all the danger and exposure, and most of the privations which the men had to undergo, but we everywhere found indications of their solicitude for the welfare of those under their command, and of their constant readiness to employ their private means in promoting the comfort of their men."

Yet to more than nine-tenths of the officers and men this was a first campaign. When they came in sight of the Russian masses arrayed on the Alma, they for the first time saw an enemy; when the shot from the Russian guns dashed past, they were for the first time under fire. Yet, under that fire, and against that enemy, they advanced with all the confidence, discipline, and determination which can attend the onset of troops long accustomed to victory. That the same discipline and spirit distinguished them under circumstances still more trying to young troops, the commissioners bear witness. Not in some peaceful, happy community, the realisation of a Utopian dream, could temperance, obedience, diligence, cheerfulness, be more conspicuous than in that camp in the wintry desert, where various and incessant horror and distress might have been expected to dissolve the ties of order, to cast submission to the winds, and to leave despair, in the form either of apathy or recklessness, sole master of the suffering host.

The only person, to whom blame was imputed, in the first report of the commissioners, was the Commissary-General. Failure to issue articles of diet, such as lime juice and tea, which were in store at Balaklava, deficiencies of fresh meat, vegetables, and fuel, and defective arrangements respecting forage, were all laid at his door, and he was charged with not being a man of comprehensive views, with not having sufficiently turned to account the resources of surrounding provinces, and with being deficient in inventive resource and administrative capacity. In reply, Mr Filder laid before the House a counter statement In the first place, he set forth the extraordinary difficulties which the commissariat laboured under; its extensive duties, the total inexperience of its officers, the absence of necessary establishments, the ignorance as to where winter quarters would be,—and then dealt with the charges in detail. The lime juice and tea had been sent for the sick, and were not more than was needful for them; when demanded, these articles were at once issued to the troops. As to the fresh meat, many of his cattle-vessels had been disabled by the storm; nevertheless, the supply both of fresh meat and vegetables had been kept up in a degree which, under the circumstances, might be called surprising. There had always been sufficient fuel at Balaklava; the only difficulty was to find means of conveying it to the camps, owing to want of transport, and that, as we have seen, was owing to want of forage. Now the Commissary-General showed that he had made ample provision for forage had the army remained in Turkey When it was ordered to the Crimea, he made contracts at Constantinople for having it pressed (very necessary for transport by sea) and despatched to him. Finding that the contractors were likely to fail in their agreement, he wrote to England for 2000 tons. Of this he only received one-tenth in six months. "Had my requisitions for hay been complied with, the deficiency which was felt throughout the winter would have been prevented, and I should have been able to maintain a sufficient transport establishment." This demand he made before the armies landed in the Crimea; he frequently reiterated it, and it was many times enforced by Lord Raglan, but without effect, till near the close of the winter. Finally, a committee of inquiry appointed later declared that the insufficiency was owing to the omission of the Treasury to send a proper supply of forage from England.

This report was followed by a second, in which several officers, notably the Quartermaster-General and the two cavalry generals, conceived themselves to be made objects of censure. And, finally, a Board of General Officers sat at Chelsea, in April 1856, "to take into consideration so much of the reports as animadverts upon the conduct of certain officers." The blame, if any, imputed to Lord Lucan and Lord Cardigan was so slight and vague that they had no difficulty in justifying themselves. General Aireys's reply may be briefly summed up. Its essence consisted in showing that, while the commissioners had imputed blame to his department for not issuing supplies in store, it was its province to provide, not for the issue, but the apportionment of these supplies. He showed that to the oft-quoted want of transport alone was due the fact that stores of clothing and other necessaries remained unissued; that no official barrier was raised between the men and the supplies; on the contrary, the issues of clothing were authorised very much faster than the men could draw it. He rightly observed that, in the altered state of affairs existing in the middle of March, it was impossible for any two persons, such as the commissioners fully to appreciate the position of the army, in the midst of the unheard-of difficulties of the winter, and concluded with a picture of the condition of the troops, and the causes of distress and perplexity by which they were surrounded.

The reader who may have followed this narrative will perhaps be of opinion that, the army once before Sebastopol, and dependent on a military system so deficient in much that is essential, no arrangement or foresight within the scope of human intelligence could have averted the disasters which followed. The inference drawn from the reports, that blame might justly be affixed in specified quarters, could not be sustained The fact that the different departments of the Army have their proper limits seemed in some measure to be lost sight of by the commissioners, as well as by the public, whose complaints were, largely based on the error that everybody ought to understand and take part in the business of everybody else as well as his own. No commander-in-chief would wish to see such an interchange of duties substituted for the restricted and specific sphere of operations and responsibility allotted to each department. To perform the duties of his own branch (including, of course, its co-operation with others when necessary) is all that can be expected from an officer; and it is the province of the superintending intellect, which knows the instruments it works with, to combine all in harmonious action. The search for delinquents pointed to this result, that all the suffering and calamity, not absolutely inevitable, which befell our troops, were the natural consequences of the unpractical and unworkable system, at once improvident and ineffective, which the nation permitted to exist for the conduct of its military business.

CHAPTER IX

EXTENSION OF THE SIEGE WORKS AND DEFENCES

Burgoyne's Proposal for our Relief—The French prefer another Mode—
Want of Fuel in the Camps—Fortress increasing in Strength—New
System of Rifle-pits—Underground Warfare—New Russian Works—
Failure of the French Attack—Great Sortie against the French and
English Trenches—The Burial Truce—Charles Gordon's Experiences—
Russians recross the Tchernaya—Niel's View of the Operations—
Burgoyne goes Home—Renewed Preparations—Another Cannonade—
The Russians slow to reply—Severity of Fire upon the Fortress—Two
Well-fought Batteries—Carnage in Sebastopol—Impatience for Assault.

I T HAS been said that the plan of attack, on the 17th October, was that
the French should assault the Flagstaff Bastion, and the English the
Redan. The first was the chief object, the second subsidiary. To establish
French troops and batteries on the Flagstaff Bastion, and maintain them
there, would have gone far to assure the surrender or evacuation of the
place; but in order to effect this, it would be indispensable to hold the Redan
also, the close fire from which would otherwise render the French operations
very costly, or impossible. But a great master of engineering science had
been labouring on these works with unceasing energy, and with formidable
effect. During the first winter months Todleben had greatly extended and
strengthened both of these works, and also the Malakoff; and the Redan was
so completely dominated by the Malakoff that the capture of this great work
also had become an essential part of the plan of attack. This had always been
Burgoyne's opinion, and he now supported it by arguing that the Malakoff
was more easy of approach than the other works; that the possession of it,
even if it should not, of itself, cause the surrender of the place, would render
the assault of the others far less desperate, while guns placed on it would at
once rid us of the fire of the Russian ships. He represented, moreover, that

the Allies would thus best attain their real object, which was not so much the capture of the town, as the destruction of the docks, arsenal, and fleet. Since the battle of Inkerman had given us possession of the heights overlooking the harbour and the Careenage ravine, this plan had obviously become more feasible, and Burgoyne had, in November and December, urged officially his reasons for desiring that the English should undertake the business, and that, as their numbers were manifestly unequal to such an extension of duty and work, the French should relieve them of the charge of pushing forward and guarding the British Left Attack, the batteries of which, however, would be held and fought by our men as before. This would set free the Third Division to perform the operations on Mount Inkerman. Immediately after the battle of Inkerman the Allies had begun to strengthen the ground there with works, one made by the French on the end of the Fore Ridge, three by the English (one of them on Shell Hill), to command the approaches, and to overlook the bridge and causeway over which Pauloff had advanced; and we had further made in front of these a first parallel, and begun a second, as approaches to the works between the Malakoff and the harbour. When this proposal was finally considered at a conference of chiefs at the beginning of February, the French preferred to leave our Right and Left Attacks to us as before, and themselves to take charge of Mount Inkerman, except that the British artillerymen and sailors already occupying our works there, should so remain. It was so settled: Mount Inkerman and the Victoria Ridge were given into the charge of Bosquet's Corps; and at the same time the plan of advancing on the Russian works from the Malakoff to the harbour, by approaches from Mount Inker-man, and of pressing the attack, not there especially, but along the whole Russian front, was definitely adopted.

Meanwhile the Allies had not been idle in the trenches, even in the time of their direst trials. The first parallel of the British Right Attack was completed, as well as another in advance of it. A second parallel was carried across the front of the Left Attack, and down the ravine on its right, barring the Woronzoff road there. The French had sapped up to within 180 yards of the Flagstaff Bastion, and now, seeing the relations of mutual defence between it and the Central Bastion deemed it necessary to include the latter also in their front of attack. Yet withal the business of the siege proceeded of necessity very slowly. What transport the Allies could muster was taken up with bringing food, clothing, and shelter. In the trenches the men stood generally ankle deep, sometimes knee deep, in snow and liquid mud; except near the cliffs, and at a great distance from the camps, the supply of fuel, in the form of brushwood, which the plains afforded, had long since been exhausted, and even the roots of the vines had been grubbed up for cooking. And this want had become a hindrance to the siege in another way. "It is very unusual," says the Engineer Journal, "to see smoke from fires in trenches, yet this took place daily." The cause of this was the want of fuel in the camps. The coffee issued to the men was in the berry, which is the best form of it when means for roasting are at hand, for wet does not injure it, and it has, of course, far more flavour when freshly ground. But when there was no fuel in camp, the men took the green coffee with them to the trenches, ground it with fragments of the enemy's shells, roasted it on their mess tins, and boiled it in them, with fuel taken from the gabions and fascines forming part of the works, and the parapets, of course, suffered seriously from these depredations. The troops, driven to these shifts, had become so few that the French could only afford about 400 by day and 200 by night for employment on the works, and the English a much smaller number, while, according to the Engineer Journal, the trenches of our three attacks, the Right, the Left, and that on Mount Inkerman, were at this time guarded only by 350 men, and on one day in January by only 290 men, being about one-twentieth of the number of the part of the garrison opposed to them, and which might have attacked them.

On the other hand, the Russians having after Inkerman abandoned the idea of using the field army for attacking the Allied position, had begun to withdraw troops from it to strengthen the garrison, and readjusted the supply between them. They poured reinforcements into the place, till they had not only made good the losses of the first weeks of winter, but enabled its commander to employ on the works a force varying, according to need, from 6000 to 10,000 men. The guns, lying in the arsenal in thousands, and the ammunition were easily brought to the batteries along the paved streets. Thus the fortress was immensely augmenting its power of resistance just when we found the greatest difficulty in holding our ground. Therefore, readers who have been accustomed to hear the chiefs in Sebastopol and their troops lauded as maintaining a struggle against unheard-of difficulties, and as exhibiting extraordinary energy and powers of resistance, may ask themselves how it was that an enemy who possessed such enormously superior forces in men and material, and who could at any time, during a period of months, have directed on some selected point of the siege works thousands of troops, that would have found only hundreds to meet them, did not muster the courage for such an enterprise when it promised deliverance to the fortress, and ruin to their foes. Yet they might perhaps have given the reason which Canrobert had already pleaded for restraining enterprise, that they were unwilling to set the great stake on a single cast, and preferred to let delay and all its evils fight for them.

With this important exception, however, the Russians showed great energy, even beyond the limits of a mere passive defence, and every kind of work demanding skill and labour they did well. Thus, Todleben developed a new feature in trench warfare, which the range and accuracy of the rifle had rendered possible. At night, parties issuing from the place dug, on selected parts of the ground between the opposing lines, rows of pits each fitted to hold a man, and having in front a few sandbags, or sometimes a screen of stones, so disposed as to protect his head, and to leave a small opening through which to fire. At daybreak they began to harass the guards of the trenches opposite, within easy range of them. The French especially suffered by being thus overlooked, and their proximity caused the enemy to adopt this form of warfare chiefly in opposing them. To direct guns on objects so small as these pits, and frequently at a great distance from the batteries, seemed but a doubtful policy, and they were therefore opposed by men, similarly covered by sandbags, from the parapets. After a time, Todleben, finding his idea so successful, expanded it; the rows of rifle pits were connected, by trenches, in parts of which shelter was given to continuous ranks of riflemen, and the defence being thus pushed out in advance of the general line, wore the aspect of besieging the besiegers. He had begun these enterprises in November, greatly aggravating the cares of the scanty defenders of the trenches. Beyond the advanced trench of our Left Attack some of these pits had been placed, screened by small stone walls, causing great annoyance both to our people opposite and to the French across the ravine, whose advanced works they partly looked into. It was on the night of the 20th November that a party of the rifles was ordered to clear these pits, which were supported by another row in rear. The occupants were driven out after a sharp struggle, with losses on both sides, and a working party made the spot tenable by our people—a service so highly appreciated by our Allies that Canrobert passed a warm encomium on it in general orders.

In November there also began, in the French attack from Mount Rodolph, a war of mines and countermines. A gallery was being driven towards the Flagstaff Bastion, when it was detected and blown in by the enemy. A mine was, however, placed in the gallery, far short of the position at first destined for it, in order to break up the ground before the bastion, and thus enable the French to effect a lodgment there. But this plan did not turn out happily; the watchful engineer opposed to them proved himself a master also of this subterranean warfare, and when the. mine was exploded; it was the Russians who succeeded in establishing themselves. on the crater.

It was on the 22d of February that the Russians undertook an enterprise which marked an epoch in the siege, and which was caused by another, the intention of which had become apparent on the part of the Allies. In front of the Malakoff, at about 500 yards from it, and on the same strip of the plain, was a conical hill, of rather greater height, and of such importance to either side which should seize it that it would doubtless have been a main object with us from the first but for our deficiency in numbers. This was the hill which afterwards became justly famous as the Mamelon. To place it, as well as the Malakoff and the intervening ground, under such a cross fire as might assure its capture, two batteries were prepared, one by the French, on a near spur of Mount Inkerman, and one in the English Right Attack. But their wary antagonist had not failed to note and appreciate the design, and was now ready with his counterstroke. On the morning of the day named, the French, who the day before had seen the Russian works end with the mouth of the Careenage ravine, now beheld new works begun on, and in extension of, a hill in front of them, being part of Mount Inkerman itself, which the enemy had seized in the course of the night, thus extending the front of the fortress to new ground, and flanking the approaches to the Malakoff and Mamelon; while the new work was itself protected by so powerful a fire that the French might well hesitate to attack it. All the 23d the enemy were again at work on it. That night, however, five French battalions, under General Monet, issued from the trenches, and while two remained halted in support, three advanced to the assault. This step had been anticipated and provided for by the Russians. Besides three battalions assigned to work on and to defend the hill, four others, being an entire regiment, were disposed for its defence, and now met the attack. They were supported by guns both from the fortress and the ships, which were brought to bear on the ground between the hill and the French trenches The combat lasted an hour; the French succeeded at one time in entering the work, but were driven out by the strong supports, and forced to retreat, bearing with them General Monet, desperately wounded, and sustaining a loss of 270 men, with nineteen officers, while the Russians lost 400. Todleben credits the French troops on this occasion with "a remarkable valour." This defeat was so far acknowledged and accepted by the French that the enemy was thenceforth left almost undisturbed to complete and arm his new work, and a few nights later he began another on a hill to his own left of it. These were in future known to the Allies as the White Works from the chalky soil they stood in. Thus, having completely abandoned Mount Inkerman after the battle, the enemy had now returned to it in a fashion which showed that he intended his occupation of it to be permanent. By this rare display of sagacity and daring, Todleben immensely increased the difficulty of the problem before the Allies. At a conference of chiefs, on 6th March, Burgoyne urged the French to attack these works as the indispensable preliminary to progress on this part of the field; but the proposal was put aside on the ground that, if captured, they could not be held under the guns which the enemy could bring to bear.

The two batteries, French and English, looking towards the Mamelon

Greek volunteers under Panos Koronaios during the siege of Sebastopol.

were pushed steadily towards completion, and on the 10th March the commanding French engineer, Bizot, advised Canrobert to seize the hill that night. Canrobert declined the enterprise, but Todleben settled the question. On this same night the Russians seized it, and morning saw the outline of a work crowning it. The question of attacking it was now more urgent than before. But Canrobert still found reasons against so decided a course, and preferred to besiege it. Consequently, the French opened a parallel against it on the Victoria Ridge, and the new batteries were also directed on it. On the other hand, the enemy held his ground, and not only completed and armed his new work, but spread rifle pits, connected with trenches, along its front and flanks.

Thus a very formidable element entered into the problem of the siege. It has been already pointed out how embarrassing to the Allies were the outposts the enemy had placed, in October, in advance of their works. Here was a tremendous aggravation of the infliction, for not only did the Mamelon cover what had hitherto been the objects of attack in that quarter, but it looked into trenches of our Right Attack hitherto secure from fire, and forbade, under heavy penalties, its further approach towards the Redan.

The French had pushed their approaches so close to the small works covering the Mamelon that they might be expected presently to seize them, when, in the night of the 22d March, the enemy cast large bodies of troops on the opposing lines. Between 5000 and 6000 men attacked the French trenches before the Mamelon, and at first penetrated into them, driving in the guards and working parties. But their success ended there; the French showed so firm a front that the attack collapsed, and the enemy fell back and re-entered the fortress, after inflicting on their opponents a loss of 600 men.

Simultaneously with the entry of the French works, 800 Russians moved out for an advance upon our Right Attack, but were easily repulsed for the time. This attack had been made on the part of the trenches next the Docks ravine. An hour later another assault (which apparently ought to have been in concert with the first) was made on the left portion of the same trenches by Greek and other volunteers. Led by an Albanian, in the dress of his country, they broke into the parallel, where the leader, first shooting one of our officers, discharged a pistol ineffectually at the magazine, and was then killed himself. The assailants moved along the trench from left to right till the guards and working parties, having been got together, met and drove them back upon the Redan.

At the same time with this last, another assault had been directed, with 500 men, on the advanced trench of our Left Attack, close to where the ridge was cut short by the ravine, and penetrated to the third parallel, where they were attacked by the nearest bodies of those guarding the trenches, and driven back like the rest. In these fights the officer commanding the guards of the Right Attack was wounded and captured, as was the engineer of the Left Attack, with about fifteen men, and a quantity of intrenching tools, dropped by the working parties when they took up their arms. In all, we lost seventy men. The enemy left about forty dead in front of our Right Attack, ten killed and two wounded in the trenches of the Left; and his losses, in all, that night were 1300 men.

If the Russians aimed, in this sortie, at establishing themselves in the French lines, it was so far a failure. But the object of such an enterprise is mostly to inflict hasty damage and discouragement on the enemy, and to gain a temporary facility for executing some of the defensive operations; and on this ground the Russians might claim a certain success, for in the following night they connected the pits in front of the Mamelon by a trench, which their engineer extended to the verge of the ravine. Thus he had succeeded in forming and occupying, within eighty yards of the French, an intrenched line, supported by, while it covered, the Mamelon.

A truce was agreed on for burying the slain, to begin half-an-hour after noon on the 24th. White flags were then raised over the Mamelon and the French and English works, and many spectators streamed down the hillsides to the scene of contest. The French burial parties advanced from their trenches, and hundreds of Russians, some of them bearing stretchers, came out from behind the Mamelon. The soldiers of both armies intermingled on friendly terms. The Russians looked dirty and shabby, but healthy and well fed. Between these groups moved the burial parties, collecting the bodies and conveying them within the lines on both sides. At 450 yards from the scene rose the Mamelon, its parapet lined with spectators. Five hundred yards beyond it, separated by a level space, stood the Malakoff, its ruined tower surrounded by earthen batteries; and through the space between it and the Redan appeared the best built portion of the city, jutting out into the harbour, and near enough for the streets, with people walking in them, the marks of ruin from shot, the arrangement of the gardens, and the line of sunken ships, to be plainly visible. About forty bodies were removed from the front of the English Right Attack, among them that of the Albanian leader, partially stripped, and covered again with his white kilt and other drapery. In two hours the business was over, the soldiers on both sides had withdrawn within their lines, the flags were lowered, and the fire went on as before.

This was the only considerable attempt as yet made on the trenches, but small losses from fire occurred in them almost daily and nightly. At one time the men killed had been taken at night to the front of the works, and there buried, and a strange experience fell in consequence on a young engineer, destined to a place in the esteem of his country far beyond that of any other soldier of these latter generations, Charles Gordon. In carrying a new approach to the front, these graves lay directly across it, and he described how the working party had to cut their way straight through graves and occupants, and how great was the difficulty he found in keeping the men to their horrible task, which, however, was duly completed. He had a brother, Enderby Gordon, on the staff of the artillery, to whom he used to relate his experiences; among others, of strolls he was in the habit of taking at night far beyond our trenches, one of which led him up close to the outside of the Russian works, so that he could hear the voices of the men on the parapet. A singularly ghastly incident of these burials took place about this time. One night two men had carried the body of a comrade, just slain, on to the open ground for interment, and had finished digging the grave, and placing the body in it, when, as they were about to fill it in, a shot from the enemy, who had perhaps heard them at work, killed one of them. The survivor laid his comrade's body beside the other, buried both, and returned to the trench.

In the period to which this chapter relates several events of military importance had occurred, to have chronicled which, at their respective dates, would have broken the narrative of the siege. On the 6th December the troops which Liprandi had established in the valley of Balaklava were withdrawn across the Tchernaya, leaving only detachments of the three arms in the villages of Kamara and Tchorgoun, and a field work with guns to guard the bridge at Traktir. On the 30th December a considerable French force advanced up the valley, while the 42d Highlanders moved by the hills

British bombardment of the fortress of Bomarsund on the Aland Islands, Baltic Sea, during the Crimean war. Drawing from 1854.

above, swept the residue of the enemy over the stream, and shelled the guns out of the bridge head, and the troops out of Tchorgoun. After destroying the Russian huts and forage, and capturing their cattle and sheep, the troops returned to their camps. Access was thus once more gained to the Woronzoff road, and in time a good road was made connecting it with Balaklava.

In January two French officers arrived in the Crimea, both destined, though in entirely opposite ways, to exercise an important influence on the course of the war. The Emperor Napoleon, regarding the appointments already made to the command of Corps and Divisions by Canrobert, under the pressure of circumstances, as provisional merely, had summoned General Pélissier from his Government of Oran, and placed him in charge of the 1st Corps, that besieging the lines before the town; and it will be seen how powerful was the impelling element introduced with the presence of this masterful spirit into the attack on the fortress. And, on the 27th of January, General Niel, the engineer who had just conducted operations against Bomarsund, and who was regarded as the military counsellor of the Emperor, arrived in the Crimea on a special mission. The nature of this, kept secret at the time, will appear in the next chapter; but he at once expressed his ideas of the military situation. Regarding it, from the engineer's point of view, as a siege, and what should consequently follow the rules of a siege, one of which was that a necessary step towards the capture of a fortress is its investment, so he believed that all the efforts of the Allies must be vain until they should have intercepted all communication between Sebastopol and Menschikoff's army. "Believe, Monsieur le Marechal," he wrote to the Minister for War, "that nothing can be done without investing," and with this opinion his language at the conference was in unison. And, no doubt, to have severed all communication with the city must have been effectual in the end, if practicable; but the event showed that the measure was not indispensable. That the Russians feared such a step was shown about this time. Omar Pasha had been for some time assembling, at Eupatoria, bodies of his Turks from the Danube. The town had been surrounded with works of earth and loose stones by the French officer at first left in charge of the place. These, thrown forward to a salient in the centre, bent round on both flanks to the sea. About 23,000 Turks and thirty-four heavy guns were within these works, when the Russians, alarmed for their communications with Perekop, delivered an attack upon the place with a large force drawn from Menschikoff s army, and said by Todleben to number 19,000 infantry, with a strong cavalry and numerous artillery. Both flanks of the works of the place were defended by a French steamer, a Turkish, and four English steamers lying in the bay.

On the 16th February the Russians appeared before the place. They spent the night in throwing up cover for their batteries, and by morning had seventy-six guns, twenty-four of them of heavy calibre, ready to open at from 600 to 800 yards from the works. At daybreak the cannonade began, and when the fire of the place seemed to be overcome, three columns of attack, supported by field batteries, advanced on the centre and flanks of the defensive line. Two of these were stopped by the fire of the steamers and of the place; the third, on the right front of the Turkish line, finding cover in the walls of the cemeteries there, assembled under their shelter, and advanced more than once almost to the ditch, but were easily repulsed; and with the last attempt in this quarter the enterprise came to an end, and the Russians drew off at once towards the interior. They lost 769 killed and wounded; the garrison, 387.

Even had they carried the works, it is difficult to perceive how they could have proposed to maintain themselves in the place, under the fire of the ships. It was probably his experience of what this fire could effect, and against which no return could be made, that so convinced the Russian commander of the hopelessness of the enterprise, as to render the assault weak and futile in comparison with his forces. No further attempt was made on Eupatoria during the war. This failure, following on the others, was visited on Menschikoff by withdrawing him from the command of the Forces in the Crimea, in which he was succeeded by Gortschakoff.

In February the Russians, finding that the line of sunken vessels across the harbour had been much broken up by the waves, sank six more, in a line inside the other; and on the 6th March an English battery on Mount Inkerman brought some guns, with hot shot, to bear on two warships in Careening Creek which had greatly annoyed the French, and drove them, one much damaged, round a sheltering point.

An important figure also disappeared from the councils of the Allies. In February the new Government, in order to appease a vague desire (part of the general discontent and impatience agitating the country) for any change which might quicken the siege operations, had decided on the recall of Sir John Burgoyne, and General Harry Jones had in that month arrived in the Crimea as his successor. But Lord Raglan desired to keep his old counsellor by his side at a time when so many important engineering questions were pending; he continued to be present at the conferences, and to issue plans and suggestions, till the third week in March, when he departed for England.

The defence of the place lost a redoubted champion, on the 19th March, when Admiral Istomine was killed in the Mamelon. He was buried by the side of Korniloff, in a tomb made by Admiral Nakimoff with the intention of lying there himself, but he now ceded the place to his illustrious comrade.

With the advance of spring the situation of the Allies (though the siege seemed as far as ever from its end) had become greatly more favourable. Not only had the climate grown mild, not only were the plains, clad in renewed verdure, once more easy to traverse, but the time of privations was long past, and almost seemed a bad dream; the men were well fed, well clothed, and well housed; the horses had been restored to condition and duly recruited in numbers; a city of huts, like those to be seen at Aldershot, spread over the Upland; the railway brought vast stores from Balaklava to the plateau, from whence they were forwarded to the depots of the camps by a growing land transport. Colonel MacMurdo, armed with independent purchasing powers, had come out to superintend the formation of that transport corps, manned both by old soldiers and recruits specially raised, and had so used his opportunities that horses, trained drivers, escorts, and vehicles, were being rapidly assembled and organised. All this demanded a great outlay, insomuch that on one of the Colonel's many large requisitions the Secretary to the Treasury, Sir Charles Trevelyan, had written: "Colonel MacMurdo must limit his expenditure." When the paper returned to the Colonel with these words, he wrote below them: "When Sir Charles Trevelyan limits the war, I will limit my expenditure." Equal improvement marked the condition of the French, and vast stores of guns had been brought up and mounted in the batteries early in April, with, for the English ordnance, a supply of 500 rounds for each gun, and 300 for each mortar. We had thus accumulated the means of a sustained and tremendous cannonade, in which 378 French guns would take part, and 123 English, proportionate to the extent of trenches and batteries occupied by each; but the English guns were for the most part so much more powerful that the difference in weight of metal was not great. On these, 466 Russian guns (out of nearly 1000 on the works) could be brought to bear. And it was certainly expected, as before, on both sides that, as soon as the cannonade should have produced its effect, the Allies would be prepared to assault. So all three armies believed; so Lord Raglan believed. But, as has been said, General Niel, the counsellor of the Emperor, had no faith in any measures which did not include an investment. It had been evident that some influence had been at work which had held back the French troops from assaulting many parts of the defences which seemed to offer fair chances of capture; and circumstances, afterwards found to have existed, seem to show that the French commander did not at this time intend to push matters beyond a cannonade.

On Easter Sunday, the 8th April, orders were given for opening fire next morning. The mortars, absent on the former occasion, were now a prominent feature in the attacking batteries, placed behind lofty and solid parapets, and hurling their great missiles high into the air, to drop thence into an enemy's work, and there explode. The various character of the soil of the plains must now once more be noted, as it very seriously affected the siege operations carried on in it. On the slopes of Mount Inkerman, and in our Right and Left attacks, especially the right, the soil was thin, the rock lay immediately below, and the workmen painfully scooped an often insufficient cover, frequently by dint of blasting; and the want of earth for parapets was in many cases supplied by sandbags filled elsewhere. But on Mount Rodolph, and to its left, the soil was favourable, easily trenched, and supplying earth in quantity sufficient to rear the parapets high, and thicken them to solidity; and thus the French had been able on that side to sap up and push their trenches to within 160 yards of the Flagstaff Bastion, while our fire was still mainly delivered (though some mortar batteries had been formed in advance), as in October, from the batteries first constructed, Gordon's and Chapman's.

When the sun should have appeared next morning, a dense mist covered the plains. It lifted a little, and at half-past six our guns, as they caught sight of the opposing batteries, opened fire, and the French soon followed. The Russians were so completely unprepared that it was twenty minutes before they began to reply. A strong wind swept volumes of the smoke from the Allied trenches over the Russian works, and must have added greatly to the difficulties of the men who worked the guns there. They were slack in replying; the guns in the redoubted Mamelon fired slowly, so did those of the Malakoff, as if insufficiently manned, though really owing to dearth of powder; and a face of the Redan was silenced. On the other hand, the French breached the salient of the Central Bastion, and inflicted immense damage and loss of men on the Flagstaff Bastion. When the sun went down, the fire of the Allied guns ceased. Not so those of their mortars, which did not depend on keeping sight of their object, and all night the great shells climbed the sky, and descended on their prey. Nevertheless, the works were again in a condition of defence next morning. On this second day the White Works were reduced to silence and ruin. On the 11th the English and French batteries directed on the Mamelon extinguished its fire, and the Malakoff scarcely fired at all, while the Flagstaff Bastion had been again and again reduced to the direst extremity. Therefore, in momentary expectation of an assault, the Russian troops were kept at hand in, or close to, the lines of defence, and as a consequence suffered heavily. They were subjected to terrible trials, from which the Allies were exempt, for the hurricane of iron which, besides ruining works, dismounting guns, and exploding magazines, swept without intermission through the whole interior space of the fortress, where it had already razed the barracks and public buildings of the suburb to the ground, and choked the streets of the city with destroyed masonry, could not but tell heavily on uncovered troops.

A remarkable incident occurred at this time. In the trenches on the furthest point of our Left Attack, on the verge of the ravine, two batteries had been constructed, but not armed. On the night of the 11th guns were conveyed to one of them, across the open ground, and these on the following day were placed on their platforms. These batteries were on much lower ground than the Redan and the Barrack Battery on the one side, and the Garden Batteries and Flagstaff Bastion on the other. Nevertheless, this battery of four guns opened fire on the 13th on its formidable opponents. From their commanding heights, they very soon concentrated on it the overwhelming fire of about twenty heavy guns. The contest was hopeless, but it was maintained. For five hours the English guns, gradually reduced to one that remained in a condition to fire, replied, not without effect. Then, this last gun disabled, nearly all the gunners struck down, the parapets swept away, the remnant of men were at length withdrawn. Out of forty-seven men, forty-four had been killed or wounded.

In the night the damage was repaired, and the four guns were put once more in fighting condition. And the battery no longer fought singly in the front line; its neighbour was armed with six guns. On the 14th they opened and brought on themselves a terrible stress of fire. All day (with one relief), and even into the night, they maintained the fight, when, with many guns disabled, many men killed and wounded, and the parapets once more knocked into shapeless heaps, they were withdrawn from the works, which were not again manned. This episode, while it did little (that little, perhaps, in the way of attracting shot from the enemy which would otherwise have been directed on other points) towards a general result, enabled Todleben to score a substantial and indisputable success in the midst of his calamities elsewhere. Yet these English gunners had not fought quite in vain; they are still remembered as having set a rare example of valorous devotion.

Ten days did the terrific storm of iron hail endure; ten days did the Russian reliefs, holding themselves ready to repel attack, meet wounds and death with a constancy which was of necessity altogether passive. On the 19th they saw the fire of the Allies decline, and settle into its more ordinary rate; they saw, too, that the sappers were again at work with their approaches, and reading in this the signs of a resumption of the siege, and the abandonment of the policy of assault, they once more withdrew their sorely harassed infantry to places of shelter and repose. Then they began to reckon their losses, which amounted for the ten days, in killed and wounded, to more than 6000 men. The French lost, in killed and disabled, 1585 men; the English, 265.

During these days and nights the great ballroom of the assembly rooms in Sebastopol was crowded with the wounded incessantly arriving on stretchers. The floor was half-an-inch deep in coagulated blood. In an adjoining room, set apart for operations, the blood ran from three tables where the wounded were laid, and the severed limbs lay heaped in tubs. Outside, fresh arrivals thronged the square, on their blood-steeped stretchers, their cries and lamentations mingling with the roar of shells bursting close by. Many more were borne to the cellars of the sea-forts; and those capable of removal to the north side were conveyed thither to permanent hospitals. In a church near the harbour the mournful chant of the office for the dead resounded continually through the open doors of the building. It was there that the funeral service was celebrated of officers dead on the field of honour. Such is the picture drawn by eye-witnesses of what was seen of the results of the conflict in the more remote parts of the city. Nor was the change to the country outside the fortress much for the better. A Russian, passing from thence to St Peters-burgh, there testified that the route from Sebastopol to Simpheropol was so encumbered with dead bodies, dead horses, and dead cattle that the whole line was infected with pestilential vapours, and, being impassable for vehicles, could only be traversed on horseback.

All these days great impatience had prevailed in the English camp. It was asked why the cannonade had been begun if not to be followed to its legitimate conclusion. The key to the mystery is to be found in the following chapter.

CHAPTER X

IMPORTANT EVENTS ELSEWHERE

Death of the Czar—The Vienna Conference—Louis Napoleon's Plan—He intends to go to the Crimea—Lord Clarendon sent to dissuade him—The Emperor visits the Queen—Terms proposed at Vienna—Austria frames a Proposal—The Emperor abandons his Intention—English Advocates of Russian Interests—First Embarkation for Kertch—The Expedition recalled—Conference of Commanders—Canrobert resigns the Command.

THE BEARING of the Czar Nicholas, so haughty and arrogant at the outset of the war, had undergone a notable alteration. Following on the defeats on the Danube, that of the Alma wrung from him, in his communications with Menschikoff, utterances almost of despair, mingled, however, with expressions of determination to oppose his evil fortune to the bitter end. Then came the terrible slaughter of Inkerman, almost pressing hope out of him. But some new comfort dawned with the news of the sufferings of the Allies in the beginning of winter, and it was then he uttered a saying, famous at the time, that there were two generals who were about to fight for him, "Janvier et Fevrier." But, as we have seen, in this last month came the defeat at Eupatoria. It is generally believed that this blow, aggravated to his proud spirit because inflicted by the despised Turks, was fatal. A very few days after receiving the news, while he was still engaged in issuing orders to his generals, and reviewing his troops, his splendidly powerful frame suddenly collapsed. On his return from the parade ground on the 27th of February, a difficulty of breathing was manifest, paralysis of the lungs ensued, and on the 2d March he died. Survivors of that time may remember a terrible cartoon in Punch of the Czar dead upon his camp bed, while a skeleton, in Russian garb and helmet, pressed its hand on his breast, with the inscription, "General Fevrier turned traitor." The French sent the news to the general commanding in Sebastopol by a flag of truce; but he kept it secret, until it should be confirmed from St Petersburgh. It came, accompanied by a message from the new Czar, to tell the defenders that, "passed away into life eternal, the supreme chief of the orthodox warriors blessed from on high their unequalled constancy and valour."

It was soon seen that Alexander II. was under the influence of the war party, for a manifesto issued on the day of his accession was not merely warlike, but menacing, and though his prudent minister, Nesselrode, sought in a circular to diminish its effect, the friends of peace found nothing in the change of sovereigns to encourage them.

In the meantime the conference of the Powers, broken off months before by Russia's rejection of the four points which formed its basis, was revived. Prince Gortschakoff, cousin of the general, had been sent as Minister to Vienna, and had managed so to represent the refusal as to afford ground for again assembling the delegates. Since the withdrawal of Russia from the Danube, Austria had no longer an interest in joining in the war; nevertheless, she had in December come to a fresh agreement with France and England for putting pressure on the Czar. But, up to the end of his life, Nicholas had declared that he would consent to no limitation of his naval power in the Black Sea. When, therefore, Nesselrode announced, on the 10th March, that the new Czar would join in the Vienna Conference "in a sincere spirit of concord," this assurance, receiving no confirmation from what else was known of Alexander's views, did not inspire much hope of success for negotiations in which the Allies were determined to insist on that condition. But they were quite willing to give the cause of peace another chance, and the conference began on the 15th March, Lord John Russell being the representative of England.

Meanwhile, other influences had been at work which seriously affected. the conduct of the war. It has been said that General Niel was regarded as the military counsellor of Louis Napoleon, and also that he considered the interception of communications between Sebastopol and the interior as indispensable to the capture of the place. This view was so natural to an engineer, that he must be considered to have arrived at it of himself; and when we find the Emperor also holding that opinion, it is more likely that he derived it from Niel, than that Niel derived it from him. However that may be, it had fixed itself in Napoleon's mind, which was much given to patient and persistent brooding and cogitation over ideas; and when, under this process, they had so far taken shape as to inspire in him a paternal interest, he also acquired in them a profound belief. Turning over in this way the idea of investing Sebastopol, he had probably at first sent Niel to the Crimea to test it on the spot, with instructions, in case he should adhere to it, to take steps to prevent such operations of the siege as would involve serious risk and loss, which would, of course, from their point of view, be incurred in vain, and would needlessly diminish the forces to be employed in the field. As has been seen, some restraining influence had become apparent in the course of the following operations. But the Emperor's meditations on the subject did not stop here. Possessed with the necessity of driving the Russian field army off the lines of communication between Russia and Sebastopol, and bestriding them with what would then become an army of investment, he combined with it this other idea, that if, when these operations should be approaching completion, he could place himself in person at the head of the Allied Forces in the field, and deal the finishing stroke, such a military achievement would tend greatly to assure his hold on France. After .this, passing out of the regions of theory, he began secretly, as if for another purpose, to assemble a large army of reserve at Constantinople, and also to construct the plan of the intended campaign, although he had no acquaintance of any kind with war.

The plan was this: the Allies were to form three armies. One was to continue to guard the trenches and push the siege. Another, under Lord Raglan, was to assemble in the valley of Baidar (east of Balaklava), and to push its advanced posts towards Bakshisarai. The third, under Louis Napoleon himself, or a general appointed by him, composed of troops taken from before Sebastopol, and the reserves from Constantinople, was to be landed at Aloushta, on the south-eastern face of the peninsula, nearly in point of latitude abreast of Bakshisarai. This last army was to march, over a pass of the Tchatir-dagh Mountain, upon Simpheropol. Should the Russians concentrate on that point for the defence of their central depot of supply, Lord Raglan, moving on Bakshisarai, was to combine his action with that of the other army by threatening the Russian right or rear. But should the enemy, abandoning Simpheropol, concentrate in the neighbourhood of Sebastopol, the French Army from Simpheropol would advance upon it by Bakshisarai, while Lord Raglan, in concert, would attack the heights of Mackenzie's Farm. The Russian army, if defeated, would be driven off the line of communication, the Allies would sever it, and Sebastopol, deprived of supplies and of reinforcements, must speedily surrender.

The Emperor's determination to proceed himself to the Crimea, and undertake the conduct of a plan of this kind, was announced, in a letter he wrote to Lord Palmerston, on the 26th February. The reason he put forward for desiring to go himself was the necessity of placing over all the Allied Forces a chief whose influence would secure unity of command. "You will tell me, perhaps," the letter said, "that I might entrust some general with this mission. Now, not only would such a general not have the same moral influence, but time would be wasted, as it always has been, in memorandums between Canrobert and Lord Raglan, between Lord Raglan and Omar Pasha." If England would find ships for the necessary transport animals, he would find the additional men required for the enterprise.

This proposal not only startled our Government, but filled it with dismay.

But it was felt to be a difficult matter to argue against a scheme which had taken such strong possession of his mind. It happened that he was about to visit the camp at Boulogne; and the opportunity was taken to send Lord Clarendon thither to discuss the matter with the Emperor in person. It was a momentous crisis in the alliance; for in the absence of the chief of the State, the gravest attempts to subvert his authority were to be feared in Paris, where, moreover, the spirit which supported the war, always feeble, might die out without him; while, on the other hand, a failure, or even a check, in his operations in the field might be fatal to power resting on such foundations as supported his. Moreover, it was strongly impressed on Lord Clarendon that the Emperor was (as the Prince Consort's diary records) "entirely mistaken in the belief that his going to Sebastopol would be popular with the Army generally, or that he would even be well received by the troops in the Crimea. They adhered to him as Emperor, but did not like to be commanded by anyone but a professional man, and they looked upon him as a civilian."

Louis Napoleon received Lord Clarendon very cordially, and explained his plan of operations, to which, as a problem of strategy, the trained diplomatist made no brusque opposition, but at once assured him that everyone to whom it had been made known was impressed with its sagacity. Where it was open to question, he said, was in the means for executing it. These were then discussed at large; delays were inevitable; if the Emperor were to go at once, he might be detained there much longer than he expected; and it was suggested, as a fresh difficulty, that the English and Turks would view his assumption of the supreme command as promising to confer on the French the chief share of credit in the new campaign. Lord Clarendon was so far successful as to induce him at least to postpone his departure.

A fortnight later came a proposal from the Emperor that he and the Empress should pay a visit to the Queen. The notice was short, because he still intended to go to the Crimea at the end of April. Fresh opportunities of inspiring him with doubts of the expediency of that step were foreseen in this visit, and on other grounds also it was cordially welcomed. On the 16th April the Imperial guests entered London, on their way to Windsor. All classes in the capital greeted them with extraordinary enthusiasm. There was a background in the recent past well fitted to bring his present position into striking relief. He had lived here a powerless exile, unregarded except by the great world, where he was, indeed, well liked, but nevertheless looked on as a dreamy adventurer. His wildest dreams were now realised, and when the master of France, the ally of England, the most powerful antagonist of Russia, after passing through cheering crowds in Pall Mall, entered King Street, he there emphasised the contrast between now and then, by pointing out to the Empress the modest lodging (now bearing on its front the record of the fact) where he had lived in the days of his exile. At Windsor a reception no less gratifying, in a quieter and deeper form of welcome, awaited them, and their whole visit was an unbroken triumph.

Meanwhile the conference was holding its sittings at Vienna. Its proceedings were not of a kind to confer credit on any of those who took part in it. On the side of the Allies, the terms offered were absurdly easy in comparison with the vast efforts they were making, and if accepted, would have left neither to France nor England anything to be proud of. On the other hand, the part played by Russia was hardly consistent with common sense, or even with sanity. Russia always has a breed of negotiators who, without making themselves conspicuous for exalted views, are quick to perceive advantages, and the use to which they can be turned, and who are nothing short of audacious in their mode of conducting the contests of diplomacy. Too much alive to the triumphs of mere cleverness, they often seem to make some empty victory at the conference board an all-important object. The article on which her Envoy now rejected all compromise was that which would limit the Russian Fleet in the Black Sea. On this point he took ground that might have been maintained had the naval power of Russia proved in any degree successful against that of the Allies. Judging by his pretensions, it might have been thought that her fleet was still holding the Euxine; but in view of the actual condition of that fleet, great part of it at the bottom of the sea, the rest penned up hopelessly in the harbour of Sebastopol, his language was preposterous. Again, by seeming to accept the terms offered, he might have procured an armistice, and with it an apparent triumph—Russia would have had time to rally from some of her disasters, to recruit in many ways, while a period of inglorious delay might well have tended to disgust the Allies with a war never popular in France. But he preferred, with the haughty, even insolent, air absurd in any but the victorious, to cast away the opportunity that stood between his country and a continuance of ruinous disaster. The conference broke up without any result but this, that Austria made a last effort at compromise, in the form of a proposal that Russia should maintain in the Black Sea a naval force not greater than that which she possessed there before the war, and that the Allies, including Austria, should enforce the condition by war against her if she were to evade it. To which an observation in the Prince Consort's memorandum is the best reply: "The proposal of Austria to engage to make war when the Russian armaments should appear to have become excessive is of no kind of value to the belligerents, who do not wish to establish a case for which to make war hereafter, but to obtain a security upon which they can conclude peace now."

On the 18th April a Council of War met in the Emperor's rooms at Windsor, at which were present the Prince, Lord Palmerston, Lord Panmure,

Lord Hardinge (Commander-in-Chief), Lord Cowley (Ambassador to France), Sir Charles Wood, Sir John Burgoyne, Count Walewski, and the French War Minister, Marshal Vaillant. "All present," says the Prince's report of it, "declared themselves unanimously against the Emperor's scheme of going himself to the Crimea, but without obtaining from him the admission that he was shaken in his resolution."

But on his return to Paris the Emperor found that, while the visit to his ally had greatly increased his popularity at home, the failure of the negotiations at Vienna had gravely added to the difficulties of the situation, and, on the 25th April, in a letter to the Queen, he announced that his intention to go to the Crimea must be abandoned. But his scheme for the conduct of the war was all the same persisted in.

The Austrian proposal, though of course completely unacceptable to our Government, had been sufficiently plausible to gain the approval both of the French plenipotentiary and of Lord John Russell, a circumstance which proved very embarrassing to Lord Palmerston and his colleagues. For the leading members of the late Government, which had sanctioned the expedition to the Crimea, were about to support a motion for an unsatisfactory peace. The Government had to meet, on one hand, the attacks of those represented by Mr Disraeli, who, desiring the prosecution of the war, denounced the conduct of our plenipotentiary; and on the other, of those who always embarrass a Government in war by insisting on the necessity of making peace. "Mr Gladstone," says Sir Theodore Martin, in his life of the Prince Consort, "developed the views of the members of the Aberdeen Cabinet who had seceded from Lord Palmerston's Government. The burden of his speech was to urge peace on the terms offered by Russia. . . . He acknowledged that he had approved the demand by his colleagues, under Lord Aberdeen, for a limitation of the Russian Fleet; but contended that Russia, having abandoned the pretensions which originally led to the war, to continue it was no longer justifiable. What we now asked for in the way of limitation was, he argued, an indignity to Russia. All the terms which we had originally demanded had been substantially conceded, and if we fought, not for terms, but for military success, let the House look at this sentiment with the eye of reason, and it would appear immoral, inhuman, unchristian." But the people held fast to the facts; they recognised that Russia could have no other reason for maintaining a fleet in the Black Sea than to employ it against Turkey, and that the Russian pretension must not be tolerated; and they upheld Palmerston.

The design of the Emperor may perhaps be considered to have borne only its natural fruit in the irresolution of Canrobert, notably when he refused to attempt the gain of a substantial result from the late tremendous bombardment. The dissatisfaction thereby excited in both armies was now aggravated by another event bearing the same character. On the 23d April the Allied generals once more agreed on delivering an assault, which was to take place on the 28th, after two days' preparative cannonade. All was being got ready when, on the 25th, the French Admiral Bruat received instructions from the Minister of Marine to assemble all available steamers at Constantinople for the embarkation of the Army of Reserve for the Crimea. With the prospect of immediately receiving this large reinforcement, it seemed to Canrobert that a hazardous attempt to assault in the interval would be to incur an unwarrantable risk. Lord Raglan reluctantly concurred; but, as some compensation, another enterprise was now agreed on. It had long been recognised that the route on which the Russians in the Crimea principally relied for supplies was that conducting to the eastern shore of the Sea of Azof; when landed at Kertch, they were conveyed by a good and direct road to Simpheropol. An expedition against Kertch had, therefore, long been contemplated by the Allied generals, and it was now to be executed forthwith. On the 3d May the troops, French and English, were embarked, and went to sea. But here a new element entered into the conduct of the war. On the 25th April the Crimea was placed in telegraphic communication with London and Paris. In the night after the expedition sailed, Canrobert received a telegram, sent the day before by the Emperor, saying that the moment was come for the expedition against the Russian field army, and that as soon as the reserve from Constantinople should reach him he was not to lose a day in beginning the enterprise. Therefore, to the extreme dissatisfaction of Lord Raglan, Canrobert, by a fast steamer, recalled the French part of the Kertch expedition, the whole of which was consequently again put on shore in the Crimea on the 6th. It was also by telegraph that General Niel, hitherto without a place in Canrobert's army, was appointed its chief engineer, in place of General Bizot, killed in the late cannonade.

These events had pressed hardly on Canrobert. He felt that the English must regard him as weak and vacillating and unreliable. Much of this apparent defect of character may have been due to the cold shadow of General Niel. But there is no doubt that inherent indecision was generally imputed to him, among others, by General Niel himself, who wrote to the Minister of War that Canrobert's nature had exactly the appearance of decision when a resolution had to be taken a long time beforehand, but always drew back when the moment for execution came. "Who," writes the Prince Consort to a friend, "who will rekindle the spirit of the French Army which has been dashed by Canrobert's irresolution and want of firmness?" The sense of a natural defect, terribly aggravated by circumstances, and of his consequent unfitness to bear the heavy burdens which the command and the alliance laid on him, grievously tormented the French general; and his troubles were further increased when, in the middle of May, the Emperor's plan, in full detail, was brought to him by an officer from Paris. According to it, Pélissier was to be left in charge of the siege, Canrobert was to command the field army and a joint force of French and Turks, taking up the whole business of the siege, was to set free the British Divisions for the operations in the field. When the three commanders-in-chief came together to confer on this plan, Lord Raglan, objecting to the separation of the two field armies by the distance, and the difficulties of country between Aloushta and Baidar, proposed that both should assemble at Baidar, and to this Canrobert was induced to agree. But on another point an insuperable difficulty arose. Both Canrobert and Omar Pasha declared that they could not take charge of the English trenches. On the other hand, Lord Raglan could not leave the task of guarding his siege material and his port of supply to a part only of his own troops, and therefore, though he had looked forward with great satisfaction to exchanging the monotony and perplexity of the siege operations for the proposed command in the field, he could see no course possible except to remain where he was. Neither could Canrobert see a way out of the dilemma, and he wrote to tell the Minister of War of the new difficulty. But he did more than this: the countermand of the Kertch expedition, and his failure to give effect to the Emperor's plan, broke down what of strength still rested in his overwrought spirit, and on the 16th May he sent his resignation to the War Minister by telegraph, requesting to be again placed in command of the Division that had been his at the beginning of the campaign, and strongly urging that Pélissier should replace him, as fitter than himself to deal with the difficulties of the situation. Though this step was quite unexpected, his resignation was accepted by the Emperor, and with the appointment of Pélissier to the chief command (for which he had already been designated in case of need), a new epoch in the war began.

CHAPTER XI

THE NEW GENERAL

*Errors in the Emperor's Theory—Pélissier's View of the Problem—
His Previous Action in May—He declares his Determination—Niel
remonstrates in vain—Displeasure of the Emperor—Course taken by
Vaillant—New Russian Work—The French attack it—And capture it—
Expedition to Kertch—Its Complete Success—The Extended Position—
Ancient Remains—Valley of Baidar*

THE OFFICER who now took command of the French Army was of a singularly strong and marked character. Its distinguishing element was hardihood: hardihood in thought, in dealing with others, and in the execution of his projects. His comrades had formed an extraordinary estimate of his determination. Marshal Vaillant, comparing him with Canrobert, said, "Pélissier will lose 14.000 men for a great result at once, while Canrobert would lose the same number by driblets, without obtaining any advantage." General Changarnier bore stronger testimony: "If there was an insurrection, I should not hesitate to burn one of the quarters of Paris. Pélissier would not shrink from burning the whole." But it would do him great injustice to imagine that he was merely a man of dogged resolution. He was not only a soldier of great experience and distinction in Algerian warfare, but took strong, clear views of strategical problems, and expressed them in a correspondingly strong, clear style, indicative of great sagacity. And there lay before him, when he assumed the command, a problem not easy to solve, yet demanding immediate solution, and of vast importance. It was whether to put in execution the project of the Emperor and Niel, or to devote all his forces to pushing the siege.

Now there is no doubt that the design of defeating the Russian field army, and severing the communication between the interior of Russia and Sebastopol, would, if successful, have speedily caused the surrender of the place. So far the view was sound. But its two advocates erred in insisting on treating it as if it were the only project which rendered success possible, and in denying that the siege operations contained any promise of victory. For there were several circumstances which clearly pointed to the probability, nay certainty, of the capture of the south side of Sebastopol on the plan

Aimable-Jean-Jacques Pélissier, Duc de Malakoff, marshal of France.
Photograph by Roger Fenton.

hitherto pursued. The enemy had never taken from the Allies an inch of ground on which they had once established themselves. If the Russians had not abandoned all intention of attempting to raise the siege by an attack with their field army, the Allies were confident of defeating any such enterprise. There were signs that if the material of war in Sebastopol showed no token of exhaustion, yet the trained seamen who worked the guns were greatly reduced in numbers. The besiegers' fire could always establish a superiority, constantly increasing, over that of the place. And, finally, the enemy's losses must, from the nature of the case, continue to be immensely greater than those of the Allies. In the preceding month the garrison of Sebastopol had lost more than 10,000 men, and there were good grounds for believing that the whole of the Russian Forces now in the Crimea scarcely numbered more than 100,000 men. It was certain, therefore, that should the Allies persevere with the siege, the day, though not yet near, would come when the enemy's fire would be overpowered, his works stormed, and the south side rendered untenable.

Pélissier's mode of grasping this problem is first shown in a letter which he wrote to Canrobert while that general was still Commander-in-Chief. He first expressed his belief that the Allies, by pressing the attack on the works, could certainly render themselves masters of Sebastopol; "difficult," he says, "but possible." Therefore he proposes, before all things, to push the siege to extremity, without regard to what was outside of it. Nevertheless, in case an exterior operation should be "inexorably commanded by the Emperor," he has his plan for that. But he presently shows that this was merely a concession to the weakness of another, by explaining that, before anything of that kind can take place, the Russians must be shut up so completely in their works that no sortie need be feared, and that the first operations must therefore be the capture of the Mamelon and the White Works at any price. "If there are to be operations in the field, they must only take place after we have restricted the Russians absolutely to their defences, and have thus achieved security for our base of operations." He meant by this to insist on the necessity of driving the Russians from all those works which, to the great annoyance and injury of the Allies, they had pushed out beyond the general line of intrenchment. He had given a practical illustration of this view, on the 1st May, when he was still only the commander of the 1st Corps in front of the town. Todleben had, on the 23d April, effected some large lodgments of rifle-pits between the town ravine and the next one on his right of it, and in the ensuing week, employing a great number of labourers, and a strong force to protect them, had formed these into an important work, closed and partially armed, and so close to the French trenches and so menacing to them, by stretching towards their flanks, that it would have immediately become a most serious addition to the difficulties of the siege. Pélissier so strongly represented to Canrobert the necessity of driving the Russians out of it at all hazards that he was allowed to have his way. In two hand-to-hand encounters of considerable forces on both sides, on the 1st and 2d May, the French were so completely successful that they not only took the counterguard, but converted it into part of their own siege works, within 150 yards of the main line in front of it, with a loss to them of 600, to the Russians of 900 men.

In a letter to Bosquet, written immediately after he took command of the army, Pélissier discusses the alternative plans. The difficulties offered by the ground which the enemy's field army occupied, the want of information respecting its strength and positions, the danger of operating through long defiles with large forces the perils of a retreat in case of failure, these and other reasons caused him to reject, or at least to postpone, the Emperor's scheme—"without regret," as he phrased it. "I am very determined," said this clear-seeing man, "not to fling myself into the unknown, to shun adventures, and to act only on sound knowledge, with all the enlightenment needful for the rational conduct of an army." He then announces his intention of extending the part of the army not engaged in the siege along the valley of the Tchernaya, so as to get air, water, elbow-room, and consequently health, and from thence to study the country for future operations, by reconnaissance's, and force the enemy to spread themselves. "But," he adds, "all this is only the prelude to an operation much more important and more decisive in my eyes, the storming and occupation of the Mamelon and White Works. I do not disguise from myself that the conquest of these counter-approaches will cost us certain sacrifices; but whatever they cost, I mean to have them." Then, after detailing the features of his plan, he observes, "All this may be thorny, but it is possible, and I have irrevocably made up my mind to undertake it." Here, then, was a general who had occupied the firm ground of knowing what he meant to do, and setting about it with an unchangeable purpose. But he did not keep his opinions for his generals only. Niel noted the new commander's course with great disquietude, and even felt justified, in the strength of being the Emperor's emissary, to offer to his chief, in a note written in reply to a request for his view of affairs, a strong remonstrance. He said his views remained the same as always; that to attack without first investing the place would lead to nothing except after bloody struggles; that he could not understand why the Emperor's plan was to be abandoned; and that the persistence of Pélissier in his projects would entail every kind of disaster. Scarcely had Pélissier received this when he telegraphed thus to the Minister of War, for the Emperor's information: "The project of marching two armies, from Aloushta (See inner map on Map 3 for Aloushta). on Simpheropol, and from Baidar on Bakshisarai, is full of difficulties and risk. Direct investment, by attacking the Mackenzie heights, would cost as dear as the assault of the place, and the result would be very uncertain. I have arranged with Lord Raglan for the storming of the advanced works, the occupation of the Tchernaya, and finally, for an operation on Kertch... All these movements are in train." This he explained fully in a letter to Vaillant next day, and asked for complete latitude of action. When we remember that Louis Napoleon was an absolute sovereign, that he had just raised Pélissier to the chief command, that he was the fountain of honours and advancement, and that, if he had set this self-willed general up with one hand, he could pull him down with the other, it must be admitted that, in thus opposing the cherished' scheme of his master, Pélissier showed himself an uncommonly strong man.

To the Emperor and his Minister, absorbed in contemplation of the excellences of their plan, and hoping to hear that it was in process of accomplishment, this uncivil treatment of it caused something like consternation. The stout warrior at one end of the wire was arousing great perturbation and resentment in the Imperial theorist at the other. At first some angry messages were flashed to the Crimea—one from Vaillant to Niel, relating to the expedition to Kertch: "This news to-day is a great trouble. What! generals and admirals, not one of them thought it his duty to consult the Government on an affair of this importance!" Then the Emperor sent a rebuke to his unappreciative subordinate: "I have confidence in you," he said, "and I don't pretend to command the army from here" ("But you do!" was probably Pélissier's comment); "however, I must tell you my opinion, and you ought to pay regard to it. A great effort must be made to beat the Russian army, in order to invest the place. To gain space and grass is not sufficient just now" (this in sarcastic reference to Pélissier's reasons for extending the army). "If you scatter your forces, instead of concentrating them, you will do nothing decisive, and will lose precious time. The Allies have 180,000 men in the Crimea. Anything may be attempted with such a force, but to manoeuvre is the right course, not to take the bull by the horns; and the way to manoeuvre is to threaten the weak sides of the enemy. The weak side of the Russians seems to me to be their left wing. If you send 14,000 men to Kertch, you weaken yourself uselessly; it is to avow that there is nothing serious to attempt, for one does not willingly weaken one's self on the eve of battle. Weigh all this carefully." But, whether weighed or not, these arguments had not the slightest effect on the mind of this resolute, even refractory, man. It might be all very well for an Emperor to amuse himself with making plans; it was for a general to conduct operations. Seeing all this, and knowing how indispensable was Pélissier, Vaillant took a very judicious course. He desired Niel to aim at moderating Pélissier's too strong style of expression The General was to be made to understand that the most complete confidence was reposed in him, and to be adjured to assume that as a basis in everything he might write. Whether Niel ever found an opportunity of discharging this mission seems doubtful, for he is shortly afterwards found uttering a lamentable wail, in a letter to the Minister. "At yesterday's meeting," he says, "General Pélissier imposed silence on me with indescribable harshness, because I spoke of the dangers which characterise vigorous actions with large masses at great distances apart. We were in presence of English officers; I saw he was irritated, and I wished at any price to avoid a scene which would have rendered my relations with him impossible." No matter whose emissary he was, Niel must know his place. There was no doing anything with so intractable a chief; he had his own way, and the French Army had a commander.

Pélissier's two first steps towards the execution of his projects, namely, an attack on an important outwork and the expedition to Kertch, took place at the same date, the 22d May, when he had been six days in command. The first of these was caused by a new enterprise of the indomitable Todleben. Between the Central Bastion and the bastion near the Quarantine Bay the line of defence was a loop-holed wall, strengthened behind with earth, but much battered by the heavy fire directed on it. Seeing its precarious state, Todleben resolved to cover it with a salient earthwork on a ridge in front, where he had already placed rows of rifle pits. Between these pits and the French trenches was a cemetery, lying in a green hollow, having in its midst a small church, surrounded by crosses and headstones. Once peaceful as any country churchyard in England, it had now for months been an arena of conflict, where riflemen had crouched in the grass of the graves, or lurked in the shadow of the tombstones. The French trenches were already close to its southern wall, when Todleben, on the night of the 21st, began his outwork with characteristic vigour. Two thousand four hundred workmen were busy with spade and pickaxe, while 6000 infantry, and many guns bearing on the ground in front, guarded them. But the French also were making a trench that night; therefore both parties had an interest in keeping their batteries quiet. But morning showed that while the French, with their working party of ordinary strength, had made about 150 yards of trench, the Russians had made more than 1000 yards, besides a supplementary work close to the head of Quarantine Bay. And these works were not to play a defensive part merely; when armed, they would rake the French trenches, and form a new and serious obstacle to the progress of the siege. Therefore Pélissier ordered that the new works should be attacked that night; the enemy was equally resolved to defend them; and it so happened that about 6000 men were devoted to the purpose on each side. All the guns, Russian and French that could aid the infantry were laid on their objects, ready to open. At nine on the night of the 22d the fight began, and continued without intermission till three in the morning. There was a glimmering moon, and against a low bank of clouds the flashes of the guns marked the hostile lines; the rattle of small-arms resounded through the night, and at times a cheer, rising out of the gloom, showed where a charge had been led, or some advantage won. Many times had each side gained a temporary success; but as the French

Volunteers of the Flying Squadron firing from a British raft at the shipping at Taganrog

could not remain in the work by day, under the fire of the place, the Russians still held it in the morning, though it had cost them dear. They had lost 2650 men; the French, 1800.

It so happened that the neighbouring bay of Kamiesch had presented, on this same 22d, an unusually busy scene, for the troops destined for the expedition to Kertch were embarking there. From the ships they heard the conflict raging at no great distance. In the morning they sailed on their enterprise. Unluckily for the Russians, one of their posts, from a tower of observation, saw and signalled that large forces were in movement from the harbour. Gortschakoff imagined that they were about to be landed on the coast for an attack on his forces in the field. He concluded he could spare no troops for another fight in the trenches from his army, which lay between Mackenzie's Farm and the heights of the Belbek. Therefore, only two battalions were to hold the new work. If the French should prove to have had enough of fighting the night before, these would suffice to protect the completion of the work; but if attacked by superior numbers, they must withdraw. The French did come on again that night in great force, drove out the guard, and converted the line of trench into a parallel of their own. This night the losses were about 400 on each side.

The much-talked-of expedition to Kertch (See inner map on Map 3) had a very practical object. The eastern point of the lozenge which the outline of the Crimea forms runs in a long, narrow isthmus towards the Circassian coast of the Black Sea, from which it is separated by the narrow straits of Kertch, and these give access, from the waters of the Euxine, to those of the inland Sea of Azof. Into this sea the River Don empties itself, and thus the resources of large districts on its banks, and of Circassia, can be swept into the isthmus; and the superiority of this route, compared with that along the wretched roads of Southern Russia, and through the barren country by Perekop to Simpheropol, had made it the great line of supply to Gortschakoff's army. The Sea of Azof was thronged with craft, occupied in transporting stores to great depots on the shores of the isthmus. Taganrog, on the shore of the Sea of Azof, near the mouth of the Don, was a considerable town, and in former days had even, from its pleasant situation, been thought of for the capital of. Russia. The whole region was at this time specially full of business and activity.

The ships reached the straits of Kertch on the early morning of the 24th. They bore, in all, French, Turks, and English, 15,000 infantry, and five field batteries. There were about 9000 Russians in the isthmus, of which 3000 were cavalry. There were batteries guarding the straits, armed with sixty-two heavy guns, and some forty others, unmounted, of large calibre. And there had been plenty of time to prepare for an attack, since the fiasco of three weeks earlier had warned the enemy. It might have been expected that, with such means at his disposal, General Wrangel, who commanded in the isthmus, would have made at least some show of resistance. But seeing how exposed his forces were, in their straitened position, to be cut off by a landing in their rear, he made haste to withdraw them, at the same time destroying his coast batteries, while, of fourteen war-vessels, ten were burnt by their crews. The Allied Squadrons therefore passed into the straits without molestation. The landing of the troops was effected the same night, in a bay a few miles from the town of Kertch, which they entered early next morning, while a flotilla of vessels of light draught passed into the Sea of Azof. There they captured or destroyed all the great number of vessels engaged in transporting supplies for Gortschakoff's army, as well as vast quantities of corn, flour, and stores. At one point they came on the wrecks of the remaining four steamers of the Russian Naval Squadron, destroyed by order of its commander. A complete clearance of everything that could aid the Forces in the Crimea was made throughout the shores of the Sea of Azof. At Taganrog, the depot of the immense supplies brought down the River Don, where some semblance of opposition was made by the garrison, the destruction of the stores on the beach was accomplished under cover of a fire from the boats of the flotilla. The fort of Arabat was bombarded and taken. Meanwhile the large men-of-war of the Allied Squadrons, outside the straits, made for Soujouk-kale and Anapa, strong places on the Circassian coast, which at their approach were abandoned by their garrisons. These operations were concluded by the second week in June, and the result was thus summed up by Pélissier, in a letter to the War Minister: "We have struck deep into the Russian resources; their chief line of supply is cut. I did well to concur in this expedition, so fertile in results. Confidence is general, and I view with calm assurance the approach of the final act." In fact, the expedition had fulfilled, in no slight degree, the Emperor's policy of investment.

Meanwhile the clearance of the crowded Upland had been effected. At daylight, on the 25th May, Canrobert, with two Divisions, and cavalry and artillery, passed the Traktir Bridge, drove the Russians from Tchorgoun, and destroyed their camp and their barracks. The force then recrossed the stream, and took position on its left bank, holding an armed work at the bridge. Italy, having some time before joined the alliance against Russia, had despatched General La Marmora, with a small army of 15,000 men, including some cavalry and artillery, to the Crimea. These troops now occupied ground on the French right, across the road from Baidar. In rear of all a large force of Turks from Eupatoria took up the same line of heights across the valley of Balaklava which they had occupied on the 25th of October. The land on which the Army was encamped had at this time resumed its smiling aspect, except, indeed, the ground between the Turks and Balaklava, where the small paradise which had greeted us on our first arrival had been completely destroyed. It had then been one large and well-stored garden. Plums and apples grew overhead, the clustering vines were thick with green and purple grapes, and between the vineyards was a rich jungle of melons, pumpkins, tomatoes, and cabbages. All this had given place to the grim features of war. But elsewhere the grass had sprung up, mixed with flowers in extraordinary variety and profusion; the willows again drooped their leaves over the Tchernaya; even the field of Inkerman resumed its green carpet, all the richer, perhaps, for the battle, and turf like that of our south downs once more covered the Upland. A most remarkable feature of the southern coast of the Crimea is the rare beauty of the colouring of its iron-bound coast. Those cliffs, so implacable in the storms of winter, are dyed with the loveliest rose-colours, pearly greys, yellows, dark reds, and rich browns, with purple shadows, in the most effective combinations. On a summit of these, in full view of the Black Sea, stands the Monastery of St George, with its long low ranges of building, its green domes and turrets, reared on solid basements of masonry, white like the rest of the edifice. Here the brotherhood, clad in black gowns, with tall cylindrical caps, from which black veils descended behind, continued to pray and chant; here, too, lived in peace some Russian families, including that of the late commandant of Balaklava; and here was established our telegraph station. Near this was the site of an ancient

The Monastery of St. George and Cape Fiolente - looking west.
Print by William Simpson, c1855.

temple of Diana; Cyclopean remains exist there, the palace and gardens which contained the famous Golden Fleece had looked from hence over the sea; and it must have been in the valley below that "Medea gathered the enchanted herbs, which did renew old Aeson." There were tokens, too, of inhabitants compared with whom Medea and Aeson are moderns. Across a gully, which led to a cove used by our troops as a bathing-place, lay a ridge which might have been the roof of a tunnel. But the many footsteps at length wore away the soil of ages, and it was apparent that a huge Saurian had been in some way swept across the gully, and become fixed there; and it was his skeleton, hidden even in Jason's time, that was now laid bare to the view of British riflemen.

Crossing the valley of the Tchernaya, in grass and flowers to the horses' knees, and ascending the green hillsides of Kamara, beyond the Sardinian outposts, the explorer came on expanses of tall coppice, with trees of larger growth, which enclosed glades like those of a park. Here were some British marines, whose lines had fallen in a place pleasant as the meadows of Devon, in front of which rose a wooded mountain, its craggy peaks breaking through the verdure. A wood path, winding amid tall trees, led to the next summit, which disclosed a magnificent landscape. Below lay the valley of Baidar, stretching from the edge of the sea-cliffs to the distant mountain range—a tract of flowery meadows sprinkled with trees and groves. In the midst of the valley stood, at some distance apart, two villages, their roofs gleaming red through the surrounding trees; but no labourers, nor waggoners, nor cattle gave life to the scene, nor had any corn been sown for this year's harvest.

The villages were not only deserted but, as some visitors had ascertained, quite bare of all tokens of domestic life. Turning back along the sea-cliffs, the silent, deserted, beautiful region came to an end on reaching the fortified ridge above Balaklava; here were the troops busied with their camp duties, mules and buffaloes toiling with their loads; and up the hills beyond Kadukoi, above the Turkish camp, the bearded pashas, sitting in open, green tents, smoked their long-stemmed pipes in that blissful calm which such matters as wars and the peril of empires could not disturb.

CHAPTER XII

A SUCCESSION OF CONFLICTS

The Emperor persists in his Plan—Pélissier opposes it—The Objects of the Attack—Assault of the White Works—Assault of the Mamelon— The Struggle for it—Assault of the Quarries—The Emperor still persists—Error of Pélissier—His Second Error—His Insufficient Reason—Failure at the Malakoff—Failure at the Redan—A Partial Success—Todleben wounded—Pélissier's Persistency in Prosecuting the Siege—Vaillant sides with Pélissier—Death of Lord Raglan—His Funeral—Sufferings of the Defenders—Russian Plans of Battle— Russian Advance for Battle—Battle of the Tchernaya—Retreat of the Russians—Russian Losses in the War.

MEANWHILE THE energy of the French General was impelling him, in complete accord with his British colleague, towards one of his main objects. This was to storm the White Works, the Mamelon, and the work between the English trenches and the Redan known as the Quarries. Todleben many times asserts that the Flagstaff Bastion, and other works in front of the town, had frequently been reduced to so desperate a condition from the artillery fire that an assault on them must have been successful, and that the loss of any of these would have entailed the surrender of the place. That the matter did not so present itself to Pélissier's mind is evident from the fact that, with all the means of forming a judgment which the proximity of his siege works to the town defences, and his frequent attacks on the enemy's outworks gave him, he deliberately adopted the course of attacking the proper left half of the Russian line of defence, that covering the suburb; and a necessary preliminary was to wrest the outworks just mentioned from the enemy. With this view, the arming of fresh batteries, and the storing of the great quantities of ammunition necessary for a sustained cannonade, once more went on in the trenches.

But if Pélissier was constant to his own ideas, so was Louis Napoleon. Unable to condemn the previous operations after they had proved so successful, he had, nevertheless, given them but a cold approval, regarding

Council of War held at Lord Raglan's Head Quarters, the morning of the successful attack on the Mamelon. Left to right: Lord Raglan, Omar Pacha and Marshal Pélissier. Photograph by Roger Fenton.

them indeed as false fires leading his General astray. And now he despatched a telegram to Pélissier in these terms: "For the well-being of France, and for the glory of our arms, you are at the head of the finest army which perhaps has ever existed. You are certain of a deathless fame, but great things must be done for it. The conduct of the siege is even more the business of the chief engineer than of the general-in-chief; but the chief engineer has addressed to you these observations : 'If you push the siege without investing the place, you will only obtain, after bloody conflicts costing you your best troops, what would have come of itself after the investment.' In conformity with the British Government, which writes in the same sense to Lord Raglan, I give you a positive order not to devote yourself to the siege before having invested the place. Concert with Lord Raglan and Omar Pasha measures for the offensive, whether by the Tchernaya or against Simpheropol."

But before receiving this, Pélissier had sent a telegram to the Emperor to a very different purpose: "To-day I am going to see Lord Raglan, who shares my ideas, in order to settle the last dispositions for the attack by storm, which ought to place in our power the White Works, the Mamelon, and the Quarry before the Redan. I calculate on beginning this operation on the 7th, and on carrying it right through with the utmost vigour." And the telegram he proceeded to act on was his own.

At three in the afternoon of the 6th June the siege batteries opened. Our own guns, as before, were mainly directed on the Redan and Malakoff and their dependencies; but our battery of heavy guns, increased now to twenty, on the right of the Right Attack, and some of the mortar batteries more in advance, were brought to bear on the Mamelon, crossing their fire with that of the French batteries on Mount Inkerman.

The work known as the Quarries was situated at about 400 yards in front of the Redan, at a point where the gradual downward slope was broken by an abrupter dip, and it thus stood on what was comparatively a small eminence. The ground there had lately been occupied with heaps of stones and rubbish, but these had been replaced by a regular work, though retaining the old name. This work, thus covering the Redan, had been itself covered by rows of rifle screens. But, on the night of the 19th April, Colonel Egerton,[5] with a detachment of the 77th, without firing a shot, drove out, or killed with the bayonet, the occupants of these pits, and repulsed the troops supporting them, so that now our advanced line of trench in the Right Attack was face to face with the Quarries. As soon as the French should have secured the Mamelon we were to attack this work, and there establish ourselves.

All the works about to be attacked contained only a small proportion of the troops that were to be employed in their defence. The number sufficient to line their parapets, with a reserve within to make good losses, having been provided, the supports, in much greater force, were drawn up at some convenient spot near by, ready to reinforce the defenders, and to meet the auxiliary attacks which would approach the work from its flanks. The White Works, backed on the harbour, were supported by a battery at the end of the Careenage ravine, and the reserves were placed some in a small ravine in rear, some on the other side of the Careenage ravine.

The fire of the siege batteries was tremendous beyond all precedent. Five hundred and forty-four great guns bore on the Russian works, and were

---

5 Killed the same night, later.

opposed by a nearly equal number. The effect of the fire of the Allies was soon manifest. The work on the Mamelon was terribly crushed, chiefly, says Todleben, "by the English guns, which made up for some slowness of fire by remarkable precision of aim." The White Works were less considerably damaged, and could keep up a fire till evening. The works of the main line of defence also maintained the struggle, except the Malakoff itself, the right face of which, says Todleben, had been so knocked about by the English guns as to be reduced almost to silence. With dusk the Allied batteries ceased firing, but their mortars continued to throw their huge shells throughout the night. Nevertheless, the Russians, under the inspiration and the eye of Todleben, had made good their damages by morning.

On the 7th the cannonade was resumed with the same terrible effects as before. The Mamelon was reduced to absolute silence, the parapet of its right face was almost levelled, and after two hours the Malakoff was no longer in a condition to support it. By six in the evening the White Works and their auxiliary battery were ruined, and the parapets thrown into the ditch.

Half-past six was the hour fixed for the assault— a time which would allow daylight enough to secure possession of the works, while darkness would come soon enough to- cover the working parties against the fire of the supporting batteries. The Russians could perceive the troops for the assault crowding into the trenches, and prepared to meet them. But the French had approached so near to the defences before the town that the part of the garrison on that side was still maintained in greater strength than that which defended the suburb. At the appointed hour Bosquet sent two brigades at the White Works, which, encountering only half a battalion in each, captured both so speedily that a reserve battalion, hurrying up from the ravine behind, was too late, and was swept away in its turn. Then two other Russian battalions, crossing the Careenage ravine, ascended to the scene of contest; but Bosquet, in anticipation, had sent two battalions down the ravine, which, ascending its bank on their right, took these Russian reserves in rear, and captured a great part of them. No further attempt was made to retake the works; though three other battalions of reserve were despatched by the Russians, they reached no further than to the battery on the point. During the night the French connected these works with their own trenches.

At half-past five the French columns for the attack of the Mamelon were formed at the entrance of the Docks ravine. To each battalion General Bosquet addressed a few words of encouragement. Preceded by their vivandiere, who was well mounted, and wore a white hat and feather, the Algerian Zouaves headed the march, next came the French Zouaves, then the Green Chasseurs, attended by their vivandiere, and several regiments of the line followed, the whole moving down to the point where the trenches in

A Zouave. Photograph by Roger Fenton.

which they were to await the signal to attack were entered from the ravine.

Crowds of spectators from the camps were assembled at points commanding a good view. The Mamelon, always conspicuous, was the cynosure of all eyes. Admiral Nakimoff rode up the rear slope of the hill about six, and leaving his horse at the entrance, passed into the work. Suddenly loud shouts caused him to look over the parapet, when he beheld three French columns advancing to the assault, and driving before them the sharpshooters who had lined the covering trench. The Turcos formed the right column, the 50th regiment of the line the centre, the 3d (French) Zouaves the left. Led by one man,

Colonel Brancion, who kept throughout in advance, the centre column, went straight up the slope, passed the line of intrenchment which crossed it, and in a few minutes was crowding the edge of the ditch. Presently the leading troops were seen on the parapet, still led by Colonel Brandon, who leaped into the work, where he was instantly slain. At the same moment the Turcos, passing the intrenchments which extended to the left of the work, ascended the slopes towards its rear, when the defenders, with the Admiral, abandoned it almost without a struggle, and hurried off towards the Malakoff, while the tricolour was presently seen fluttering over the Mamelon.

The captured work was of the kind called a lunette (though a very irregular one), two sides meeting in a salient, and open in the rear, so that not only could reinforcements be poured quickly in, but the batteries of the main line could sweep the interior if occupied by the enemy. To cover their working parties, who would now close and fortify the open rear, the foremost assailants pressed out in pursuit, even up to the verge of the Malakoff, the guns of which at once opened on them, while the rifles of the garrison blazed along the parapets. For a quarter of an hour the scene was wrapped in smoke; then the Russian reinforcements, arriving in strength, drove the French back upon the Mamelon. The Russians, in their turn, followed up their success, pressing into the Mamelon, and after a short struggle the French gave way, and ran down the hill to their own trenches. Ample provision of reserves had been made for this contingency, and reinforced by these the French again went up the hill and into the work, which they captured and held, and round which their musketry continued to sparkle in the darkness, while their comrades constructed the necessary trench across the rear of the lunette, converting it into what was henceforth called, in obedience to a general order, "the Brancion Redoubt."

The entry of the French into the Mamelon was to be the signal for the English to attack the Quarries. Troops of the Light and Second Divisions were assigned to this purpose, in number 700, for the immediate assault, with 600 in close support, and the 626. Regiment in reserve, with strong working parties, the whole under Colonel Shirley. The stormers, operating by the flanks of the work, easily drove out the defenders, not only from it, but from the collateral trench extending thence across the ridge. But the work, unenclosed, afforded no protection from the fire of the Russian batteries behind it, which came into play, till their infantry, sallying from the Redan, engaged the assailants on the ridge outside. The combat swayed to and fro at intervals, as often as the Russians made a fresh sally, throughout the night, but all the trenches fought for remained in possession of the British.

Morning disclosed not only that Pélissier had accomplished the object of driving the enemy everywhere from their outworks, and restricting them to the main line of defence (for they had abandoned the auxiliary battery on the edge of Careening Bay), but that the advanced positions they had occupied had been converted into the front line of the siege works, connected by trenches with those in rear. In accomplishing this the French had lost in all, killed, wounded, and prisoners, 5440 men; the English, 693; the Russians, 5000. But, besides these losses, in the six days' cannonade, from the 6th to the 10th June inclusive, the Allies lost 750 men; the Russians, 3500. The French had taken in the works seventy-three guns.

The Emperor, clinging as was his wont persistently to his idea, did not on account of this success cease to harp on the one string of his plan for operating against the field army. It was not till seven days after the action that he telegraphed to Pélissier saying that, before congratulating him on his success, he had wished to know the cost. "I admire the courage of the troops," he continued, "but I wish you to observe that a general action, which would have decided the fate of the Crimea, would have cost no more. I persist, then, in ordering you to make every effort to take the field." In reply, Pélissier reaffirmed his conviction that his course was the right one. "In this situation the complete execution of your orders is impossible. It is to place me, Sire, between insubordination and discredit. . . . The army is full of confidence and ardour; mine equals my devotion; but I pray your Majesty either to free me from the straitened limits imposed on me, or to permit me to resign a command impossible to exercise, in concert with my loyal allies, at the end, sometimes paralysing, of an electric wire." And to Marshal Vaillant he wrote: "The silence of the Government and the Emperor respecting me, and, above all, respecting my troops, and their brilliant feat of arms of the 7th, has surprised and afflicted me. The telegraphic despatches received since have still more painfully impressed me." And, finally, on the night of the 17th: "I have waited all day for an answer to my important despatch of yesterday, but have received none, and the combinations settled with our allies are taking their course. To-morrow, at daybreak, in concert with the English, I attack the Redan, the Malakoff, and their dependent batteries. I have firm hope."

Up to this time Pélissier has appeared as a commander not only singularly resolute, but singularly clear of view. But now, with the great attack of the 18th pending, he committed two acts, not of resolution, but of waywardness, and in which his accustomed clearness of view showed itself to be suddenly obscured. He was already displeased by a difference of opinion between himself and Bosquet (who wished to postpone the assault until the progress of the works should leave less of open ground to be traversed under fire by the assailants), when that general gave new cause of offence. A plan of the Malakoff had been found on the body of a Russian officer, and brought to

Bosquet, who had omitted to forward it to the General-in-Chief. Hearing of this, Pélissier, not content with demanding it with violent reproaches, removed Bosquet from the command of the forces with which the fresh attack was to be made, sending him to the corps on the Tchernaya, and replaced this experienced commander, so well acquainted with the ground, by another just come from France, and knowing nothing of the local features and circumstances.

This was a very grave error, impossible to justify. Niel wrote to Vaillant about it: "Canrobert says it is not an eagle, but a vulture which he has put in his place, and that he regrets what he did. It is impossible to describe the wrath of Bosquet; the proceedings of which he is the object are incredible." The general who replaced him, Regnaud de St Jean d'Angély, Commander of the Imperial Guard, had just thirty-six hours in which to study the very difficult ground and the siege works, and to place himself in relations with troops who did not know him, and who regretted their old chief.

The other error was even worse. Pélissier had arranged with Lord Raglan that the cannonade of the 17th should be renewed at dawn on the 18th, and should last for two hours, in which time it was calculated the enemy's guns might be silenced, and their works, after the repairs of the night, once more ruined. The attack was therefore to take place at five, or half-past. On the 17th, the batteries opening over the entire front from Quarantine Bay to Careening Bay produced their effect as before. Evening saw the Barrack Batteries, the Redan, and Malakoff, with their dependencies, and the works thence to the harbour, all disabled, with vast losses within them of killed and wounded. But suddenly, without a word to Lord Raglan, Pélissier changed the plan. He resolved to dispense with the preliminary cannonade next morning and to assault at daybreak. He communicated this change to his colleague in a despatch as definitive, and resting on grounds that could not be disputed. Lord Raglan heard of it with deep concern, but concluded that it was better silently to accept and conform to the change than to protest. Nevertheless, considering the issues involved, it is a question whether he would not have done well in declining to co-operate, except on the jointly arranged plan. The change was lamented by the English artillery officers, who had been very confident of rendering the Russian batteries nearly harmless in a very few hours.

These aberrations of Pélissier have never been quite accounted for. Kinglake suggests that they were due to the extreme anguish of mind inflicted by the Emperor's telegrams, and even states the time during which the perturbation lasted as eight days. In his despatch to Lord Raglan, Pélissier gave as his reason for hastening the hour of attack that the assembly of his troops in the trenches, as had been found on trial, could not after daylight be concealed from the enemy, who would therefore be prepared to meet them. But the cannonade would have already prepared them; moreover, the hour before dawn is that in which all menaced garrisons specially expect attack. Therefore nothing was so essential to success as to stop the fire which would bear on his troops in the open ground, and Pélissier's reason was not such as ought for a moment to have swayed him.

Before dawn, on the 18th, Lord Raglan and his staff assembled in an advanced trench which seemed suitable for observation, and would have been so, had it not been the focus of fire from the Redan and Malakoff. From thence could be seen our troops, detailed for the assault, and their supports, crowding the advanced trenches; and the movements around the Malakoff were, with daylight, also discernible. The day had been chosen as one on which the memory of Waterloo might happily give place to a joint victory of French and English. Instead of this, it was marked from the outset by a series of blunders and misfortunes.

First, the French troops, destined to form the right column against the Malakoff, found, on reaching the trenches in the night, that the post they were to take up was still occupied by another part of the attacking force. Much delay and confusion was thus caused, and under the brilliant starlight, the enemy, already roused to more than common vigilance, perceived the preparations for attack. At two in the morning his bugles sounded the alarm; the reserves closed up to their posts, the embrasures were opened for action, and field-guns were placed in the Malakoff and elsewhere to fire on the columns of assault. Next, the French general who was to direct the assault against the left of the Russian line mistook a casual shell for the signal of attack, and advanced prematurely. But it is not likely that these mischances greatly affected the result. The repairs and renewals, which by the extraordinary energy of the garrison and its leaders had been accomplished in the few hours of darkness, enabled them to pour such a storm of shot from every part assailed that no serious impression was made anywhere. Under the overwhelming fire from the ramparts, the spaces of open ground to be traversed by the assailants were thickly strewed with the fallen. For the most part the attacks, made on the part of the French with, in all, 25,000 men, resolved themselves into an exchange of rifle fire between the assailants spread out around the works, and the defenders aiming from the parapets, and aided by the field-guns as well as by the regular armament.

Lord Raglan, though it was seen that the attacks were thus far failures, felt bound to take his part in the enterprise. He was himself under a very hot cross-fire, especially of that now obsolete projectile called grape. It was formed of bullets the size of small apples, piled symmetrically, and tied round an iron spindle rising from the centre of a wooden disc of a size to fit the bore of the gun. With the discharge the tie was broken, the bullets flew together with a noise like that of a covey of partridges, while in rear the spindle, retarded by the pressure of air on the disc, came on separately with a whistling sound of its own. But round shot also dashed plentifully in, and one, after killing a sapper, left a gunner lying headless, as if guillotined, in the trench, and knocked off the arm of an officer. The grape, besides other damage, prostrated the commanding engineer with a wound on the forehead, and many officers, arriving with intelligence or seeking orders, were killed or wounded. It was from this place that the order had been given to our troops to attack. Upon them, as on the French, a tremendous fire of all kinds was poured. The several columns that moved out were almost annihilated, and the parts of them that still went on were held fast by a belt of abattis in front of the ditch. General Campbell and Colonel Yea, who each led a column, were killed; the ladder party of twenty volunteers lost eleven; of 120 sailors, fifty-two fell; and the stormers generally in equal proportion. Nothing that could be called an assault, of a kind that even faintly promised success, took place anywhere; and after a conference between Pélissier and Lord Raglan in the Victoria Redoubt, they considered what they had seen and learned to be so discouraging that, between seven and eight o'clock, all the attacking troops were recalled to the trenches.

Meanwhile a partial success had been achieved on our left. General Eyre, with a brigade of 2000 men, descending the Picket House ravine, had driven the Russians out of buildings and a cemetery at the foot of Green Hill. Here they were immediately under the Garden Batteries, which all day poured on them a destructive fire; and an infantry force descending from thence, and lining a breastwork in the valley, exchanged volleys with our troops, who forced them to regain the shelter of their works. Eyre, himself wounded, and his troops held their ground till nightfall, with the loss of 600 men and officers, and the cemetery was then fortified by our engineers, who afterwards handed it over to the French.

The losses in the actual assault, during which the besieging batteries ceased firing, were heavily against the Allies; but, taken in conjunction with those caused by the cannonade of the 17th and 18th, the French lost 3500 men; the English, 1500; the Russians, 5400. Of the six generals and commanders, French and English, who led the six attacks, four were killed and one disabled.

The spirit of resistance shown by the Russians was such as their nation may well be proud to recall. But it was only rendered possible by the reliefs of fresh un-harassed troops always available from the army outside. When, however, at the moment which the Russians were giving to exultation and thanksgiving, the cannonade recommenced in all its terrors, the spirit of the soldiery gave way, and many of them made for the harbour, fighting with their own people there for the boats and rafts with which to escape the iron storm that searched the crannies of the south side. And they soon had other cause for discouragement. Slightly wounded on the 18th, their sagacious, unresting, resourceful, and indomitable engineer, Todleben, was disabled on the 20th by a shot through the leg, and was carried from the fortress, not to return during the siege.

Considering his own share in causing the disaster, Pélissier showed at least his characteristic hardihood in reporting the issue of the attack. The same day he telegraphed to Vaillant thus: "From causes which cannot now be discussed, our attack of to-day has not succeeded, although part of our troops set foot in the Malakoff. Our allies not having attained, in spite of their vigour, a footing in the Redan, I ordered a withdrawal to the trenches."

The "causes" alluded to in this telegram were set forth, in a letter, as the mistakes made by General Mayran, in attacking too soon, and by General Brunet, for remissness in his preliminary arrangements for the assault. When told that both these generals had fallen in leading their troops, he uttered what the French chronicler Rousset calls truly "a cruel word," and which, he says, shocked the staff: "If they were not dead, I would send them before a council of war." To Vaillant he utters no words which would admit that he was himself to blame. He points out that mistakes made on an open field of battle would entail consequences much more serious than in an assault from the trenches, where the defeated troops were at once sheltered and rallied. Not only a defeat, but even a drawn battle in the field, would paralyse the Allies, far from their ports and resources, and encumbered with sick and wounded. Therefore, he is still for prosecuting the siege. "I cannot console myself for the failure at the Malakoff otherwise than in repairing it by energy, and, above all, by method." Niel also wrote to Vaillant, in a tone much more moderate and hopeful than was his wont. But nothing, apparently, could remove Pélissier's natural prejudice against one who criticised and opposed his measures, and who had the ear of their master. On the 26th there was a conference of French generals, when Niel, in endeavouring to argue in favour of a certain direction of the siege works, was thus met, according to his own report of the scene: "The General-in-Chief said to me, 'I forbid you, in the most formal manner, to add anything to the reading of your note, and if you infringe my orders, I warn you I shall resort to rigorous means.'" The check Pélissier had met with had not softened his spirit, or rendered him more conciliatory; and when, in compliance with a hint from Vaillant that the Emperor complained of the small attention paid to the Imperial views and messages, Pélissier wrote to Louis Napoleon, he set forth his conception of the situation no less clearly and decisively than before, and weighed the Emperor's plan against his own without any sign of giving way.

"We must look even more carefully to the chances of a reverse than to those of a victory. Before the fortress our failures do not change the situation; they leave us to-day where we were yesterday; but in a battle in the field the losses and disorders will be multiplied in proportion to the distance from our base." He then discusses the problem in a very masterly way, and winds up thus: "I am too devoted to my country, too anxious to serve the Emperor according to his views, to be suspected of being governed by obstinacy; it is simply sincerity and devotion which actuate me ... Believe that if I do not enter into the projects which have your sympathies, Sire, it is because I should risk the fortunes of your Majesty, which are the fortunes of France." Probably it will be thought that Pélissier gave no greater proof of the firmness of his character than when he thus adhered to the much-questioned plan, in executing which he had just sustained a heavy defeat. The letter made a strong impression on the Emperor. He had been with difficulty dissuaded from displacing Pélissier and giving Niel the command. But he now showed this letter to Vaillant as no less remarkable for its substance than its form. And Marshal Vaillant himself plays a very fine part in the correspondence. He gives excellent counsels, admirably and often wittily expressed, to the Emperor, to Pélissier, and to Niel. He admonishes Niel to conciliate Pélissier; he advises Pélissier to trust Niel. And now he declared for Pélissier's plan. "There can be no question of field operations now," he writes to Pélissier; "that would be to abandon the certain, which, I allow, is not brilliant, for the uncertain, which may be disastrous. It is the fortune of France which is played for before Sebastopol. At least, let it be well played for, ... I have often told the Emperor that the time for diversions is past; that we grasp the fortress too closely to distract ourselves with exterior operations, in which a check might have terrible consequences." And to Niel he says: "To undertake a campaign with the cholera for company, and a great siege at our back, would terrify me; I could understand it in May; in July it is no longer possible." So the siege went on; only Pélissier practically confessed his mistake by now resolving to push his approaches (as he had phrased it in his letter to the Emperor), "as methodically, as prudently, and as closely as possible."

There can be little doubt that the event of the 18th June pressed heavily on Lord Raglan. He had never appeared to be a commander who took his responsibilities anxiously; indeed, to some observers, it seemed that they scarcely impressed him in due proportion to their gravity. But the suppression of feeling may itself have been costly. Five days after the failure of the assault, an officer of his staff wrote: "I fear it has affected Lord Raglan's health, he looks far from well, and has grown very much aged latterly." He wrote to tell Pélissier he was unwell, "but nothing serious." On the 26th he spent the morning in his correspondence, which he always conducted most industriously; but when he concluded it that day, he had written his last letter. Cholera, not in its cruel or violent form, declared itself; he sank gradually away, and, on the 28th, died peacefully in the presence of his military household. Next day his colleagues came to take a farewell look of him, when the stern Pélissier, who had always evinced a great regard and even affection for his English colleague, showed a new side of his character. "General Pélissier," says an officer who was present, "stood by the bedside for upwards of an hour, crying like a child." And the tribute he paid him in a general order was highly appreciated in all the camps, and is so evidently genuine in expression, that it may well serve to show in what estimation the deceased commander was held by his colleagues.

"Army of the East, No. 15, General Order.

"Death has suddenly taken away, while in full exercise of his command, the Field-Marshal Lord Raglan, and has plunged the British in mourning.

"We all share the sorrow of our brave allies. Those who knew Lord Raglan, who know the history of his life, so pure, so noble, so replete with service rendered to his country, those who witnessed his fearless demeanour at the Alma and Inkerman, who recall the calm and stoic greatness of his character throughout this rude and memorable campaign, every generous heart, indeed, will deplore the loss of such a man. The sentiments here expressed by the General-in-Chief are those of the whole Army. He has himself been cruelly struck by this unlooked-for blow.

"The public grief only increases his sorrow at being for ever separated from a companion-in-arms whose genial spirit he loved, whose virtues he admired, and from whom he has always received the most loyal and hearty co-operation.

"A. Pélissier, Commander-in- Chief.

"HEADQUARTERS BEFORE SEBASTOPOL, 29th June 1855."

The funeral was a very striking spectacle. Covered with a white flag, showing the red cross of St George, and borne on a gun carriage, the coffin journeyed slowly, from the farmhouse which had been the English headquarters, across the plains. The generals and staffs of the four Armies, English, French, Turkish, and Sardinian accompanied it, as it moved between saluting batteries and lines of troops extending to Kazatch Bay, the place of embarkation. Crowds of boats, with naval officers, there awaited its transfer to the Caradoc, the steamer in which Lord Raglan had come from England, and which was now to take home his remains. His destined successor, General Simpson, was already on the spot, and at once assumed the command of the army.

On the 10th July Admiral Nakimoff, who had commanded the Russian Squadron at Sinope, and had been one of the foremost chiefs of the defence, was mortally wounded in the Malakoff. He was buried, with imposing ceremonies, on the City heights, near the tombs of his colleagues, Admirals Lazareff, Korniloff, and Istomine, all slain in defending the fortress.

All through July the defenders of Sebastopol beheld the works of the besiegers creeping steadily on; and while the ordinary fire caused them a daily loss of 250 men, they knew that the interval must be short before they would again have to pass through the terrific ordeal of another cannonade, with the now ascertained result of seeing their artillery silenced, and dreadful losses inflicted on the garrison. At the burial truce, which followed the 18th June, a young Russian officer said to one of our staff,[6] who had been speaking of the losses of the Allies, "with great bitterness of manner and voice choked with emotion: 'Losses! you don't know what the word means; you should see our batteries; the dead lie there in heaps and heaps. Troops cannot live under such a fire of hell as you poured upon us.'" In that bombardment the Russians had lost from 1000 to 1500 a day, and a renewal of the terrible time was now approaching. Supposing, then, that the thought of retreat to the north side could not yet be entertained, the question was urgent whether to persevere in the passive defence or to bring up their field army for a general attack upon the enemy. It seemed that the chief officers on the spot were alone competent to settle this, and Prince Gortschakoff was ordered, with the approval of the Czar, to convene them in a council of war, which met on the 9th of August. The majority pronounced in favour of taking the offensive, but as to the time and mode there was such a diversity of opinion as showed how little hopeful was the situation. Whether to fling the field army against the positions on the Tchernaya; or to combine with an attack there a great sortie from Sebastopol; or, as one or two desired, to evacuate the south side, and combine garrison and field army for a great battle; or whether (as Todleben held) the field army should be brought to reinforce the garrison, and both hurled against the besiegers' lines; also, whether certain reinforcements of militia should be waited for—all these found their advocates. What was decided on was to attack the Allies on the upper Tchernaya, that is to say, the French on the Fedioukine heights, (see map 3) numbering 18,000 men, with forty-eight guns, and the Sardinians, who continued the line up the stream, also on a line of heights bordering it, and held a hill on the Russian side of the river near Tchorgoun as an outpost, and who numbered 9000, with thirty-six guns; while close enough to act as a reserve were 10,000 Turks, in the valley behind. In addition to these, the French could readily bring down from the Upland a disposable force which would raise the whole Allied Army

---

6 The author of Letters from Headquarters

in this locality to 60,000. Besides the obstacle of the Tchernaya, there was a watercourse along the front of the Allies, who had further protected their lines and batteries by intrenchments.

On the afternoon of the 15th August the Russians brought their troops from the Belbek to join those on the Mackenzie Farm heights. During the following night, the right wing, 13,000 infantry, 2000 cavalry, and sixty-two guns, under General Read, moved down the high road of the Traktir Bridge, and halted opposite the French. The left wing, 16,000 infantry, seventy guns, under General Liprandi, moved in two columns; the right one, under that general, followed the march of Read; the left, under General Bellegarde, descending the heights by another path, was to halt on the road to Tchorgoun. The reserve of infantry, 19,000, with thirty-six guns, was to descend by both roads, and draw up behind Read; the great body of cavalry, 8000, with twenty-eight guns, was to follow Bellegarde; the reserve artillery, seventy-six guns, to draw up behind the infantry reserve.

Gortschakoff's plan was this: at daybreak, Liprandi was to drive in the Sardinian outposts on the right bank of the stream, while the whole Army formed to attack. Gortschakoff would then determine whether to use his whole force for the attack of the Sardinian position, or for that of the French, and, till he had determined, all were to await orders. The first step in the programme was accomplished by driving the Sardinian outposts as far as the last height on the right bank, which they continued to hold. But here a terrible disappointment, according to his own report, awaited Gortschakoff. General Read, apparently interpreting an order sent to him "to commence" as meaning "to attack," launched both his Divisions, prematurely and without a preliminary cannonade, at the heights held by the French. He carried the tete de pont with the Division on his left, the Twelfth, and ascending by the road, it reached the French lines. But it got no farther. Crushed by a tremendous fire, it was driven down the hill, and across the stream, with immense slaughter. Read's other Division, the Seventh, crossing by fords, endeavoured to move along between the front of the French and the river, in order to attack their left flank, but was soon compelled, after a feeble attempt, to regain its own bank in disorder, and though suffering a comparatively slight loss, was not again brought into action. The Twelfth Division, reformed after its repulse, was now used as a support to the Fifth of the Reserve in again attacking the French right; they again took the tete de pont, and advanced by the road and neighbouring fords across the stream and up the heights, but only to be again driven back to their own bank ravaged as before, and with the loss of General Read, who was killed. Thereupon the Twelfth and Fifth Divisions, reduced to half their numbers, were withdrawn to ground near the bases of the Mackenzie heights, and Liprandi was ordered to send a brigade of the Seventeenth Division to the assault. It ascended at the same points as its predecessors, and like them, after reaching the French lines, and undergoing heavy loss, was driven back to the other bank, its retreat being covered by another of Liprandi's regiments.

Gortschakoff, seeing that the French were being strongly reinforced (a French Division having reached the ground, and two others being on the march for it, while six battalions of Turks had come up), withdrew his troops. His cavalry and guns formed line across the valley, the infantry in rear; and thus for many hours he waited, beyond cannon shot, in case the Allies should quit their positions to attack him. But this formed no part of Pélissier's design. The Russians, whose disaster was aggravated by want of water, withdrew, and about two p.m. were seen ascending the road to the Mackenzie heights, while other columns followed the route thither from Tchorgoun, till the whole had quitted the field. The slaughter among them had been very great. Three generals, sixty-six other officers, and 2300 men were killed; 160 officers and 4000 men wounded, and thirty-one officers and 1700 men had disappeared. The French lost 1500 killed and wounded; the Sardinians, 200.

With this defeat vanished whatever faint hope the Russian chiefs might have had of retrieving, in any important degree, their failing fortunes. The employment of militia in this battle showed the approaching exhaustion of their resources. In May 1855 Lord Lansdowne stated in the House of Lords, as derived from authentic sources, that a return was made up a few days before the death of the Emperor Nicholas showing a total loss to the Russians of 240,000 men. It seems almost incredible, but the march through the muddy flats, and bad, unmetalled roads of Southern Russia, the severity of the winter there, the traversing of the wind-swept steppes of the Crimea, supplies and shelter being throughout the route difficult to obtain, and the transport of the country destroyed, had put such a strain on the troops that, out of every three men who were despatched to the army, it may be said two fell by the way. Besides losses of this kind, in the six months from March to August inclusive, 81,000 men had been killed or wounded in and around Sebastopol. There was a cemetery on the north side, called "The grave of the Hundred Thousand," whither the dead were conveyed from the works and the hospitals. The Armies of the Great Military Powers had not at that time approached to their present magnitude, and it was evident that even the comparatively huge resources of Russia must be drawing towards their end.

CHAPTER XIII

THE DESTRUCTION OF SEBASTOPOL

What Gortschakoff saw in Sebastopol—Yet he resolves to sustain an Assault—French Plan of Assault—The Final Bombardment—The French Attacking Forces—The English—The Assault—Cost of taking the Malakoff—Failure of the French elsewhere—Failure at the Redan—Predominance of the Malakoff—Incidents on Following Days—Constancy of the Garrison—Final Destruction of the Fleet.

SEEING HOW desperate was the condition of the fortress, Prince Gortschakoff had resolved, after the battle of the Tchernaya, to abandon the place. In letters to the Minister for War, of the 18th and 24th August, he expressed this intention, saying there was not a man in the Army who would not call it folly to continue the defence longer. It was with a view to operating a retreat that he pressed forward the construction of the bridge across the harbour, which was to have a roadway of sixteen feet, and to bear heavy vehicles. He also conferred with Todleben on other measures to protect the withdrawal, and, accordingly, barricades were built across the streets, and formed into armed and defensible works, in which, as a last resort, to hold in check the assailants. Preparations were also made for blowing up the principal forts and magazines.

Another great cannonade had begun on the 17th August. The French lines had now approached so close to the place that new additions to them were immediately destroyed or rendered untenable by the fire from the Malakoff and Little Redan; and the shower of small shells, easily cast into the trenches from the ramparts, and called by the French bouquets, greatly increased the losses of men. It was for the silencing of the artillery which thus hindered the French, that the Allied batteries opened in full force against the part of the enemy's lines from the Redan to the great harbour. But the town front was not included, and the English batteries suffered greatly from want of support by the works on their left.

On the 20th August Gortschakoff entered the fortress, and went round the lines of defence, upon which the fire of the Allies was just then at its height. What he saw might well confirm him in his resolution to retreat. There was no longer either a city or a suburb to defend, for both were heaps of rubbish and cinders. The parapets of the works, dried in the heats of summer, and split in huge fragments by the shot, were crumbling into the ditches. The interior space was honey-combed with holes made by the shells. Gabions and sandbags could not be procured to repair the embrasures, which remained in ruins. Many of the dismounted guns could no longer be replaced, not because there were not plenty in the arsenals, but because to mount them by night, under the deadly fire of the mortars, entailed such frightful sacrifices of men, The defenders of the works were packed in caves under the parapets; the gunners lay dead in heaps on the batteries; the wounded could not be removed by day, because the communications with the rear were now searched throughout by the fire of the Allies, and so lay where they fell, in torment, in the sun, beside the more fortunate slain. On landing, the Prince had passed the hospitals, full to overflowing, and the ambulances with the wounded, crowding what had been the squares. There was nothing to relieve the horrible monotony of destruction and devastation, except the bridge, which promised retreat from this misery, and which was approaching completion.

Yet it was after this visit that the Russian General changed his mind in the direction of what he had before termed folly. "I am resolved," he wrote to the Minister for War, on the 1st September, "to defend the south side to the last extremity, for it is the only honourable course which remains to us." Calculating that the daily loss of the garrison was from 800 to 900, and that he could bring 25,000 men from the Army outside to reinforce it, by leaving only 20,000 to guard the Mackenzie heights, he considered he might still prolong the defence for a month. Everything was against such a cruel determination; but he proceeded to execute it so far as in him lay. It did not, however, rest with him to determine the end.

The cannonade once more reduced the Malakoff, its dependencies and neighbours, to absolute silence, and enabled the French to push their works yet closer. The soil between the Mamelon and Malakoff could be cut into like a cheese, and the trenches were more easily made and better constructed here than elsewhere. The English trenches before the Redan had been stopped by solid rock; the French approaches to the Little Redan, now only forty yards from it, had also got into soil so stony as would no longer afford cover. The most advanced approach to the Malakoff was only separated from it by twenty-five yards; in the soft soil the trenches might have been pushed to the very edge of the ditch, but only with great loss, and, besides, the facility of mining below them would increase as the distance lessened. It was therefore deemed that the time for assault had come, and it only remained to determine the details. Accordingly, a council of war considered the matter.

The Attack on the Malakoff by William Simpson, 1855. This print shows the French assault on the Malakoff on 7th September 1855. French soldiers advance from the left, Zouaves from the left foreground, crossing the ditch and engaging Russian soldiers in hand-to-hand combat on the right.

After the members had delivered their opinions, Pélissier expressed himself thus: "I, too, have my plan, but I will not breathe it to my pillow." There is, however, no need to be so reticent with the reader. The French commander had learned that the relief of the troops in the works before him took place at noon, and that in order to avoid the great additional loss which would be caused by introducing the new garrisons before the old ones moved out, the contrary course was followed of marching out most of the occupants before replacing them. Thus noon was the time when the Malakoff would be found most destitute of defenders, and noon was to be the hour of the assault. Also another advantage was offered to the French. The salient of the Malakoff had been adapted to the form of the tower which it covered, and was therefore circular, consequently there was a space in it which could not be seen or fired on from the flanks; that was the space upon which the troops were to be directed. Roadways, twenty yards wide, were made through the trenches, and then masked by gabions, easily thrown down, by which the reserves could be brought up in the shortest time. The Malakoff, the Curtain, and the Little Redan were each to be attacked by a Division, supported by a brigade; and four Divisions, with other troops, were destined to attack the Central Bastion and works near it, and break from thence, by the rear, into the Flagstaff Bastion. But, first, the cannonade was to be renewed. It began on the 5th September, and this time it encircled the whole fortress, the French batteries before the town opening no less vigorously than the rest. At night a frigate in the harbour was set on fire by a shell, and the conflagration for hours lighted up the surrounding scenery. On the 6th and 7th the feu d'enfer went on, the Russians replying but feebly; on the night of the 7th a line-of-battle ship was set on fire by a mortar, and burnt nearly all night; it contained a large supply of spirits, the blue flames from which cast a lugubrious light on the ramparts from the harbour to the Malakoff, producing, says Todleben, "a painful impression on the souls of the defenders of Sebastopol."

Daylight, on the 8th, found the Russian defences completely manned, the guns loaded with grape, and the reserves brought close up. But, as the reader knows, the assault was not yet, and the result of these preparations to receive it was increased havoc in the exposed ranks of the defenders.

Many names which acquired fresh distinction in future wars are found among the French commanders on this occasion. The Division to attack the Malakoff was that of MacMahon, one of whose brigades was commanded by Decaen, the other by Vinoy; and in reserve to it was De Wimpffen's brigade of Camou's Division, and two battalions of Zouaves of the Guard, under Colonel Jannin.

Dulac's Division, composed of the brigades of St Pol and Bisson, was to attack the Little Redan. In reserve were Marolles' brigade of Camou's Division, and a battalion of chasseurs of the Guard.

Between these two was posted, opposite the Curtain, between the two bastions, La Motterouge's Division, formed of the brigades of Bourbaki and Picard; in reserve two regiments of voltigeurs, two of grenadiers of the Guard, the whole under General Meilinet, with De Failly and Pontevés for brigadiers. Pélissier's headquarters were in the Mamelon. To avoid giving warning to the enemy by signalling, the Generals set their watches by his, and on the stroke of noon, Bosquet, commanding the whole attack on this side, was to launch his troops against the lines where the defence was conducted by General Khrouleff, to aid whom, with their guns, four steamers were held ready in the waters below.

The attack on the Redan was to be directed by General Codrington. His Division (the Light) and the Second, under General Markham, were to supply the column of attack, of which the covering party, the ladder party, the working party (to fill up the ditch, and convert what works we might gain to our own purposes), and the main body, were to number 1700, and the supports 1500. The remainder of these two Divisions, numbering 3000, was to be in reserve in the third parallel. Also, in last reserve, were the Third and Fourth Divisions.

No attack on the Redan would have been undertaken by the English as an isolated operation. Our compulsory distance from that work, the want of a place of arms (that is to say, a covered space in the advanced trenches of sufficient extent to harbour large bodies of troops), the construction of which was forbidden by the rocky soil, and the still unsubdued fire from the ramparts, all condemned an assault. But it was deemed necessary as a distraction in aid of the French, and that purpose it fulfilled.

The two French Divisions for the assault of the town defences were assembled in "the work of the 2d of May." In the right portion of it, and in the adjoining ravine, was the Division of D'Autemarre, formed of Niol's and Breton's brigades; in reserve was Bouat's Division. In the left of the same work was Levaillant's Division, composed of Trochu's and Couston's brigades, which was to head the attack on the Central Bastion and the adjoining works, with Pate's Division in reserve. Cialdini's Sardinian brigade was to attack the Flagstaff Bastion as soon as the Central Bastion should be carried; and two French regiments were to cover the left of the forces attacking this part of the lines, which were all under General de Salles. The town defences opposite him were commanded by General Semiakine. The English were to await the hoisting of the tricolour and the Union Jack together in the Mamelon as the signal for their advance; the French before the town were to expect further instructions.

At noon the whole of Bosquet's first line rushed from the trenches. Not a shot was fired at MacMahon's leading brigade as it crossed with flying steps the short open space, pushed the planks over the ditch, and partly by means of these, partly by leaping into the ditch and mounting the battered escarp, crowded over the parapet. And here Pélissier's expectations were exactly fulfilled. The few defenders in the salient were completely surprised, their commanders killed or captured, and the Zouaves, who headed the attack, took absolute possession of this corner of the work. But, though the redoubt covered 350 yards in depth by 150 in width, the open space within was very small, for, behind the round tower, rows of traverses, each forming a new line of defence, partly crossed it from side to side. As soon as the Russian garrison issuing from their shelter caves under the traverses, and the reliefs swarming in, had manned these, the real struggle began, and it was desperately bloody. Every traverse was fought for, taken, and retaken, and it was not till Vinoy's brigade, directed on the eastern face, had broken in there, in rear of the traverses, and had from thence combined with the Zouaves in front in attacking them, that the enemy was at length forced out of them, and MacMahon's troops occupied the work throughout its extent. Many times the enemy brought up reserves to retake their strong-hold, but they could do nothing against the closed rear, now powerfully manned, and Prince Gortschakoff, who had come up to the foot of the slopes surmounted by the Malakoff, at length caused his troops to be withdrawn from the hopeless struggle. It was four o'clock when the conquest of the principal work was thus fully assured. Though well worth the price, it had cost very dear. MacMahon's Division had issued from the trenches with 4520 bayonets and 199 officers. Of these twenty-nine officers and 292 men lay dead, and eighty-nine officers and 1729 men were wounded. The Zouaves of the Guard had lost 311 men out of 627; Wimpffen's brigade, 637 out of 2100; in all, 3087.

St Pol's brigade went against the Little Redan, and Bourbaki's against the Curtain. Both broke into those works, but there was an interior line of defence stretching across the space from the rear of the Malakoff to the rear of the Little Redan. This was strongly defended, field batteries were brought up by the Russians, and the ships, keeping in motion, and bringing their broadsides to bear, made havoc amongst the French in the open ground. Both the brigades were compelled, with considerable loss, to re-enter the trenches, which were filled with wounded, and along which it was not easy to pass. However, Marolles' brigade was at length sent against the Little Redan, the voltigeurs and grenadiers against the Curtain, where they once more broke in, and were once more driven out. It was now that a singular feat was performed. Bosquet gave the order for two batteries of field-artillery to advance by the prepared road through the trenches, and come into action against the guns which were firing on the French from the Curtain. From their station behind the Victoria redoubt they advanced at speed, losing many horses as they went, formed up in the open space before the Curtain, and came into action with their twelve-pounders. But the ground was swept both by the artillery and musketry from the enemy's parapet. The batteries were at once crushed, and what was left of them at last withdrew, leaving most of their men and horses, and their commandant, Souty, dead on the spot. It was a new operation to essay with artillery. It was brilliantly attempted, but the heavy sacrifices were incurred absolutely in vain. The attack on this side made no further progress.

The portion of Codrington's troops destined to head the attack on the Redan moved rapidly and steadily across the open space, though suffering much loss from the heavy fire of round shot, grape, case, and musketry now directed on them from every available point, and those in front passed with ease over the battered rampart and entered the work. But the rest, with too strong a reminiscence of their mode of action in the trenches, lay down at the edge of the ditch and began firing alongside of the covering troops, who alone should have performed this duty. The supports also reached the ditch, and some of them entered the work. But the great reserves, in moving through the trenches towards the point of issue, were obstructed and discouraged by meeting the numbers of wounded men and their bearers, who were of necessity brought back by the same narrow route, a difficulty which also hindered some of the French attacks. Colonel Windham, the leader of the attacking troops, finding that his messages for support produced no result, took the ill-advised step of going back himself to procure reinforcements. It was not surprising that, before he returned, his men also had withdrawn. It is probably in reference to this that the Engineer Journal remarks, in excusing the troops, "they retired when they found themselves without any officer of rank to command them." They had been overwhelmed by the numbers which the Russians brought into the open work; and as they hurried back they suffered not less heavily than in their advance. It was unfortunate for them that the French had spiked the guns in the Malakoff instead of turning them on the enemy moving into the Redan, as they ought to have done. With the immense increase of difficulties in making way through the crowded trenches, and renewing the attack against works now fully armed and manned, the attempt was postponed till next day, when fresh troops, headed by the Highlanders, were to renew it. In the meantime our batteries once more opened with full effect on the now crowded Redan.

On the French left the two leading brigades of Couston and Trochu attacked the two works which flank on each side the Central Bastion. At first Couston's troops had some success; but the Russians, reinforced, drove both brigades back upon the trenches. A second assault was even more fruitless. Levaillant's Division was preparing for a third attempt, when Pélissier, hearing how complete was the failure, ordered the attack in this quarter to cease.

The French General had learned, soon after the Russian attempts to recapture the Malakoff had ceased, that masses of the enemy were passing by the bridge to the north side. Still he could not yet feel assured that his victory was decisive. But, in truth, even before darkness set in, the Russians, withdrawn from all their works, were collecting and moving to the harbour, under cover of the barricades; those in front of the town towards the bridge, those from the works of the suburb towards points in the harbour where steamers and boats were to transport them to the north side. By daybreak the whole of the garrison, carrying most of the wounded with them, had made good their retreat. But the means adopted to prevent the Allies from pressing into the place revealed, during the night, that Sebastopol was being abandoned. Measures had been taken by the garrison to ensure the explosion of the magazines in the works and forts at considerable intervals. Thirty-five of these were blown up successively, the first at eleven o'clock; at the same time fires broke out wherever anything combustible yet remained in the ruined city, and the glare of the conflagrations was augmented by the burning of two line-of-battle ships in the harbour, where most of the rest were at the same time sunk. All night sleep was driven from the camps by the roar of the explosions, which shook the plains as if with the tremors of an earthquake, and combined, with the red light glowing murkily against the canopy of smoke, to render the scene terrific. Soon after daybreak an explosion more tremendous than the rest seemed to blow the city and suburb against the sky, a vast cloud rising in earthy volumes and darkening the sun. Beneath it the bridge was seen to be disconnected from the southern shore, and the last of the retiring troops were descried ascending the opposing slope. Divided by the harbour, the hostile armies, from the heights, looked on the destruction of the city, which seemed a fitting conclusion to the hardships and the conflicts of the immense hosts that had contended for it. Copious libations of blood marked this final sacrifice. The French lost, in all, 7567 officers and men; Generals St Pol, Marolles, Ponteves, Rivet, and Breton were killed; Bosquet, Mellinet, Bourbaki, and Trochu were wounded. The English lost 2271 officers and men; Generals Warren, Straubenzee, and Shirley among the wounded. The Russians lost, on this last day, 12,913 officers and men; two generals killed, and five wounded.

Next day access to the Malakoff showed how completely it dominated the surrounding works. It looked into the interior of the Redan, swept in its view every corner of the suburb, was only 1200 yards from the harbour, and commanded, within range, the only anchorage of the fleet, as well as the bridge which formed the sole line of retreat for the Russians. In consideration of its importance, Todleben had lavished on it all possible means of defence, making of it a citadel, and in order to guard against an attack on its rear by an enemy who might have penetrated elsewhere, he had closed the gorge, a precaution, however, which had the grave disadvantage of assuring possession of it to the French when they had once succeeded in expelling its garrison. On the other hand, the Redan showed an open interior space, which, widening from the salient to the rear, enabled the troops assembling in its defence always to enter in great force, and to present a front more extensive than that of the assailants. These different conditions in some degree account for success on one point, failure on the other.

The explosions still continued on the 9th, when in the afternoon Fort Paul was completely blown into the air; a failure in the firing arrangement prevented Fort Nicholas from following it. On this day the dead were brought out for burial. The open space between the Curtain and the intrenchment in rear of it, and the corner of the Little Redan, were heaped with slain. The explosion of a great magazine in this latter work had opened a chasm there, which was now made the grave of the Russians; while the French killed in this part of the assault were brought out and laid on the grass before the Curtain, extending in long rows, according to their regiments, to the number of more than a thousand. One part of this space was heaped with the wreck of the two field batteries, and the bodies of the artillerymen and horses.

On the 10th the Vladimir crossed the harbour, under a flag of truce, to ask for certain of the wounded which, in the retreat of the garrison, had been left behind in a hospital. The building was very spacious, and in it was concentrated an extraordinary amount of human misery. It had afforded shelter to 2000 desperately wounded men. They had lain here two days and nights, without aid, without nourishment, surrounded by the din of explosions, and by flaming buildings, which alone dispelled for them the darkness of night. In one vast room were 700, many of whom had undergone amputation, and who were all dead of misery, lying in blood on their beds, or on the floor as they had writhed on to it. Five hundred were still alive, and were conveyed to the Vladimir. Three English officers wounded and captured in the assault were found here, who lived long enough to be conveyed to camp.

Perhaps even stronger testimony to the unhappy condition of the garrison was afforded by the provision made for sheltering the troops who occupied the works. Huge subterranean barracks had been dug under the ramparts, the earth above being supported on the trunks of trees. These dismal chambers were entered by tunnels, and it was here that the troops destined to oppose assaults found all the repose that could be given to them when not immediately called on to face the unrelenting iron storm which swept across the open space of the interior. Phrases can hardly do justice to the constancy, the military spirit, of a soldiery that could, under such conditions, readily obey the call which brought them to the last struggle, and so bear themselves in it that their enemies had everywhere recoiled, except at one point. The only vulnerable spot of the defences had proved to be that on which every resource of war had most profusely been brought to bear, and success here had been achieved almost by accident. Pélissier tersely expressed how sharp had been the crisis, how doubtful the chance, when he said, "We were four all, and I turned the king." Vast consequences were involved in the fate of the Malakoff, for the chiefs of engineers and artillery, in face of the fact that we were again brought round to the time of year at which we had first approached Sebastopol, had come to the conviction that, if the place were not taken before winter, it would, as a matter of course, be necessary to raise the siege; and they had gone on to the deduction that it was therefore indispensable to hasten its conclusion by an immediate assault.

Next day two eight-inch guns, placed on the esplanade of the town, were brought to bear on the Vladimir, hulling her several times. In the night the Russians consummated the sacrifice of all that they had fought to defend by burning or sinking the remainder of their war-vessels. Morning saw of the Black Sea Fleet no tokens except protruding stumps of masts, and fragments floating on the waters—a sight which any Turk who may have chanced to survive the massacre of Sinope must be thought to have surveyed with peculiar pleasure.

CHAPTER XIV

THE CLOSE OF THE WAR

A Further Question—Views of the Emperor and his Generals—Fresh Operations—Destruction of the Docks—The Government's Wish to push on—Vaillant's Views—Pélissier's Views—Excellent State of the British Army—A Diplomatic Difficulty—The Emperor and the Queen—New Proposal of Russia—Good Faith of Louis Napoleon—The Treaty of Peace—Strength of the British Army—The Results of the War—Russia repudiates the Treaty later—England retains Interest in the Crimea—The Graves of the Crimea—All that remains of the War.

MASTERS OF the smoking ruins, and thus far relieved from a huge difficulty, the Allies did not yet see clearly the way before them. The Russian army, now become, by its close connection with the Inkerman heights, altogether a field army, defied them from beyond the harbour; and although the objects with which the war had been undertaken were accomplished, yet the fact that the enemy still held the field could not be ignored. The question, What was to be done next? was taken up and dealt with by Louis Napoleon himself. "The Emperor wants to know your projects," Vaillant telegraphed to Pélissier; "he hopes you will not run your head against the fortified Mackenzie position, but will manoeuvre like a skilful general." Next day Louis Napoleon, in a letter to his Minister in London, set forth his views. He wished to turn the month of October to account by a forward movement of the army, its right wing in advance, so as to force the Russians to abandon their positions near Sebastopol by threatening their communications. He went on to observe, that when the Allies should be thus masters of the Crimea, they would occupy themselves with filling in the trenches, repairing the land defences, taking care of the docks and barracks, and re-establishing the harbour as a port. They would then abandon the Crimea, keeping Sebastopol only, and leaving there a garrison and a fleet. They would thus hold an important gage, until Russia, who could not hope to retake the fortress, should consent to treat; and, instead of further destruction, they should repair the establishments of the town as much as possible, in order to have something of value to offer. He also wrote to Pélissier, urging him to use the last of the fine weather in an advance upon Simpheropol, which the reinforcement of the Russian Army would render impossible next year. Niel took the same view. But Pélissier was not to be persuaded to abandon his own opinions. " I have been using my troops to feel for a way of advancing on my right. The Russians keep their positions behind the rocky heights, which extend from Inkerman beyond Simpheropol; they have garnished the gaps in them with artillery, and made them more difficult to force than the ramparts of Sebastopol. In engaging there in bloody combats, producing no results, we might throw away the good position we have gained. But I will attack if you give the order." To appear, however, to comply with the desire for action, so far as he deemed safe, he left only one French Division with the English on the Upland, and spread his army along the Tchernaya, and into the valley of Baidar; and at the same time sent a force of cavalry and guns to Eupatoria to operate with the Turks from that place against the Russian corps observing it, where some success was gained over the enemy's cavalry; and the Allied Generals were encouraged by it to augment the forces there (of which General D'Allonville commanded the whole) by a Division of French infantry and a brigade of English cavalry.

Also, a combined operation was undertaken against Kinburn, where the rivers Dnieper and Bug flow into a wide estuary, after forming highways for transport through districts affording abundant supplies. On one of these, at Nikolaieff, was a great naval station and arsenal. An English brigade, under General Spencer, and a French brigade, under General De Wimpffen, both commanded by General Bazaine, were disembarked, under cover of a combined naval squadron, whereupon the troops and ships together brought an attack to bear which in a few hours caused the place to surrender. With it the Russian Army in the Crimea lost another important source of supply.

All this time the British Ministers were not entirely at one with the Emperor. Sharing his desire for a forward movement of the armies, they strongly opposed his idea of conserving the maritime establishments of Sebastopol. In this they had much reason. It had always been evident that Russia could have no object in maintaining a war fleet in this inland sea, where her commerce between shore and shore could need no protection, except to use it in prosecuting her designs on her neighbour's territory. It was quite in accordance with logic, therefore, when we had just been rejoicing over the destruction of the Russian Fleet, that we should destroy the means of restoring that fleet now that they lay in our power. As to preserving them in order to have something to treat with, no provision on paper that we could wring from so slippery an antagonist, against the undue use of his naval power, could compare in efficacy with the step of leaving him no naval power to use. Pressed by the British Government, the Emperor consented. Between Christmas and February the French and British engineers destroyed the great docks, the remaining forts and barracks on the south side of the harbour, and the aqueducts which supplied the docks.

The minor successes at Eupatoria and Kinburn by no means satisfied the desire either of the Emperor or of the British Government for a more complete and substantial triumph. The military situation, where the Allies on the one side of the Tchernaya, the Russians on the other, stood face to face, each defying their enemy to attack, presented itself under different aspects. Under one of these, it seemed as if the Allies, pent in their corner, though they had gained the immediate prize, could not claim a victory so long as a Russian army was in the field ready to fight them. Under another, it might appear that the Allies, having destroyed that standing menace to Turkey, the Russian Fleet, with its arsenal and docks, thus attaining the grand object for which they had resorted to arms, might well be content to hold what they had gained, and to see the enemy squander his remaining strength in maintaining an army under such difficulties as he must find in doing so at the extremity of the Empire. Louis Napoleon, as was inevitable, viewed the case with reference to the effect on his own hold on France. It seemed to him that he still had to satisfy the Country and the Army. This thought set his imagination once more at work in the region of strategy. He had a vision of a great army, based on Kinburn, invading Russia by the bank of the Dnieper, and thus compelling its army to leave the Crimea and move towards the threatened territory. This project, laconically disposed of by Vaillant, seems never to have been under general discussion. The British Government, equally desirous of active operations, left the mode of execution to the generals on the spot. "It is important," Lord Clarendon wrote to Lord Cowley, so late as the 31st October, "to give positive orders to the Generals in Chief to drive the Russians out of the Crimea before the bad season sets in. If this is found impossible, at any rate we might harass them daily during the winter, so as to force them to retreat before spring. The military honour, and the political interests, of France and England require this triumph and this guarantee; we must have it at any price. Even during the winter our Fleets can so transport our troops as to harass and threaten the Russians on all sides; in any case, something may be done to increase their difficulties and diminish their prestige."

On the other hand, Vaillant, whatever his views earlier in the autumn, now thought it too late for action. He discussed all the projects for active operations. "We cannot, from our position at Kinburn, seriously threaten the Russian communications. On their right towards Eupatoria, on their left on the Mackenzie heights, the enemy are covered by obstacles, natural and artificial, which defend all the approaches to the vast intrenched camp which they occupy north of Sebastopol. Everywhere they have retired behind their formidable lines, without risking an engagement, as soon as the Allies have moved forward. The difficulties of the roads, the want of water, the absence of resources of all kinds, have forced General D'Allonville to fall back on Eupatoria, as they forced Marshal Pélissier to retire into the valley of Baidar after having pushed forward on the road to Bakshisarai. In this situation, the greater part of our Forces in the Crimea have become useless, and the measure of withdrawing all that can be withdrawn, without risk to our position there, appears to us reasonable. Should the British Government not think itself able to adopt this course, in view of adverse public opinion in England, the French Government ought in strictness to renounce it; but in maintaining all their present forces in the Crimea, these must be kept in their present winter quarters on the Chersonese, without exhausting themselves in vain and perhaps perilous attempts, which the winter must render nearly impracticable." On the original draft of this reply the Emperor wrote : "I find this Note perfect." Pélissier, too, renewed his objections to any forward movement. He disposed of the Emperor's project for operating from Kinburn by endeavouring to show it to be impracticable. He considered it necessary, in the interests of the alliance, that the French and English Armies should no longer operate together, and set forth a plan for retaining a proportion of the French Forces round Sebastopol, at Kinburn, and at Constantinople, and sending the rest back to France, while the English, with the Turks, should occupy Kertch, and operate in Circassia towards Tiflis. France would thus be ready to meet a possible endeavour of Russia to transfer the war to Germany at a time when the Crimea would otherwise still absorb the strength of the French Army. A little later he expressed himself still more strongly. "Thank God it is not difficulties which frighten me. The capture of Sebastopol— of which the chiefs of this Army, and others greater than they, were still doubtful on the 7th September— showed that I could face dangers when I saw success beyond. But here the situation is not the same. I see the obstacles; I do not perceive the success, nor even the hope of it. I should be perplexed to form a plan of campaign, still more to carry one out... If, then, the Allied Governments should decide on operations such as I have been discussing, I should be obliged, to my eternal regret, to decline the honour of directing them."

No doubt Pélissier was one of the most resolute of commanders; yet it may nevertheless be doubted whether he was not swayed by influences apart from his estimate of the military problems before him, and such as have weight with less resolute men. He had undergone a tremendous strain, such as might well diminish his ardour, while the conflict hung so long in the balance. He had at last achieved a triumph, all the more brilliant because of the failure of his allies. It might well seem to him that such further successes as were to be gained in this remote region could hardly exalt the fame of him or his Army. His officers were openly showing their desire to receive at home the compensations for all their trials which there awaited them—a desire which he may have shared more than he was conscious of, for he was growing old and heavy of frame. The notion of a campaign on the Rhine, a much more conspicuous and attractive theatre of war, was generally entertained in the army. French surgeons had prognosticated a decline in the health of the troops under existing conditions, and their apprehensions were even now beginning to be realised in a visitation of typhus. Above all, the French people were tired of the war, and ready to welcome back their army.

On the other hand, those responsible for the condition of the British army had turned the sharp lessons of the campaign to singularly good account. Our troops in the Crimea were now fed, housed, and clothed in the best way, and their health was as good as at a home station. The strength of the army was increasing every month. In November it numbered 51,000, of which 4000 cavalry and ninety-six guns, besides a Turkish legion, raised by the British Government, of 20,000, and a German legion of 10,000. Our Land Transport corps could speedily be made adequate to the needs of these large forces in a campaign in the field. Our army medical system now so greatly surpassed that of the French that a commission was sent from Paris expressly to study it. The comparison between the two armies had become enormously in our favour. Our fleet, too, had been vastly augmented in force and efficiency. In these circumstances, it was natural that the British people should prefer another campaign to any treaty of peace which should fail to fulfil their just expectations.

It was at this time that a diplomatic difficulty arose very threatening to the alliance, and which brought the variance in the desires and interests of the two Allied nations strongly into view. After the fall of Sebastopol Austria had once more come forward with proposals for peace. These were, from the British point of view, such as we ought not to accept. But Russia had at this time so established her influence with high officials in France that they had first concerted with Austria, and without reference to England, what these terms should be, and had then laid them before the British Government as what must be accepted without modification. Palmerston was not the sort of Minister to allow his country to be thus dealt with, and intimated that England intended to maintain her claims as a principal in the negotiations. The communications between the two Governments grew sharper in tone, and at length Lord Palmerston signified to the French Ambassador that, rather than be forced into the acceptance of unsatisfactory terms of peace, England would continue the war with no other ally than Turkey, and that she felt herself fully in a condition to enter on such a course. Never had the alliance, throughout the war, been so strained as now. The Emperor endeavoured to restore concert by writing a letter to the Queen, recommending the Austrian proposals to favourable consideration. The Queen's reply, pointing out, in the most friendly spirit, the difference of position in the two Governments, and consequently in their points of view—the Emperor responsible to nobody while in England the advisers of the Sovereign must recommend only such steps as can be defended in Parliament—contains this passage : "I cannot conceal from your Majesty my fears, founded upon information on which I can rely, that the language held at Paris by men in office, and others who have the honour to approach you, in regard to the financial difficulties of France, and the absolute necessity of concluding peace, has already produced a very mischievous effect at Vienna, at Berlin, and at St Petersburgh; and that it is very possible that Austria may by this time be disposed to draw back from her ultimatum, and to seek to obtain more favourable terms for Russia." It appeared, from the Emperor's subsequent expressions, that the nature of the British objections to the Austrian proposals had been misrepresented to him by persons about him who desired peace on any terms—the source of that desire being perhaps explained by a passage in a letter of the Prince Consort, where, discussing the aspect of affairs in France, he speaks of the "stockbroking propensities of its public men." But Louis Napoleon himself was thoroughly loyal to the alliance, and now, says Martin, "took means to let it be known that, however this note might be sounded for purposes of the Bourse, he would be no party to a peace of which England did not approve. If the war had to be carried on, France would not be found backward." "Whatever I think right," he said to Lord Cowley, "I will do, and I shall not be afraid of making my conduct understood in France."

Nevertheless Russia must have felt great confidence in the agencies she had set to work in Paris, for she not only conveyed to the French Government her determination to accept no proposals that should come in the form of an ultimatum (that is to say, accompanied by a threat of joining the alliance) from Austria, but put forth a proposition of her own, of the most preposterous tenor, respecting the limitation of her power in the Black Sea, the point in which the British people were most interested. She caused it to be proposed "that the Dardanelles should be closed, and that no ships of war should henceforth enter the Black Sea except those of Russia and Turkey, which should be maintained there in such numbers as the two neighbours should agree between themselves, without a voice on the part of the other Powers." That the wolf should thus be left to arrange matters with the lamb would have been a very singular outcome to the costly efforts by which Russia had been reduced to her present condition, and her audacity in still maintaining such pretensions shows how strong was her reliance on the influences at work with the corrupt officials of the French Empire. But her game of brag was nearly at an end. Austria had at last laid before the Allied Powers a carefully prepared treaty, which, though short in some respects of what England had a right to claim, had been found to be what the British Ministry could accept, and this had now been sent as an Austrian ultimatum to St Petersburgh, the period for the Russian reply being limited to the 18th of January. The Emperor of the French had made it understood that he was prepared either to make peace on these terms, or to continue the war with increased vigour, and he suggested that a council of war should meet in Paris to settle the course of action for the following spring. In consequence, British, French, and Italian officers, convened for the purpose, held their sittings in his capital, while the intention of Russia was still undeclared.

The alliance, thanks to the good faith of Louis Napoleon, having thus proved firm, the hollow pretensions of Russia vanished like a bubble. Her exhaustion left her no choice but to accept. Her losses, never accurately known, had been stupendous. Up to the end of August those in the Crimea alone were estimated at 153,000 men, while hundreds of thousands, drawn from the recesses of the vast Empire, had died of the hardships of the march. Altogether it was confidently believed that her total loss during the war was not less than half a million of men.

On the 16th of January she accepted the Austrian terms as the basis of conference, and on the 25th February the Plenipotentiaries of the Powers met at Paris. Their first act was to settle the conditions of an armistice, which was to last till the 31st March. After that, the first point taken was the neutralisation of the Black Sea, and the article opening its waters to the commerce of all nations, and interdicting it to ships of war, was passed with unexpected facility. Another article which excluded Russia from the bank of the Danube was more strenuously contested by her representatives; but this also was finally agreed to. Also, an article was included which admitted Turkey to a participation in the public law and concert of Europe, and prohibited the other Powers, singly or collectively, from interference in questions between the Sultan and his subjects, or in the internal administration of his Empire.

The Treaty of Paris was signed on the 30th March. It was well known in the congress that, but for England, the conditions imposed on Russia would have been far easier. And though they were still too easy, yet England might congratulate herself on having obtained so much in circumstances so adverse. For the Emperor was perhaps the only man in France who held firmly to the alliance. The French nation had no strong interest in the affairs of Turkey, and was now ready to believe, and to proclaim, that it had been made the tool of England. And Louis Napoleon himself had already obtained from the war all that was necessary for his purpose, in the victory of the Tchernaya, and the brilliant finale of the Malakoff; while the unfortunate condition into which his army in the Crimea had fallen during the winter supplied an ample reason for desiring peace. Nevertheless he continued to act in thorough unison with his ally, and again declared that he was ready to recommence the war if Russia should refuse her concurrence to the treaty. The feeling with which the two nations regarded the close of the war was thus expressed by the Prince Consort: "Peace is signed. Here it has been received with moderate satisfaction; in Paris with exultation." That they should have cause for even moderate satisfaction was by the British people rightly attributed to the firm, patriotic spirit of Palmerston, who, amid all the clamours of the Peace Party and the Opposition, steered right on, winning a popularity which, when he appealed to the Country in the following year, returned him to power with a largely increased majority.

On the 2d April the Upland was for the last time shaken by the thunders of the artillery of the Allies. This time it proclaimed in salutes the tidings of peace. To those who have noted the difficulty with which we put even a small army in the field in these days, the dislocation of all our establishments which attends the operation, and the paucity of reserves, there is something almost marvellous in the strength of our Forces in the Crimea at the close of a war in which we had lost 22,000 men. At Christmas 1855 we had there still greater forces of men than those already enumerated, with 120 guns; and in the middle of April 18,000 fresh troops were mustered at a field-day in Aldershot camp. The land transport, the commissariat, and the hospital system of the Army were all in excellent working order. But they did not long remain so. Upon the return of the Army, the reduction of its establishments was effected in the usual reckless fashion. We soon reverted to our customary condition of military inefficiency, and during the next thirty years nearly all that remained to us as the result of the experience which we had gained in the war were the present excellent system of our military hospitals, the great example of these established at Netley, the framework of the Land Transport corps, which still survives in the Army Service corps, and Aldershot camp.

For a whole generation the world continued to have the benefit of the war in the enforced quiescence of Russia. Her wounds were too deep to permit her during that time to attempt measures of aggression, or to indulge a desire to disturb the peace of the world. And this result proved that the point of attack upon her had been rightly and fortunately selected. The small proportion of coast line she exposes to the descent of an invader, the immense distances from the extremities to the heart of the Empire, the scarcity of roads, the rigours of the climate, all rendered the attack of the Western Powers upon Russia a nearly insoluble problem. But on the other hand, when she had once resolved to bring all her might and all her resources to bear on the defence of Sebastopol, these conditions turned against her, and rendered her course absolutely ruinous. Her fleets were at once imprisoned in their ports, her troops were obliged to traverse enormous spaces to reach the point of conflict, the length and bad condition of the lines of communication rendered the supply of the Army difficult and extravagantly costly, the winter brought untold losses to the columns moving through mud and snow, and exposed to piercing winds. The requisitions for supplies and transport disorganised Southern Russia, and ruined its husbandry. A speedy victory of the Allies, however complete, would have left the great resources of the enemy untouched, and the victors without an object. In such a case, it is difficult to say how or when the war would have ended, or how long the Western nations would have endured to see it drag on. But, in the course of the long siege, every failure on the part of the Allies, every gleam of hope which induced Russia to send fresh reinforcements to the Crimea, only served to prolong the terrible stress which was exhausting her.

Therefore the war was worth all it had cost. Its effect was not merely to defeat, but to disarm and disable the enemy. But to this advantage there was a limit. It had always been felt that Russia would not submit to the treaty longer than it could be enforced. A condition compelling a Power to refrain from certain acts on which it is bent will be repudiated at a fitting opportunity. It was when the Germans were in Versailles that the Minister" of the Czar issued a Note repudiating the Treaty of Paris. That was a moment when the other signatories were in no condition to enforce it, and Russia set about, among other things, the restoration of Sebastopol as a naval station, with its docks and arsenal. A Black Sea Fleet was once more to ride in its harbour, and was to be again a standing menace to Turkey. On the 18th May 1886 the Tchesma ironclad was launched by the Czar in person at Sebastopol; and on the 28th May 1890 it was announced in the Times that "the official trials of the Imperial Russian ironclad Sinope" (ominous name!) "were completed at Sebastopol last week, and the results were considered highly satisfactory. This formidable warship, one of the most powerful in the Russian Navy, has been built at Sebastopol, and forms one of the Black Sea Fleet." Thus had the great war been rounded off into an episode, having no further connection with the future. Other great wars have been fought out since, with more permanent influence on the destinies of nations; new and pressing interests have arisen; old alliances, with their obligations, have been dissolved; and, amid the shiftings of European policy, Russia once more makes ready for her opportunity.

But the interest of England in that Upland, and those valleys, on which her eyes and thoughts were once so earnestly bent, has not yet entirely ceased. Their soil still holds a multitude of her sons, the memory of whom has not altogether died out. In spots outside the several camps to which the dead could be most readily conveyed, in the precincts of battlefields, in the neighbourhood of conflicts in the trenches, a great number of burial-grounds had been formed, which were afterwards enclosed with some kind of fence, and garnished with memorials. A commanding point of the exterior range of hills, which extended between the camps of the British Divisions and their siege batteries, was known as Cathcart's Hill, because the general who fell at Inkerman was buried there, with many others. It had become the chief cemetery; it was enclosed with a lofty wall, and the graves, carefully tended by the comrades of those who lay there, were marked with headstones and crosses, and more considerable mementoes. Englishmen visiting the plateau in recent times noticed that the fences of these grave-yards had become ruinous, and that many of the bones were scattered. When this became known at home, it was resolved that all the remains which had not yet mixed with the soil, and reappeared in the grass and the flowers, should be transported, along with their memorial stones, to Cathcart's Hill, the cemetery on which should be placed in repair, and provision made for so maintaining it. All this was effected a few years ago. The Englishman who may still be attracted to the spot reads there names once well known in England; and looking on the neighbouring hills and hollows, where so protracted a strife was waged, and where so many thousands fell, he sees the points which mark the Russian lines of defence, with the famous Malakoff and Mamelon standing up in all their former defiance; while beyond, against the blue of the Euxine, are the streets and domes and churches of the city, risen from its ashes. New batteries protect the shore, the docks once more resound with the clang of labour, the port is filled with the barks of commerce, and guarded by the vessels of war. Yet a few years, and all those who still remember how passionately the thoughts and wishes of the people of England were once directed on this spot, will themselves have departed, and nothing will then survive to remind the world of this long and desperate conflict of giants except a page in history.

Printed in September 2021
by Rotomail Italia S.p.A., Vignate (MI) - Italy